BACK IN THE
USSA

PASSIONATE POSTS AND EXPATRIATE NOTES

BORIS DRAGUNSKY
PhD, PE

ISBN: 978-1-962402-98-9 (hardcover)
        978-1-962402-97-2 (paperback)

Published by

Fideli Publishing, Inc.
119 W. Morgan St.
Martinsville, IN 46151
www.FideliPublishing.com

A Word about the Title: *A word about the Title: Yes! It's a play off The Beatles hit song: "Back in the USSR." As such, it is a parable and a playful poke in the ribs to my adopted country that I dreamt of so much—to be mindful guardians of our liberties and the Western Civilization at large.*

Famous political philosophers of 20th Century Strauss and Voegelin warned in 1950's that the political stability and economic prosperity of postwar America hid a deeper angst and a fear that the center would not hold. Liberal democracy in the United States required, they believed, a reinvigorated idea of purpose.

At the moment, America seems to be at a crossroads—caught between extremes with no visible political discourse. It is no longer the USA I had finally reached in 1977 and not the USSR… yet. And though the Alt-Right comes at so many of us like a bulldozer with their pundits and rallies, history of my country of birth should teach us all that it is the small insidious chipping away at our liberties from the left, from the "Woke," Cancel Culture and Anti-Zionist/Anti-Semitic propaganda that ultimately pose the greatest danger.

Either way this missive is a call to all of us to, "Let reason prevail," and to light the path, in our small way, to help to make it so.

To my grandchildren:

Arielle, Arnold, Jordan, Izabella, Noah, Simon and Talia.

So they may learn and not forget

Acknowledgments

Acknowledgments are invariably about gratitude and recognition. So, I would like to take this opportunity to acknowledge my best friend and passionate wife Emilia for her years of support, loyalty, encouragement and faith in me. I would also like to recognize with a full heart all the friends, family, associates and mentors in my life who have, over the years, formed so much of the fabric of this story, and especially those who were encouraging me to do this writing.

This is also a tribute to the blessed memories of my parents, grandparents, aunts and three uncles fallen in the war in their 20s. As well as to my Uncle David, whose life story is on the pages of this book, and whom, over the course of my life, I have been proud of, ashamed of, and reconciled with at the end. The closeness to him and his inner circles played an important role in my awakening, discovering and witnessing the rotten spirit of the Soviet system and its duplicity.

My deepest gratitude goes to the editors and publishers, Robert J. Ahola, of blessed memory, and Robin Surface who believed in this story when it was just a whisper, untangled my thoughts and brought it to life.

Table of Contents

Introduction

This book is a refreshing hybrid—inasmuch as it is both a love letter to America and a cautionary tale, a painful recollection of what is known in the West as World War II (and in Russia as "The Great Patriotic War")… as well as the Cold War in what was once the Soviet Union. Along the way, it will also prove to be an astute, tough-love approach to America seen from the perspective of a Russian-born Jew who left the USSR forty-eight years ago to come to the one country that he'd always felt a part of, body and soul.

Beginning with a letter written while he was stuck in Chicago traffic, Dr. Boris Dragunsky's message to his grandchildren serves as the perfect "philosophical rationale" for taking us all on this journey, following the ingrained axiom that: "Those who do not learn from history are doomed to repeat it."

This book is a compelling portrait and a jeremiad as well— that, as Eleanor Roosevelt once observed, "Freedom makes a huge requirement of every human being. With freedom comes responsibility." Written with humility and yet with an unapologetic point of view, Dr. Dragunsky offers this memoir and his perspectives of a changing world in hopes it will encourage his progeny and others to keep the flame of freedom and their own identity alive…and never to take democracy for granted…remembering the words of American President Dwight D. Eisenhower, "History does not long entrust the care of freedom to the weak or the timid."

A passionate political observer and patriotic expatriate to America, Boris Dragunsky, PhD, licensed engineer, is a former refugee from what was once the USSR who managed to emigrate to the USA in 1977, navigating the Minotaur's Maze of geopolitics to escape a totalitarian system and become a free citizen of the one nation that is held (up to now) as the beacon of democracy and the standard of personal freedom by which all other countries are measured.

As such, Boris Dragunsky's fascinating saga is a non-linear tale that opens in 1941 as the ultimate paradox between two evil totalitarian systems: a repressive, Stalin led, Bolshevik-infused Soviet nation under attack by Nazi Germany's Operation Barbarossa. In it we find the earliest reminiscence of a small lad, impressionable but with an iron-clad collection of memories of an embattled Moscow in the heat of World War II. From a family with a celebrity General for an uncle, Boris is also a proud Jew and, as such, quickly learns that both he and his family are looked upon, by accident of birth, as somewhat suspect and to be kept at arms-length; they are privileged but in a limited way. Boris reflects on his country at war as a confusing ménage of the majority willing to die for the Motherland while others become Nazi collaborators gladly participating in killing their Jewish neighbors or the infamous Soviet General Andrey Vlasov, who switched sides to the Wehrmacht in hopes of getting rid of Stalin's dictatorship.

When Boris's father Zalman is drafted into the Soviet Army, young Boris is brought up by his mother Sonya (Polunovskaya), who provides him with real-life lessons on how to navigate the hardship and dangerous war years of his youth; ones of deprivation, innovation and a somewhat surreal environment that only happens when a global conflict is brought to one's very doorstep. Through this insight into the youthful days of Boris Dragunsky, we behold a world transformed—from one of an almost idealized patriotism, a healthy disdain for "the West," and a love of Russia's Motherland father figure (a beloved "Dear Comrade Stalin")…to a slow erosion of both trust and respect for the Soviet Socialist system.

Bombarded by impressions in legion fraught with myriad contradictions, Boris soon finds that canny observation is the only way to survive in his complicated world. Shielded from peril to some degree by his Uncle David's sterling reputation, Boris soon comes face to face with the perils of being a Jew in Soviet Russia. Along the way, he also discovers the great deception: everything he'd ever learned about the superiority of his Socialist Mother Russia was a body of lies—a totalitarian myth spun off Pravda's Orwellian Ministry of Truth.

Determined to put the pieces of the puzzle of global politics together on his own, Boris learns everything he can about the West, especially the USA, where the heart of freedom is said to reside. Through his close friend networks and Western "broadcasts" such as the *Voice of America,* samizdat literature and love of the truly original American musical art form of jazz, Boris discovers an alternate reality—and through that a glimpse of what the "real world" is really meant to be: a safe-haven in a new nation that he comes to love. This leads us toward the climax of the initial chapters, where young Boris goes through a slow but relentless transformation: from a dedicated son of the Soviet Union, blind to its many perversions—its Stalin-inspired tyrannical leadership, its GULAGs, its social paranoia and murderous persecutions—to a courageous counter-culture rebel and more, a vocal outspoken Refusenik.[1]

This process over the next dozen years proves both perilous and painful as Boris learns from his father, (who returned from the Manchurian front) and his Uncle David about the monstrous torture and execution of their parents, sisters and other relatives—74 souls in all—at the hands of their Nazi occupiers, simply for being Jewish. They also mourn the loss of two younger brothers—one a tank commander and another a volunteer student during the Moscow defense.

Young Boris also suffers through the death of his mother on his 16th birthday. And yet through it all, he grows and develops as a human being. Through Boris's eyes, we experience firsthand the evolution of an independent thinker and determined political rebel, one who embraces his Zionist roots as an antidote to the draconian Communist purgatory that became the Soviet Russia of the 1930s throughout the 1970s.

As a prelude, the early chapters culminate in his 20-year dream of escaping from the Soviet Union and final arrival in Houston, Texas in August of 1977, followed by his ultimate move to Chicago, Illinois.

As Boris comes into full manhood, the emphasis of his new life reveals a Soviet refugee, grateful US citizen and founder of a successful engineering consulting company. It is also a portrait of the life of a dedicated American

---

1   *Refusenik.* 1) A person in the former Soviet Union who was refused permission to emigrate—in particular a Jewish person forbidden to migrate to Israel. 2) A person who refuses orders or obey the last, especially as a protest. In both cases, our author fits the bill.

patriot, captured in his many experiences in his new country, his attempts to get the rest of his family to the USA, and his growing dedication to his Jewishness, Zionism and the Jewish homeland, Israel. It is also a lucid social and political commentary expressed in a series of letters, articles and personal observations that are often provocative, outspoken and astute…but always penned with a sense of purpose: to awaken, enlighten and fill with hope, even as it acts as a cautionary tale to the moral collision-course toward which modern America may be headed. In this very original series of stories, life experiences, recollections, notes and letters, you'll also find a well-researched and meticulously documented set of socio-political perspectives that cover a period of 48 years, from his arrival in America to the present time.

~The Editors

CHAPTER ONE

A Letter to My Grandchildren

In hopes they will read, understand, question and share with their friends

May 18, 2022

Today, my wife Emilia and I are driving from our North Chicago suburb of Highland Park to the city to have a dinner with our friends, whom we invited to my celebration. It is early in the evening and traffic is heavy. As is often typical of Chicago, we are crawling along—providing time to reflect upon many things, including my journey to America. And as my thoughts drift, they take me to this very day 45 years ago—May 18, 1977. Yes, I am celebrating what happened to me, down to every minute detail: the day I consider the most significant in my life, my second "birth day"—the day when I was blessed to be let out of the Soviet Union, to set my course to the "Free World," and to finally be given a chance to begin my second life.

What my life in Russia had been and why I left it behind, what I was looking for, and my observations of the old and new surroundings—these are a few of the things I will attempt to address as a part of my message to my grandchildren and their peers, and to all the readers who, I hope and pray, will find in this written offering something of interest. And if I accomplish my goals at all, it will also serve a second purpose: as a jolt to the conscience, a challenge to perceptions and ultimately a piece of writing worthy of the readers' time.

I am not a professional writer. Regrettably, I've never kept diaries or daily journals. Still my life is, and has been, a complicated mosaic pieced together with memories both indelible and acute. I put them in place with the sting of passion and as an act of love. So it will be, that on these pages, I will try to paint the mural of my journey of eight-plus decades on planet Earth, as I recall, as best I can, the events of my life from my memory as well as with the help of available records kept by others—beginning in the USSR and ending in the USA and Israel.

Originally, I had chosen to put my story in a letter format, especially since I have always found that kind of literature—in the form of fragments written by others—to be the writings that contained the most credibility, sincerity and accuracy of expression. But as times change, and circumstances with them, this book has become something of a hybrid.

So, whenever I find I have a moment to reflect upon my life, my first reflex is to flashback to May 18, 1977, and the point when I was finally permitted to leave the place where I was born and lived for almost 40 years: Moscow, the capital city of the USSR. Today, you know it as the capital of modern Russia. But then it held a different significance, one that was doubtless more sinister and imposing in our lives. Even as we lifted off from Sheremetyevo International Airport on that spring morning, I felt the pall of uncertainty about where my journey would end, until I reached that inflexion point where I'd finally breached Soviet air space and was soaring over Western Europe.

So, there I was (and there we were) on May 18. 1977. An early, sunny morning, in mid-air aboard Aeroflot Flight 129 from Moscow to Vienna, when I heard the words that seemed like a dream, as the gentle voice of a female flight attendant came over the loudspeaker and announced: "Please fasten your seat belts. We'll be landing in Vienna in 20 minutes."

Then it happened, just as she finished, that phenomenal feeling of decompression, of the air being sucked out from the place where I had been sitting for the last three hours. I was literally gasping for air (but in such a wonderful way; in that convergence where hope and fear collide, just as your dreams come true.) And so the thought struck me at last: *Am I really landing outside and out of reach of the Soviet Union? Am I at last, and for the first time in my life, truly free from its grasp? Who am I, and what was the Soviet Union I just left behind? How can I explain it to anyone who's never experienced it before? Was it truly, as Churchill once described, "A riddle wrapped in a mystery inside an enigma?" Or was it something far more sinister, dire, corrupt and utterly misunderstood?*

In an attempt to overcome the fear of uncertainty, I kept telling myself that in order to be free I had to release myself from that environment of daunting serf mentality ingrained in the Russian psyche, or so it seemed, from the beginning of time, knowing that if I had remained in the USSR for the rest of my life I would have, as I had witnessed for so long, become numbed by my own constant sense of oppression and lose my humanity.

The great Russian writer Fyodor Dostoevsky once observed, "The final measure of humanity is the ability to love." The opposite of that was what I was seeing unfold before me. In his book *1984*, George Orwell described the ideal (totalitarian) Communist society when he said: "If you want to see the future, imagine a boot stamped on a human face forever."

Whether it was Joseph Stalin or Leonid Brezhnev in charge, the basics of the Soviet system I knew would remain intact. So, I took a page from *Exodus* when Moses went to Pharaoh and said (after 400 years of slavery), "Let my people go." (I could not free all Soviet Jews, but for that brief window in time, I had found a way to free myself...so I seized it with all my heart. *Carpe Diem* Boris Dragunsky!) It was a leap of faith I simply had to take.

What would it really be like, this nation where I now sought sanctuary: America? The USA! This standard bearer of freedom to the world! I asked myself the rhetorical question: Is this the beginning of an end for me? Or the end of a beginning? (If it was to be half as good as I'd always hoped, it would be Heaven on Earth.)

When one is conditioned, as I had been for virtually all my life, learning what it is like to be free was easier said than done. With this freedom would come a responsibility, something called Citizenship 2.0. As I arrived on US shores, I vowed two things then and there: 1) to be the best American I could be, and 2) to someday tell my story...so that others will know that freedom is a two-sided coin whose flip side is the danger that it could be lost at any time. Citizenship requires a constant vigilance that John F. Kennedy once used as an expression of faith in us all: *"Let every nation know, whether it wishes us well or ill, that we shall pay any price, bear any burden, meet any hardship, support any friend, oppose any foe in order to assure the survival and the success of liberty."*

When I finally arrived in America in 1977, it was—despite its well-publicized political differences—as the Pledge of Allegiance described it: "One nation, under G-d, indivisible, with liberty and justice for all."

Over the years, however, I have seen this country that I love become a nation divided into rival camps where reasonable people—center right or center left—have become caught in a power struggle between extremes. The question then for all of us becomes: "Where do we, as individuals, draw the line?" Which is more dangerous to our nation: intense nationalism and a desire, however misguided at times, to preserve the "American Way of Life?" Or a new "Woke" America where the Cancel Culture is working on a slow erosion of our freedoms? Is America still, as promised, "The Land of Opportunity?" Or are we on our way to becoming a place where mediocrity has replaced meritocracy and we sponsor and support villainy in the name of the false spring of equality; where excellence has no reward and vile actions have no consequences; where gangs rule Chicago streets and roving bands of looters wreck the city of Portland, Oregon; where America under Presidents (like Obama) make nuclear deals with rogue nations like Iran, even as it turns its back on proven allies like Israel (as we did in the UN in 2017)? Are we a nation of laws and traditions, or one where the rules no longer apply to all of us—where debts are not paid, obligations not met, and a responsible citizenry with a love of country has been replaced by those who consider entitlements a birthright and universal Socialism the wave of the future? Is freedom of speech still a sacred covenant protected by the First Amendment? Are we at risk of losing our Democracy altogether?

For me this moral collision course is not an aberration, but a foreshadowing of things to come.

What I have done in some recollections, thoughts and letters that comprise the rest of this book, is address that debate and what I believe has become our most pressing moral dilemma as a nation and for western civilization itself. I do so, not to create even further division, but to set down warning signs for us all: it is the act of the true citizen, not only to inspire, lead, and motivate, but also to question, challenge, and be a moral conscience for the nation that we love. Loyal opposition is not a meaningless term, nor is civilized debate.

In so doing we must constantly remind ourselves, as President Ronald Reagan once did: *"Freedom is never more than one generation away from extinction. We didn't pass it to our children in the bloodstream. It must be fought for, protected, and handed on for them to do the same."*

That is what I hope to do with this book: offer a perspective from an adopted American son who has seen both sides of the coin, one that is still spinning—one that, unless we keep our heads, might easily come up tails.

~ Boris Dragunsky

CHAPTER TWO

Born in the Storm

"Russia is a riddle, wrapped in a paradox, inside an enigma."

~ Winston Churchill

One of my early memories that stayed with me forever is the recollection of holding my mom's hand in the crowd standing outside the freight-like car of a just-bombed train and watching the panic that ensued. This was our failed attempt to leave Moscow and avoid the Germans after the Nazis invaded the Soviet Union in June of 1941. As the Wehrmacht was advancing toward Moscow, my mother had arranged last-minute passage on a train for us, along with her parents and sick sister to evacuate farther East in the country, as far as we could get from the death and destruction of daily combat. But war was already at our door and also at our throats, because soon after we left Moscow, our train was struck by low flying Luftwaffe planes. I clearly remember the train cars next to ours catching fire and the terror we all felt at the proximity of such death and destruction.

Somehow, we were lucky and managed to return to my grandparents' home on the northern outskirts of Moscow, where we anticipated every knock at the door was going to be coming from German hands. Meanwhile, as the Luftwaffe bombed our city, I recall seeing skies filled with the lights of anti-aircraft projectors...even as one of the bombs fell on a nearby streetcar rail, resulting in a piercing sound-effect that left my caught-outside grandpa Solomon concussed and deaf for a while. I also somehow remember the conversations within the family about our next-door neighbor, an active

Communist at the train terminal who resided in a rather dirty home, who all of sudden was putting a lot of effort into washing and painting his place. He explained by saying, "Germans are tidy people." He apparently wanted to be ready, just in case.

Fortunately for us, the Wehrmacht troops were pushed back by the Red Army before they made it to the city. They were first sunk in the heavy rains flooding the unpaved roads into Moscow and then frozen to death in an early winter—one of the coldest on record.

My other memories take me to hospital surroundings. I was just over two years old and about to have my arm amputated. I had cut my right forearm on rusted barbed wire and it had become infected, swelling to three times its size. There was no such thing as an antibiotic in sight. Penicillin had just been invented in 1941 and was still in experimental stages in the United States. (It didn't come to the USSR for another seven years.)

"There's nothing more we can do," the doctors told my mother, "It looks like gangrene is setting in. So, we recommend amputation. Otherwise we can't guarantee his survival."

Presented with this Solomon's dilemma, my parents decided to take a risk. For the entire year that followed, I underwent a series of operations that finally saved my forearm, wrist and hand...but not without consequence. For the next several years, I was plagued with a crippled right hand and presented with certain limitations as to the way I was able to negotiate my surroundings. But children are adaptable and quickly learn to navigate the world that they are given. The same cannot always be said for adults, as the world around them hardens.

My father, Zalman, came to Moscow in his twenties and labored to the best of his ability to support his mother, father, three brothers and a younger sister still living in Svyatsk, a small village situated in the borderland where Russia, Ukraine and Belarus formed into a triangulated territorial corner. Like most men, Zalman was drafted into the Soviet Army at the start of the German invasion called The Great Patriotic War. Shortly thereafter, he was shipped off as a grunt to the Eastern front to fight in Manchuria, in what was then the anticipated campaign against the Japanese.

My mother was the bedrock and breadwinner in our family during those long four years, taking care of her parents, her handicapped sister and me. This involved a daily search for basic food, with the even hard-to-get potatoes being our main staple. In a year or so, my memory brings to mind having on our table such things as condensed milk and canned stew meat (not necessarily a viable kosher combination). They were delicious to my youthful palate! The latter two were of American origin and came to us obviously as complements of the US's Lend-Lease Act. My indulgence in the sweet American condensed milk during my childhood later became a reliable source of a decent income for American dentists.

Other things I learned early on were matters for discretion; things to be kept under the radar, if they were mentioned at all. One of them was our Jewishness. The word Jew was whispered within the family and among other Jews, but by the society we lived in it was only used in a derogatory context.

TASS (the Soviet News Agency) had convinced us all that spies were omnipresent, and turning in anyone suspicious to the authorities was patriotic. We saw it happen often enough, though the reasons were often unclear. Several people from our neighborhood were interviewed at the NKVD,[2] and shipped off to the GULAGs or worse, nevermore to return.[3]

During that time, my mom Sonya was the one upon whom all of us relied—just as Joseph Stalin was our leader *(Vozhd)*, our Dear Comrade General Stalin (commonly known in America as Uncle Joe) our paterfamilias, our bulwark against all evil in the world. There he stood in newsreels and print, our man of all trades, General Secretary, Premier, Commander in Chief: Joseph Stalin (*Stalin* being a Russian pseudonym for steel), square-jawed, prominent mustache, a look of determination in his cool cerulean gaze, pipe smoking, standing erect, a tower of power, ever-attired in his modest trade-mark tunic (Сталинка). Later he would hold his own with Churchill, Roosevelt and the other heroic free-world leaders of World War II, as they met in places like Yalta, Teheran and Potsdam, and came to critical concords about how to finish off the Nazi hordes. How could we not feel a comfortable certainty with this man? For most of us, Comrade Stalin had been the only

---

2   NKVD. Russian Army Secret Police from 1931 through 1946. It was renamed by the MVD (and MGB) run by Lavrenti Beria until 1953—basically the same organization with a different structure reflective of current leadership at that time.

3   The term, *GULAG,* is a Russian acronym which translates into English as "State Directorate of (Correctional) Camps." The GULAG system consisted of over 30,000 camps located primarily in remote areas (mostly in Siberia) and used as a slave labor force.

national leader the Soviet people had known for nearly 24 years, counting by the time WW II had come to an end.

(And for a little boy of my tender years, he was a superhero. For us he was like Superman, Batman and Captain America all rolled into one.)

In a point of historical irony, the entire Bolshevik Revolution, the appeals to the peasantry and workers in the cities, the establishment of communes and all that they implied were so embedded in the Russian character that it was virtually impossible to extract the man from the way of life. For nearly a thousand years, the average Russian peasant had been so entirely inculcated into a serf mentality that anything resembling personal freedom was a concept that eluded them entirely. The language of their servitude might have altered slightly, but it was still the same old game: one of repression, poverty and lack and worse.

Once the war ended, and the German/Japanese Axis powers surrendered and we emerged victorious, our troops came marching home with honors and parades in Red Square. My family believed, or was led to believe, that the dark curtain that hung over us during the war-time years would be lifted. But no such period of relief was to follow.

Of course, I had no other points of reference, no contrast at an early age. This was the only world I knew, my dark reality: nothing for a young child to endure, but children are resilient. Later in my youth, this resilience was replaced by education—and exposure to new ideas alien to the teachings of Marxism-Leninism and the Communist Manifesto. My Mother Russia was a place of dread—of hideous retribution, of poverty, lack, and brutal reprisal for the slightest of offenses. Soon enough, our beloved Father Comrade Stalin turned out to be a Hydra-headed monster of repression, one who'd designed a terrorist state unprecedented in world history. One with spies everywhere—lurking in every nook and cranny of our lives.

Stalin's Russia (1924–1939) — The Backstory

Even today—unless you're a diligent student of history—few people in few nations in the world know how close this planet came to complete domination by a pact between Nazi Germany and the World Communist Movement epitomized by Joseph Stalin's Union of Soviet Socialist Republics (reconstituted out of blood, torture, political sabotage, assassination and show trials of all his opposition). It was called the Molotov-Ribbentrop Pact and it would have reversed the course of world history had it been permitted to fulfill its course of shared power and mutual non-aggression.

To archivists of political records, to superficial historians and victims of selective memory Adolf Hitler's Third Reich, its blood-lust for world conquest, and its carefully structured pogrom against European Jews combined to grab all the headlines, taking most of the blame for World War II and the dragon's share of the calumniation in the annals of Global Villainy! (That is precisely how Stalin would have wanted it…and in some ways he had a hand in spinning that perception.)

In fact, the ideological mosaic constructed in the USSR prior to World War II is far more complex, sinister, and dire than anyone might imagine. A bit of backstory is required to provide a better understanding of the pandemic of political insanity that gripped the pre- and post-Depression Era of the 1930s.

To summarize, Russia (the name most often used to identify first the Russian Empire and later the Soviet Union) in a nutshell: Up to and even through part of World War I, Tsarist Russia under Alexander III and the Romanovs was still a feudal empire and arguably the most backward nation in Europe. With the most deeply imbalanced social structure in the newly industrialized 20th century, it was still controlled by royals, nobles, and a few rich industrialists who rode roughshod over a deeply downtrodden mass of city dwellers, repressed union workers and peasant farmers, virtually all of whom were still *de facto* serfs, chained to the land they tilled and toiled on for the duration of their otherwise underprivileged lives. All this and more was "red meat" for proponents of Karl Marx and *The Communist Manifesto*: an idealized portrayal of a socialist state where the people (in a happy network of communes) controlled their own destiny. The irony in all of this is that Socialism, by definition, is a form of government where the state controls *everything*: ergo—as expressed in its darkest potential—the very manifestation of Statism.

Originally in the idealized worlds of Marx and Engels, the philosophy had tremendous mass appeal, especially among intellectuals and political idealists. Given the folly of World War I, a useless war started by a quarrel between a bunch of old guard royal houses of Europe, any new political system carried great appeal.

So...Why the History Lesson?

That's what I wondered when I first started writing this chapter, and then I realized that author George Santayana was right: "He who does not learn from history is doomed to repeat it." As Gallop poll found:

- As of 2025, only 54% of Americans are more positive toward Capitalism than Socialism, down from 60% in 2021.

- Socialist sentiment is increasing among younger generations with favorability among Generation Z at 49%.

- Over a quarter of Americans (26%) support the gradual elimination of the Capitalist System in favor of a more Socialist State with a surge in support among younger generations (31% of Gen Z and 35% of Millennials).

- 18% of Gen Z and 13% of Millennials think communism is a fairer system than capitalism and deserves consideration in America.

- 39% of Americans are likely to vote for a Democratic Socialist (as it proven by the recent mayoral elections in NYC and Seattle), with the sentiment increasing among younger generations.

- Only 53% of Gen Z and Millennials believe the Declaration of Independence better guarantees freedom and equality over the Communist Manifesto.

- Democrats are the only partisan group of the three that views Socialism more positively than Capitalism (66% to 32%). Independents are modestly more pro-capitalism (51% vs 38) while Republicans are overwhelmingly so (75% vs 14%).

To all this and more I have to protest: **"What perversion of logic is driving you to come to these conclusions? "**

Please read the rest of this book and educate yourself before it's too late!

After the Russian Revolution in 1917 and the rise to power of the more radical Bolsheviks in 1919 after a bloody Civil War, Vladimir Lenin emerged as our nation's version of George Washington, and Premier of the newly formed Union of Soviet Socialist Republics (USSR). A spiritual disciple of Karl Marx, Lenin was the intellectual inspiration of the new socialist/communist regime. But by 1921, his early mandates such as 8-hour workdays, guaranteed primary education, redistribution of land to the peasants and universal suffrage had been gutted or made more severe by the Bolshevik-inspired Left Communists who thought his reforms were too mod-

An idealized portrait of Vladimir Lenin, circa 1923

erate. Served by a large Politburo of possible heirs, Lenin, though only in his fifties, was already a man in fragile contact with this life, much of this due to the poor medical practices of the era.

Having barely survived an assassination attempt in 1918, he still struggled with lead poisoning from bullets left in his body. These caused a slow-leaking sepsis that doubtless had catastrophic effects on his system.

By 1923, he had already endured a series of strokes that left him barely able to speak, prompting him to make fewer and fewer public appearances. During that time, Lenin had come to rely on his newly appointed Secretary General, a young soldier of the Communist revolution named Joseph Vissarionovich Stalin, whom he looked upon as a dull but loyal keeper of the flame.

Born in Georgia in 1878, Joseph Stalin came from a poor cobbler family and was often a sickly child; but one with a pugnacious disposition. Fighting his way through school he showed great promise as a student. He even studied for the seminary and planned, at one time, to become a priest in the Eastern Orthodox Church. Joseph was also a journalist, as well as a political idealist, who innately understood the power of propaganda. He learned this when, for two years, he was editor of *Pravda*—a small Communist Party newspaper at the time.

Unlike some of the superstars in Lenin's central committee, Stalin had actually tasted hardship, and had gotten his hands dirty in the fields and undergone reprisals in the form of two prison sentences, including one three-year fatal banishment to the work camps in Siberia in 1915 for his political activism, which included bank robberies and extortion as means of fund raising. Pulled out for military service in the Russian Army in 1916, Stalin was disqualified as "unfit for active duty" due to a withered arm that had crippled him as a small boy growing up in *Gori* (Georgia).

A tiger in so many other ways, Stalin gained Vladimir Lenin's confidence early on as a central figure in the Bolshevik struggle for the soul of Russia during the Civil War (1918-1921) and earned a reputation for work ethic and a devotion to the cause once the revolution was won and the Red Russians finally took over the country. Despite becoming Lenin's strong right arm, Stalin (never the warmest of figures) was looked down on by the shinier members of the Politburo, and it was only at Lenin's insistence that he was allowed to keep his post.

After a year of severe illness, paralysis and mental diminishment, Vladimir Lenin died from a fourth stroke in January 1924, leaving his inner circle, including various protagonists who engaged in the power struggle to become his successor: alongside Stalin were Leon Trotsky, Lev Kamenev, Alexei Rykov, Nikolai Bukharin, Grigory Zinoviev, and Mikhail Tomsky. Of them all, at the time of Lenin's death, Stalin might have easily been considered out of favor. This was especially true since, only a few weeks earlier, he had resigned as General Secretary as a gesture of apology but had been reinstated immediately by Lenin himself for offenses considered too trivial to be of merit.

This had been very much due to the fact that Lenin's wife, Krupskaya, loathed Stalin to such a degree that (with the help of Trotsky and others) she apparently forged and published a dictum attributed to Lenin condemning Stalin as a vulgarian, "too crude, tactless and blunt," and otherwise undeserving of party leadership of any kind. (All qualities Lenin, while he was alive, had been willing to overlook, but his death left Stalin visibly short of allies.)

Among the successors, only Grigory Zinoviev shared a close personal history of mutual hardship and a legacy of trust with Stalin. Meanwhile, Lenin favorite, Red Army founder and hero Leon Trotsky especially looked down upon the "stodgy bureaucrat" from Georgia, viewing him as unworthy of either concern or any modicum of respect.

To their peril in 1924, the other members of the Central Committee voted to allow Stalin to stay on in his post as Secretary General, where he would be taking on the dirty business of running the day-to-day operations of the newly formed Soviet government, military, communes and secret police. At the time, this title was not that of the nation's leader. That fell to Lenin's heir-apparent, Alexei Rykov, who assumed Lenin's mantle as Chairman of the People's Commissars of the USSR, and de facto Head of State. It was a role he officially held until 1929, even though he had long since lost all leverage inside the party to Stalin, who was a master at disenfranchising all his opponents, until all power—from the military to the treasury to the secret police—resided with him.

It was also in 1924 that Stalin formed a governing Troika with old friend Grigory Zinoviev and Lenin favorite Lev Kamenev. They were to be the power base that would temporarily run the USSR until new elections could be held—but these elections ultimately never took place.

In the midst of all this jockeying for position, two philosophical factions formed. One with Stalin, Kamenev and Zinoviev at governance, and the other, a Left Opposition, was headed by Leon Trotsky, Mikhail Tomsky, Alexi Rykov and others. To provide a picture of how radicalized the new Russia had become, The Left Opposition, led by Trotsky and Tomsky, felt that the Stalin-Kamenev-Zinoviev Troika had become too Capitalistic, too statist and economically pragmatic in their structure. Instead, they wanted the New Communism to radicalize even further with little or no centralized power, a loose confederation of committees, and a mission to convert the rest of the world while ignoring issues at home. (This was a flawed position from the get-go and Stalin knew it.)

Born of a very wealthy Ukrainian Jewish family, Leon Trotsky was a true aristocrat, a social scion, and something of an intellectual snob. Commissar Trotsky, a military hero of the Bolshevik Revolution and an early protégé of Lenin, was also still something of a show-pony for USSR foreign relations, and became the traveling face of the Soviet Franchise, while leaving the Stalin-Kamenev-Zinoviev Troika behind for what he believed would be an inglorious end.

Acting as the Soviet Union's Foreign Minister in principle, if not in fact, Trotsky hobnobbed with European dignitaries, made passionate speeches, wrote articulate expositions of Marxist philosophy, charmed the public at

Portrait of Leon Trotsky, circa 1919.

Classic photo of Soviet Premier Stalin, 1941.

large and remained one of the most popular figures in Russian politics…all of which had absolutely nothing to do with the establishment of a genuine power base inside the Kremlin.

Meanwhile, he left Joseph Stalin behind to keep the cult of Lenin alive, while made sure the name of Vladimir Lenin became even more closely linked to his own. Lobbying to rename Petrograd, Leningrad, it was Stalin who became the architect in principle, if not in fact, of Lenin's Red Square Memorial in Moscow.

It was Stalin who advanced the aspect of Marxism known as Leninism, and it was Stalin who slowly, relentlessly and ruthlessly assumed total control of the Politburo's Central Committee and, through that, rule of the Soviet Union by systematically eliminating any viable competitors through a series of token elections, uncovered "plots," arrests, show trials, "suicides," assassinations and executions over the next 12 years. All of that left him the de-facto supreme leader of the Union of Soviet Socialist Republics.[4]

Beginning with treating the Left Opposition as a dog-whistle to Communist Party hardliners, Stalin carefully conspired to eradicate all threats to his personal power. He even turned on his old friends and allies like Zinoviev, until there was no one left but him…and a Central Committee populated by toadies, sycophants and cronies.

---

4   In fact, only Leon Trotsky—out of the country at the time the purges began—remained at large, in exile, and perpetually hunted down by Stalin's assassins, fleeing from country to country with a price on his head. Something he managed to do successfully for over 15 years…finally being hatcheted to death in Mexico City in 1940.

By the late 1920s, Joseph Stalin had assumed absolute control of the Soviet Union, a conglomerate of socialist republics that he governed with an iron fist. He followed up with two badly failed Five-Year Plans, viciously crushed a peasant rebellion and established arguably the most elaborate and insidious spy system in the modern world, which included infiltrations of some of the major nations of Europe, and especially the Roosevelt administration in the depression plagued United States of the 1930s.

While cultivating and charming what Lenin had frequently referred to as "useful idiots" among socialist intellectuals in America and Europe with cocktail parties and warm and fuzzy tours of "showcase" communes replete with happy workers and Kommissars with sunny dispositions, Stalin had implemented a behind-the-scene terrorist state unequaled in modern history.[5]

Nothing epitomized this more dramatically than his cultivation, expansion and fortification of the Soviet Secret Police.

Known as the NKVD (*Kommissariats* of Internal Affairs), this small but elite group of enforcers had been originated by Vladimir Lenin after two assassination attempts on his life, as a kind of Russian Praetorian Guard. Joseph Stalin saw it as something else entirely: a well-trained, draconian control mechanism populated by his handpicked henchmen and purblind loyalists.

During Stalin's rise to power in the 1920s the NKVD was expanded ten-fold, both in size and authority, until it became the military/political trip-hammer by which he tyrannized an entire nation. Although the NKVD might logically be compared to the Gestapo inside Hitler's Third Reich, there was really no comparison. The Gestapo's repressive tactics—though ruthless and terrifying—were mostly conducted with surgical precision against Jews, homosexuals and Communist seditionists inside Germany and its acquired territories. (This was nothing the average German citizen, and especially Nazi party members, had to fear. This was what the Nazis were selling, but was nowhere near the truth.) On the other hand, under Stalin, the NKVD was an equal opportunity oppressor and a statist bludgeon under which no one was safe. In both theory and practice it became the hammer depicted on the USSR's hammer and sickle emblazoned flag.

---

5   Vladimir Lenin was once famously quoted as saying: "Whenever we wish to advance The Cause (of world Communism) we can always find 'Useful Idiots' in the West to help us."

Starting as early as 1925 with arrests and imprisonment of political opponents with its broad-sweeping show-trials, sham three-man (troika) panels and often mysterious deaths of key party members, the NKVD became nothing more than Stalin's personal secret police, his *own* Praetorian Guard, and an extension of his will. As such, it came to be known for its brutal repressions and draconian punishment of everyone—from influential Soviet Jews to defective Commune Leaders…to anyone who published even a paragraph critical of Stalin or anyone who could be suspected as a critic, to disgruntled factory managers, to progressive trade-unionists, or anyone anywhere who muttered a single sentence with even a hint of doubt about the Stalin regime.

All it took was a rumor, innuendo, a cross comment or anti-communist inflection—and people disappeared! Informers were rewarded. Dissenters were disappeared…and their families threatened, brutalized and watched. They were brought into NKVD headquarters for questioning, or placed before troika panels and sentenced to work camps in Siberian GULAGs, or subjected to torture and imprisonment and worse: some were simply executed without ceremony. Neither infrequent nor isolated incidences, these were matters of wholesale repression and state terror with victims numbering in the millions—earning for Joseph Stalin a reputation as arguably the most paranoid dictator in world history. (If you're looking at pure body-count, no one—not even Adolf Hitler—comes close.)

In the moment, and seemingly in perpetuity, Stalin had done a masterful job of combining positive party propaganda with statist control and terror, so much so that the rest of the world came to perceive him as the opposite of who he truly was. So iron-clad had been Stalin's grip on power that by the mid 1930s he was looked upon worldwide as the consummate "strong man," both respectable and popular among the world leaders of that time…except for the rare few political observers who understood the true subtext of the totalitarian nightmare—The Great Terror— he had created.

By the late 1930s—after disseminating the old and sometimes skeptical of him communist cadre, killing a third of the Communist Party members and more than half of the Central Committee—only one obstacle remained to challenge Stalin's strangle-hold over the Soviet Military.

One of the mind-boggling questions I asked myself for many years while still living in Moscow was: What in the world possessed Hitler and the Third Reich, while still fighting the British and not able to break them, to start a war against the Soviet Union? _is was a nation with a population three times that of Germany and territory 33 times larger. It spanned eleven time zones, and had a military (on paper) three times the size of the German Army, Navy and Luftwaffe combined. Only when I came to the West and had access to records discovered and described by American and European historians was I finally able to understand what actually motivated the Nazis to make such a bold and fatal for them move.

In the restructured USSR of 1937–38, a dichotomy had arisen: Joseph Stalin had carefully constructed the largest and (on paper) most powerful military in the world. It was populated by a general staff who were fiercely proud, individualistic, and philosophically independent—all qualities the Secretary General viewed as a threat to his authority. To Stalin's way of thinking this particularly stood to reason, since his political adversary Leon Trotsky, a military hero of the Revolution, was still at large. He was in exile, evading demands for extradition, bounding from country to country to country and eluding capture while writing reams of anti-Stalinist exposés and waiting in Mexico for the Supreme Leader to stub his toe.

So, in order to preclude this possible perfect storm, the Soviet Secretary General manufactured a Military-Fascist plot purported to exist among a handful of top Red Army generals, with particular focus on its most luminous public figure, free-thinker, and legendary icon to the average Russian, Marshal Mikhail Tukhachevsky. In very real terms, this would have been comparable to the arrest and trial of superstar US Generals Douglas MacArthur or George S. Patton. Though the charges were entirely trumped up, to Stalin's perverse way of thinking, it was a necessary final step.

Historically, most world dictators have been overthrown by military juntas. So the Red Army's most popular general was the perfect target. Then in a logical broadening of the Great Purge—once Tukhachevsky had been arrested, tried an executed—he was followed by score of other generals who were summarily given sham trials, incarcerated and put to death in the following months. All of this was fraught with allegations of ties to the Third Reich, the Wehrmacht and German high command.

This was trumpeted daily the state-controlled media, and seemed to have fed rather well into Stalin's propaganda machine. For a time, the average Russian may have even bought the ruse. But, to Joseph Stalin's perverted logic, "Too much is never enough." So, he followed up over the next two years with a most ruthless and absurd purge of the Red Army, which involved the court-martials, trials, torture, imprisonment and/or executions of more than 30,000 officers, including the execution of 81 out of 103 of the Red Army, Navy and Air Force's highest-ranking officers. Practically everyone above the rank of major was eliminated, leaving the Soviet military utterly gutted and virtually rudderless. To compound the folly, Stalin reinforced his paranoid need for adulation by populating all the high officer ranks with NKVD operatives, mindless minions, political *apparatchiks* and paramilitary *politruks* whose only talent was indoctrinating the troops with daily inculcations of party propaganda accompanied by a long list of "penalties" should they under-perform—not exactly morale builders for an army that consisted primarily of peasant lads from the communes and lower-class city dwellers who were already under-educated, inadequately trained and poorly fed.

Very few of the original general and admiral corps of the Russian military remained…just enough, it seemed, to provide a global showcase for the Communist cause. Given Stalin's absolute lock on information, little news of his purges ever reached the outside world. So, even to his closest contacts, all appeared to be well.

By force of sheer statistics, the Soviet military—Red Army, Navy and Air Forces—had become the largest and most formidable in the world. On paper, the Red Army had 1.8 million men, compared to Germany's 1.4 million. It had 6,800-plus tanks compared to the Wehrmacht's 2,800+plus, and more than 30,000 aircraft (fighters and bombers) compared to the Luftwaffe's approximately 10,800. A formidable force by any standard of measurement—this "paper armada" appeared to make a non-aggression pact between these two military juggernauts a very good idea. Thus was born the Molotov-Ribbentrop Pact that caused the whole world to shudder.

CHAPTER THREE

"The Faustian Pact" that Almost Destroyed the World

"One Death is a tragedy. A million deaths is a statistic."

~ Joseph Stalin

At this point in history, it is almost inarguable that the Soviet Union under Stalin had been the prime supporter of the repair, redemption and rise of the Third Reich, as exemplified in the wake of the Treaty of Brest-Litovsk. From 1919 on, the newly formed USSR sought to counter the draconian terms issued to entirely demilitarize the German Reich by the Allies at Versailles. They did so for good reasons: First, many European nations including Great Britain and France were terrified by the violent, bloody overthrow of the House of Romanov in Russia and, as such, politically aligned against the new Bolshevik regime. They even conspired to reverse the revolution as late as 1921.

Second, feeling the pressure of world opinion against them, the leaders of the Soviet Union were looking for allies from every available sector—especially a downtrodden Weimar Republic vivisected by the Treaty of Versailles. They did so through a series of clandestine agreements. Evidence of this took place when the reborn German military formed a secret partnership with the USSR. In 1922, during the unofficial Rapallo Accords, the Germans and the Bolsheviks agreed to restore diplomatic relations. While publicly they were signing economic agreements, negotiations were unofficially underway for mutual cooperation in the development of chemical weapons, air force and tanks, as well as training military pilots and tank crews.[6]

The Saratov Region school of chemical warfare was the most secret Reichswehr facility on Soviet territory. It gave the Germans excellent opportunities to test future chemical weapons in vast open fields, something that would be difficult to hide in a densely populated Germany. Tests at the facility were carried out from 1928 through 1933, and consisted of spraying poisonous liquids and toxic substances using aviation and artillery and the decontamination of territory.

A German aviation school secretly established near Lipetsk, just 250 miles from Moscow, carried out tests of all new aircraft, aviation equipment and weapons. It also trained both German and Soviet pilots—oftentimes together. The planes were purchased by the German Defense Ministry through third party countries via intermediaries and were then delivered to secret German strongholds inside the USSR. The first batch consisted of 50 Dutch Fokker D.XIII fighters that were delivered to the Lipetsk air center in pieces, and German technicians there assembled the planes.

In another secret agreement signed in 1926, the two nations collaborated in setting up a German tank school in the USSR. Situated near Kazan, 500 miles from Moscow, the Kama School operated along the same lines as the other two academies: in complete secrecy, funded mainly from the German side and providing joint training for both Soviet and German tank crews.

From the outset, the Red Army and Air Force high-commands would have known about the future militaristic intentions of their German partners. On the weapons ranges at their joint bases, officers often fired at dummies dressed in Czech and Polish uniforms. German tank prototypes tested in the Soviet Union were carefully designed to fit onto French and Belgian railway cars. German ambitions became even clearer in 1933, when Hitler became Chancellor and accelerated rearmament to unprecedented levels.

Even so, it was an amicable run of cooperation between the two countries that continued until the Spanish Civil War in 1936, where Hitler made a series of aggressive moves to empower the forces of Francisco Franco and

---

6   Ian Johnson, *The Faustian Bargain: The Soviet-German Partnership and the Origins of the Second World War*, 2021

the fascists with men, training and material. Feeling stabbed in the back, the Soviets countered with support of the Republican forces…so much so that it became a major cause of the rift between the two nations—at least until Soviet Foreign Minister Vyacheslav Molotov saw an opportunity to make repairs, and the Molotov-Ribbentrop Pact was proposed as a benefit to both sides.

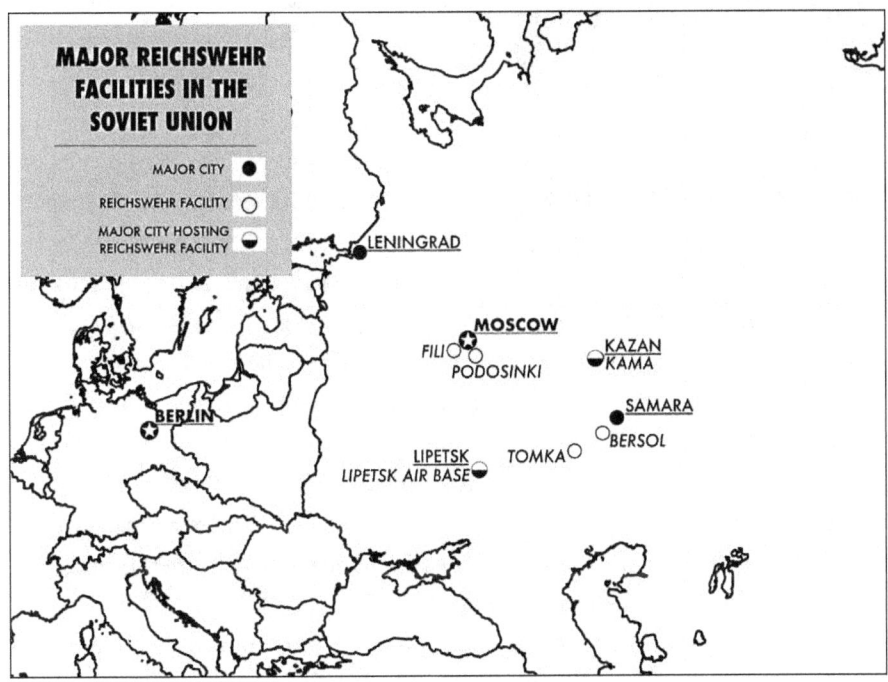

German Military Bases and Training Centers inside the USSR:
Set up in 1922–23.

Acting as Russia's Minister of Foreign Affairs for over a decade, Molotov was an old school Bolshevik with an uncanny knack for survival inside the Kremlin, which was no small feat. He had bargaining skills that might rival those of Talleyrand or Disraeli. Joachim von Ribbentrop, his opposite number inside the Third Reich and a longtime ally of *Der Führer*, had already shown his chops by brokering the Alliance of Steel with Mussolini's Italy in 1938.

Coming first to political and economic accords during the summer of 1939, the Soviet Union and the Third Reich secretly agreed in a shadow arrangement to split much of Eastern Europe between them, leaving little to guesswork and making clear the course of their true malice aforethought.

Under the terms of the Pact, Germany would annex, or bring under its sphere of influence, Lithuania, Czechoslovakia, Eastern Prussia, and Hungary. The USSR would expand its hegemony to encompass Finland, Estonia, Latvia and Romania. Poland would be partitioned between them, with Russia taking the Eastern half.

Although some puppet regimes had already been installed in nations such as Lithuania, most of the other nations in question didn't get the memo. So, the question (in quiet circles) remained, which nation would move first and upon what target?

Buoyed by the fact that Molotov had quite apparently outmaneuvered von Ribbentrop—and the pact would succeed at all levels—Stalin decided, in November of 1939, to test the waters by taking a territorial bite out of his fat, friendly, peaceful

Generalleutnant Mauritz von Wiktorin (left), General der Panzertruppe Heinz Guderian (centre) and Soviet (Jewish) Kombrig Semyon Krivoshein (right) in Brest-Litovsk after the partition of Poland in 1939.

neighbor directly to the Northwest: Finland.

After some dummied-up negotiations that tried to implicate Finland in an act of aggression—a conjuration believed by absolutely no one in the world—the Soviets managed to convince the British and the Americans that it had zero territorial designs on their sparsely populated, largely agrarian Nordic neighbor. By 1939, US President Franklin Roosevelt was so paranoid about the rise of Nazi Germany that he would have believed anything the Soviets told him. So, reassured by Molotov and his own Secretary of State Cordell Hull that Stalin would keep his word, Roosevelt bought the ruse entirely. Even though the USSR ordered massive buildups all along the 1,180-mile border from Leningrad to the Barents Sea. The Finns and their Nordic neighbors knew better and tried to warn the world, but no one listened—absolutely no one at all.

On the surface of it, Finland appeared to be low-hanging fruit. An agrarian nation of 3.5 million people, its major industries were fishing, farming and furniture design and manufacture. Its militia consisted of an army of 150,000 men, half of whom were reservists, made-up of Finnish farm boys and middle-aged retirees, few of whom had undergone more than rudimentary combat training. Finland also had no more than 86 tanks, 320 artillery pieces, 114 combat aircraft, and soldiers were primarily armed with bolt-action rifles dating back to World War I. This was no problem for the Russian Juggernaut massing along their borders with 800,000 Red Army troops, more than 2,200 tanks, 6,000 artillery guns and about

German and Soviet officers going over the spoils of the Molotov-Ribbentrop Pact.

3,200 planes set up to saturation bomb the Finns prior to the invasion.

Encouraged by an overnight invasion and assimilation of Poland with very minimal losses earlier in the year, the Red Army generals believed they could make even quicker work of the Finns. Under the command of old guard infantry General Kirill Meretskov, who somehow managed to survive Stalin's purge, the plan was to launch a *Blitzkrieg*-like assault, using 450,000+ troops and armored personnel to form a spearhead that was supposed cut the country in half in a matter of days (two weeks at the most), annex the lower half, which included Helsinki and two-thirds of the country's population, and install a puppet government.

This would be followed by a 300,000-plus Army of Occupation to keep the peace and pacify the nation. This was to be a mere bagatelle. A piece of cake. A walk in the park. Right…right?

The *Finnish (Winter) War:* **November 1939–March 1940**

Unfortunately for the Soviet military machine, wars are not won on paper. They are fought by men. They are also led by men; occasionally men of genius. Equally, they are also often lost by incalculable acts of folly.

Even at the beginning of his campaign, Kirill Meretskov was aware that much of his Soviet Armada was comprised of raw recruits, who were poorly trained and under-equipped to endure Finland's harsh winters. The problem was mostly one of logistics—getting food, supplies and weapons of war, many of which had not been winterized for the viciously cold Finnish weather, to the men.

Meretskov tried to warn Stalin of the challenges ahead, but Stalin was convinced the real solution to a quick victory lay in more patriotic education into the true Communist philosophy, which was a job for PURKKA, which literally translated stands for Political Administration of Workers and Peasants Red Army. This had become an army of indoctrination within an army, headed by Stalin's favorite hatchet-man Lev Mekhlis, who had enthusiastically overseen his 1937 purges of the military.

Just prior to the Finnish invasion, Mekhlis dropped in with two battalions of *Politruks* ready to slather Meretskov's 7th Army with party propaganda. This meant that rather than training for combat, practicing firing weapons, or getting into good physical shape for the coming invasion, the average Soviet grunt spent his days sitting in a cold classroom enduring hours of brainwashing and being bombarded with threats of reprisals should he fail.

By contrast, the Finns were ramping up for a war they couldn't afford to lose. Every last Finnish soldier—to the man—was trained to be an expert cross-country skier, a superb marksman, and a master of camouflage. From the outset, the Finns were blessed by two things: an early heavy autumn snow, and the leadership of Field Marshal Carl Gustav Emil Mannerheim. A brilliant tactician, and arguably the most gifted master of guerrilla warfare since the Roman General Quintus Fabius, Mannerheim realized early on that he would not have a chance if he met the Soviet war machine with any kind of direct assault. So, he'd simply outmaneuver them.

Setting up what came to be known as the Mannerheim Fabian Line, he rapidly evacuated all civilians from the cities, then kept folding his own army into a motile echelon of withdrawal, allowing the Russian 7th, 8th, 9th and 14th Armies to overextend themselves. They arrived at vacated villages and empty farmhouses and got bogged down in long, snow-bound convoys while Finnish snipers picked them to pieces using winterized rifles, home-made improvised pipe-mines, mortars and machine-gun fire.

Masters of camouflage, the Finns wore winter white and posted on the heavily wooded hillsides. They hid under white cotton blankets and even homemade sheets sewn, often together in strands. To everyone's shock and utter surprise, the Russian Air Forces flew too high over the cloudy winter skies to knock out even one strategic Finnish port or industrial center, and the average Russian infantryman was provided with neither the right winter-worthy gear nor given weapons properly lubricated to be able to fire in the −50°F, Finnish weather.

Finnish Ski Troops during the "Russo-Finnish War," 1939.

As a result, Red Army rifles and machine guns—even their canons—literally froze on the spot. This meant that tens of thousands of soldiers were strung out like long lines of spaghetti stuck in snowbanks with weapons that would not fire against an enemy they could not see. To make matters worse, the vaunted Soviet mobile corps of T-26 tanks proved to be incapable of maneuvering well through the rough Finnish forests to accomplish anything. All too frequently, they got bogged down in the deep snowdrifts and could not climb out. So, they too became sitting ducks (papier-mâché ones at that) to be knocked out by Molotov cocktails and hand grenades.

By the sixth week of the Winter War, Soviet losses were nothing short of colossal. To make matters worse, the foodstuffs that had to be driven by convoy to the soldiers at the front were stranded in the rear near the Russian border. So, by the middle of January 1940, the Russian grunts were starving to death in the field, faced with the dilemma of either freezing in place or advancing on the Finnish enemy, with malfunctioning weapons, in hopes of being captured.

Outraged and offended by his own army's poor performance, Stalin was convinced that the fault lay, not in the logistical and tactical failures Meretskov had predicted, but in the fact that his feckless infantrymen needed more "inspiration." This came in the form of two more battalions of *Politruks* and *Kommissars* flown in to drive the troops ahead, not only by terrorizing them with the consequences of failure, but also with a "do or die" mandate from the Russian Premier himself.

This resulted in one of the worst examples of a Hobson's Choice in the history of warfare. The Russian soldiers were literally prodded to make headlong assaults into the face of Finnish machine guns and sniper fire, as the PURRKA fired machine guns at their feet to let them know they would be cut down by their own military should they retreat even 50 meters. Either that or, in some cases, the soldiers were doused with gasoline and promised that—should they show cowardice and retreat to the Russian side—they would be immediately set on fire by waiting PURRKA agents.

The Russian advances from that point on were so brutal and self-destructive that the combat and skirmishes along the Mannerheim Line were like a shooting gallery…with the Finnish snipers and gunners wiping tears from their eyes as they beheld the fate befalling their adversaries. Photos of Russian soldiers staggering toward Finnish positions like lost children, covering their faces in anticipation of being shot, soon became fodder for the Nordic press who published them for the rest of the world to see.

This also led thousands of Russian soldiers to realize that no matter what horror stories they had been told about the brutality of their Finnish captors, they stood a better chance of living if they surrendered to the enemy. Once they did—to their shock, awe and ultimate relief—they encountered Finnish hosts who were both compassionate and humane. Told they would, upon surrender, be tortured and then executed, many Red Army infantrymen asked if they could have "at least one decent meal" before they were shot.

Realizing the Finns had no such intentions for them, and that they were to be housed in warm billets, given blankets and fed—the Soviet soldiers started surrendering in droves. Some even sought political asylum, while others, learning they would not be shot, asked, "Could you at least shoot them?" referring to the *Kommissars* and *Politruks* who had driven them forward like cattle, using both death threats and distortion to get them to perform.

This story was possibly apocryphal but persisted as gallows humor and spread throughout the war. So complete had been the decimation of the invading Red Army that by the middle of February 1940, the Finns had either won every battle or left the Soviets with hollow victories and virtually without spoils of any kind. Plus, by the middle of March, Soviet casualties had been recorded as 126,896 killed, more than 88,000 wounded, and another 35,000 captured, with scores defecting every day.

As the cherry on top of Stalin's brutalization of his own military, the bulk of the 30,000-plus Red Army prisoners who returned to the USSR were given a hero's welcome in the summer of 1940, including a parade in Red Square and medals of valor for what was suffered at the hands of the enemy. They then summarily vanished from public view. To the man, they were secretly arrested, tried by sham troikas for treason, cowardice and worse, and were later shipped off to military prisons or to work camps in the GULAGs. Once there, they disappeared forever, never to return.

To make matters worse—no matter what the final outcome—Finland had already won in the court of world opinion. Volunteers from Sweden, Norway and Romania came pouring in weekly to enlist in the Finnish Army, which was now surfeit with abandoned Soviet tanks, machine guns, artillery and other weapons of war. Practically every foreign government had condemned Stalin's naked aggression, and even Franklin Roosevelt, whose administration had, by then, become peppered with Soviet agents, denounced the USSR as a force of evil to rival that of Nazi Germany.

So complete had been Russia's humiliation—recorded daily in the international press—that it threw Stalin and Molotov into a panic that prompted the reinstatement of whatever remained of his general corps and most of the high ranking Red Army officers who were in prison or awaiting trial.

Once Stalin decided to give command to old reliable Soviet Marshal Semyon Timoshenko, the Red Army finally started winning enough shallow victories, like capturing abandoned villages and empty farm houses, to mark some visible, if superficial, progress. Timoshenko at least displayed enough common sense to order the Soviet Air Forces to saturation bomb Finnish cities, which got them to the negotiating table by the end of March 1940.

Even though the USSR finally won a negotiated peace and managed to bite off a small portion of southeastern Finland, the aftermath of the war for the Soviet Union had been nothing short of catastrophic.

Stalin's reputation as the leader of a super power and imposing military force was, by the middle of 1940, irreparably damaged. Now exposed outside the USSR as a brutal dictator, as foul as any in modern history, the Soviet Secretary General also had to face the fact that his once-vaunted Red Army, Navy and Air Force was a fallible, bloated relic, badly in need of restoration before it was too late. But in many ways, it was already too late. The ripple effect from the Winter War carried on for the next two years and opened the door for the Third Reich to spread its territorial reach.

Although the Molotov-Ribbentrop Pact superficially held together until June of 1941, Adolf Hitler and his General Staff were already licking their chops as they realized that their Russian ally's military had been proven feck-less, fraught with distension, and corrupt to the core.

Map of Nazi Germany superimposed on that of the USSR, a "nation" 33 times the size of its attacker. Artwork and design by Simon Blaustein [my grandson].

With the United States still politically "paralyzed" and sitting on the side-lines, Nazi Germany launched a relentless campaign of *Blitzkrieg* (lightning war) against a dozen nations, from France to Libya, while bullying others into paper alliances and setting up Nazi party leadership, propaganda centers, and military strongholds from which to finish off all other opponents of the Third Reich and the cult of National Socialism. That now included the Union of Soviet Socialist Republics—and what still remained, far and away, the largest Armed Forces in the world.

Operation Barbarossa: The War at Our Doorstep!

As early as the spring of 1940, the momentum of World War II had entirely shifted in favor of Nazi Germany. With a gutting of the British Army at Dunkirk in June of that year, followed by a rapid defeat of the French (including an outflanking by legendary General Erwin Rommel of the archaic Maginot Line in just two months), the Nazi German high command was flush with a nonstop run of victories and feeling, perhaps justifiably, invincible.

By that time, the Soviet Union's Red Army and Air Forces had been knocked out of commission and were in the process of regrouping and reassessment. In fact, in the fall of that year, the USSR was demoralized and ripe for a quick strike invasion. Rather than listen to many of his top Generals, Hitler decided instead to bring Great Britain to its knees—and to the negotiating table—by a series of air and sea blockades followed by day and night bombing of strategic military bases and factories.

Wars are fraught with both egos and villains, and Hitler's No. 2, Hermann Göring, felt that his vaunted *Luftwaffe* needed to flex its muscles even further. He convinced *Der Führer* that the Brits could be bombed into submission by attacking English cities. After all, his *Luftwaffe* had a superb flight command of state-of-the-art bombers and fighters that enjoyed a 5 to 1 numbers advantage over the British. Since, prior to Churchill's taking over as Prime Minister, the British had been almost embarrassingly pliant at the negotiating table, Göring and Hitler *et al.* thought that day and night bombings would finally finish them off. So, they created a kind of aerial *Blitzkrieg* to pummel them into submission. This could all be done by air, of course, while the German Army's Generals planned a full-force ground war against Russia in the coming weeks and months—a good idea in theory.

They set about saturation bombing England, 24-hours a day, seven days a week for nearly four months. The Blitz stiffened British resolve, leading to a depth of patriotism that was a model for the world. Add to that the fact the RAF had quickly populated its Hurricane and Spitfire fighter corps with additional combat planes and that the British pilots were superbly trained to fly, and the *Luftwaffe* suddenly found it had more than met its match. With 20% of its combat pilots now coming from other countries like New Zealand, Poland, Canada and Czechoslovakia, the RAF decimated the *Luftwaffe* in a series of areal combats, picking its bomber force to pieces. These attacks left only remnants of the German air force and it never fully recovered.

Commonly known as the Battle of Britain, this two-month areal sortie over the English Channel, the coast of France and the white cliffs of southern

England is still looked upon in some circles as the probable turning point in World War II.

In retrospect, that assessment may have been a bit overemphasized. But there was little doubt that it was Phase One of a Three-Phase set of events that finally did-in the Axis Powers once and for all. The process took another three years, but this was the opening wound. It also created a ripple effect that would literally change the game in how the Nazis conducted the war from that day forward.

First of all, it had dealt a mortal blow Germany's *Reichsmarshall* Hermann Göring's prestige and influence inside Hitler's inner-circle, one from which he would never entirely recover. Second, it exposed an Achilles Heel in the heretofore overpowering Nazi War Machine. Third, it drove Adolf Hitler to a new level of paranoia, one where he felt it necessary to personally take over the day-to-day operations of the war. This act undermined what was arguably one of the most gifted group of military strategists in the annals of modern warfare, and replaced them with a paranoid amateur.

Even so, there are still those historians who would argue the fact that the *Luftwaffe* had accomplished its objectives and the Nazis had truly put their boot on Great Britain's throat when Hitler decided to change directions. His grand idea was to direct all of Germany's military might against attacking the Russian Bear. Hence Operation Barbarossa was born. It was the ultimate thrust of *Blitzkrieg* launched with the largest land force in the history of warfare. At least it looked that way…on paper!

On a Personal Note:
What was Hitler Thinking?

I dwell on this part of history as a great moment of personal discovery for me, because, as I said before, I could never quite come to grips with any sane rationale that would have prompted Hitler and the Third Reich to take such a bold, direct thrust at a nation with a population three times that of Germany, with 33 times Germany's size in territory. This nation spanned eleven time zones, and had a military (on paper) three times the size of the German Army, Navy and Luftwaffe combined. T

This especially defied logic since it had been the Soviet Union that, for the previous 20 years, had been Germany's sole secret sanctuary in the aftermath of its unconditional surrender at Versailles—and the singular nation that had helped it recover its military might. Given the generous terms of the Molotov-Ribbentrop Pact, where the two powers had agreed to mutually partition the rest of Europe to their liking, it stood to reason at the time to leave things as they were. The honoring of that alliance stood—on paper at least—to benefit them both. The answer to the riddle had to be this strange little Winter War against the Finns coupled with the practically beheaded Soviet Armed Forces. It appears it was the stone in the sling that took down the Russian Goliath with a shot.

That was the common perception in Berlin and a classic case of hubris. Historic Russia, with its 8.65 million miles of land mass, 37,000 miles of borders, spanning 11 time zones, two continents and the most unforgiving climate in the world, had always proven to be, "The Graveyard of Empires," since the 6th Century, CE. And so, it would be again—in ways that no one conceived of at the time.

To Hitler's perverse way of reasoning, launching a full-blown military campaign against the Soviet Union was a war of a different kind—more of a crusade and fulfillment of a promise made in his own autobiography, *Mein*

Kampf (My Struggle). But, where Hitler's generals had been masters of strategy and tactics, Hitler was driven by demons of racial ideology and an obsession with ethnic cleansing.

Convinced that there had been a certain level of Teutonic equanimity in fighting the Brits and their allies, Hitler was obsessed with the fact that the Soviets, and in fact all eastern Europeans, belonged to an inferior race of *Untermenschen* dominated by Slavs and Bolshevik Jews, mainly out of Moscow. This fit his Superman (*Ubermensch*) mission to purify all of Europe and create the perfect Aryan race. This mania, along with that of his inner circle, dictated much of his thinking regarding conquered territories and how they should be administered to by his victorious invading corps.

At this point, it is essential to understand Hitler's fixation on the belief that Communism (Bolshevism) was the brainchild of Jewish intellectuals, and that other political philosophy intent on world dominance. Karl Marx, though an atheist who had openly renounced Judaism, was ethnically a German Jew and the grandson of a rabbi. Leon Trotsky, the show-pony for world Communism, was unapologetically Jewish, as had been others in the Politburo. Even Lenin had a Jewish grandfather.

This was never lost on Joseph Stalin for a moment. Though he was disguising his animus against the Jews, Stalin was pragmatic enough to realize that they had become a political inconvenience. Ever aware, *vis a vis* his spy system throughout Western Europe, of Hitler's plans for the expunging of all ethnic Jews, he was careful to appear sympathetic to the cause of Jewry while, at the same time, meticulously removing Jews from all positions of power. This, of course, would not have slowed down Adolf Hitler one bit and had doubtless sharpened the blade for his strategy of attack.

Named after legendary Holy Roman Emperor and Aryan archetype Frederick Barbarossa, the entire invasion took on the flavor of an ideological crusade. Launched in late June 1941, it was strategically appropriate that this would be a summer war, favoring the German's dominant strategy of *Blitzkrieg* on land and in the air to simply overrun the outmatched, less sophisticated Soviet forces in a matter of weeks. (Sound familiar?)

I use the word "outmatched" advisedly because the Soviets and their allies outnumbered the *Wehrmacht* on paper with over 5 million troops massed along its borders from Belarus to Ukraine. The Germans brought 23 armed and armored divisions that amounted to 3 million men, which proved to be more than enough to launch a three-pronged attack and overrun the Red Army at every point of defense.

Preceded by a series of aerial bombardments by the Luftwaffe that demolished 66 Soviet air bases and knocked out nearly 4,000 Red Air Force fighters and bombers, the *Waffen-SS* and *Wehrmacht*

Soviet troops marching in Red Square on their way to the front (Circa 1941).

Panzer divisions and infantry won virtually every battle, overran Belarus and penetrated so deeply into the Ukraine that it had virtually subsumed the entire countryside in a matter of weeks.

The German Army became the superior fighting force for all the world to see, and doubtless the best trained and most ruthless war machine in the history of military combat. The German High Command's task was made much easier by the fact that Stalin and his Communist Party cronies had apparently learned nothing about motivating the average Red Army grunt.

With his general staff and many high-ranking officers back on the job, Stalin had finally seen to it that his troops were now receiving more intensive training and better preparation for battle. But it wasn't enough because the presence of the PURKKA army-within-an-army was still felt everywhere—with party *politruks* still calling the shots and intimidating the troops, promising reprisals should they fail in their duties—and carrying them out to a "T."

This was a contributing factor in the Russian military's continued poor performance. They lost more than 800,000 troops, and even more astounding, an estimated 1.5 million either surrendered or changed sides during the conflict rather than face the certain consequences of their defeat.

Ironically, this also placed a burden on the German Army, since it was totally unprepared to house and feed a prisoner population that size. Even though it tried to honor the Geneva Convention to which it had become a signatory, as many as 600,000 Soviet soldiers simply starved and froze to death in German camps while awaiting relocation.

USSR frontline courts and executions:
Set in place to eliminate perceived traitors and spies.

Nowhere was this felt more severely than in Ukraine, which by every measure received the most vicious thrust of the *Wehrmacht* spear as its *Blitzkrieg* cut through them virtually all the way to Kiev. Of all the members of the hegemony of the Union of Soviet Socialist Republics, Ukraine was most unique because in some ways it was the most Russian of Russian states. As far back as the 10th century A.D. Kiev was, for a century or so, considered the Capital of old Russia. As the centuries wore on, it was also Ukraine that always fought the hardest for its own territorial integrity. As a result, it was traditionally the least trusted and most brutalized of all the Soviet states.

Under the Stalinist regime, it seemed to suffer with the severest kind of oversight of its communes, hardship for its peasant farmers, and harsh *Politruk* governance of its villages and towns. In a sense, this made no sense at all, since Ukraine had been the USSR's breadbasket for decades and also the heart of one of its largest industrial areas. So, strategically it was one of the most important pieces of the Soviet economic mosaic—a fact almost entirely lost on Stalin and his *apparatchik* toadies.

In truth, Ukrainians had been so perennially repressed by their Bolshevik overlords that, in many cases, they proved to be willing accomplices to their newfound German captors. In some cases, victorious *Wehrmacht* regiments were even met by cheers, applause, and occasionally even victory parades by a populace who had, for a brief time at least, come to look upon them as liberators.

But...history and irony are handmaidens to outcome. By now, Adolf Hitler had gone as mad as a hatter and had lost all sense of the political cunning that had so defined him early in his career. Along the way, he ditched the rapprochement with those nations assimilated into the Nazi fold, those with pliant peoples and puppet governments. In place of that, Hitler's ideological goon squad had since resorted to a draconian enforcement of his *Ubermensch* (Superman) philosophy of building a pure Aryan race.

As part of Adolf Hitler's strategy of pacifying all territories conquered in Western Russia and Eastern Europe, he decided to enforce all aspects of what came to be known as *Die Obstplan*. Conceived and designed in secret with Heinrich Himmler, Hitler's *Obstplan* or Eastern Strategy was a methodical process of racial purification that entailed the permanent enslavement of all Slavs and inferior races (termed *Untermenschen*) through forced labor, brutal repression and complete disenfranchisement. This plan also emphasized the ethnic cleansing, i.e. annihilation, of all Jews and people of color.

Pumped up by a nonstop run of early victories that defined Operation Barbarossa, *Der Führer* overrode the advice of his high command and decided to apply a scorched earth strategy to all captured Soviet lands. This meant rather than harvesting the countryside and embracing the locals in Ukraine, Belarus and Central Russia, the *Wehrmacht* were under strict orders to seize all the crops, raze all farm houses, hamlets and communes to the ground and slaughter every farm animal down to the very last pig, cow, goat and chicken—thus leaving the locals to starve and die. (In an ultimate point of incongruity, Stalin had ordered the very same scorched earth policy be enacted on his own Ukrainian and Western Russian provinces. But in many cases, the Nazis beat him to it.)

Nazi treatment of civilians was even more ruthless, driven by the severest kind of ethnic cleansing, especially in Ukraine, Belarus and the adjacent western part of Russia, known for having large Jewish populations. Nazi party operatives and their allies quickly followed on the heels of victorious *Wehrmacht* armies to enact the Hitler/Himmler secret document to apprehend, arrest, torture and execute all Jews on the spot.

This would affect my own family in extremely tragic ways. While most of my mother's family, including her parents, who by that time lived in Moscow, my father's parents, sister and other relatives still lived in the above mentioned Svyatsk, which was caught in the snarl of Nazi occupation in the first months of war. So, it might strike you at this moment that the Dragunsky family living there might very well have been put in harm's way—and you would be right. A vicious tangle of events no one could have foreseen were yet to come. (See Chapter Four.)

It should also come as no surprise that Hitler's scorched earth *Obstplan* was fated to backfire in the most emphatic of ways, turning what might have been a compliant, complicit Ukrainian populace into an army of insurgents that jammed up Operation Barbarossa until it hit the "Winter Wall." A winter that, by a seeming act of G-d, came six-weeks earlier than usual.

It is here that the trope from George Santayana comes into to play: "Those who do not learn from history are destined to repeat it." By every appearance it seemed that the *Wehrmacht* had been ordered to press on, driving forward relentlessly with Moscow as its ultimate objective.

In her remarkable book *The March of Folly*, historian Barbara Tuchman creates a brilliant hypothesis that wars are almost always won, not by strokes of genius, but by those commanders who make the least mistakes. Just as Napoleon before them, the German Army committed the fatal error of trying to drive to Moscow before the winter set in. In a deadly pincer movement called Operation Typhoon, the *Wehrmacht* threw 23 divisions, including 5 Panzer regiments, at three different points of attack, inflicting monumental casualties on the Soviet Armed Forces at the cities of Vyazma and Bryansk. More than 540,000 Soviet troops had been captured and another 600,000 killed in action.

The Germans suffered heavy losses as well—losses in terms of numbers they could not afford. More important, the action took most of the month of October in 1941, and for much of that time the Red Army, motivated this time by a defense of its Motherland, stood its ground; so much so that by the time the Germans broke through to make their way to Moscow, the vaunted *Wehrmacht* was already splitting at the seams.

The logistical cost had become a nightmare, causing Hitler to send in reserves and additional weapons of war. Soon enough, December had arrived...

and with it a bitter frost. The Russian Winter Wall had held, and by then the United States had entered World War II.

It was the same up and down the Eastern Front of Europe. Russia, despite heavy losses, had held the battle lines from Leningrad to Smolensk. By early 1942, the German wins had become Pyrrhic ones, and the war was beginning to turn. The vaunted German Army had frozen in place; it literally had nowhere to go. It had lost all tactical volition and worse...

Meanwhile, in a reversal of fortune, Joseph Stalin had been redeemed. His stalwart stand against the Nazis had met with its reward, certainly among the Allied forces, and especially with Roosevelt and Churchill. Once again restored to prestige, he was showered with modern Lend-Lease Act weapons from the West, including British aircraft and artillery guns, American bombers and fighters, tanks and Jeeps and a host of logistical support, foodstuffs, fuel and civilian aid (and soon their armies would come). He gained all of this, plus a seat at any tripartite treaty between major powers to counter the Axis hordes and once again bring peace and stability to a troubled world. Stalin's early failures, his unspeakable cruelties to his own military, his atrocities against his own people even up to that moment were overlooked.

Politics makes strange bedfellows, as the saying goes. Heroes and villains switch seats. Yesterday's international criminal becomes tomorrow's recruitment poster Marine. So it was with Comrade Joseph Stalin, Soviet Premier, Secretary General of the most influential Communist power with the largest land mass of any nation in the world.

Of course, those perceptions would gradually shift. But at that time, and in all forms of public perception, it was a simpler world: one of patriotism and sacrifice, of heroes and noble causes, of villains to be vanquished, of a Russia to be proud of...and of small boys with big dreams and the whole of life ahead.

CHAPTER FOUR

The Holocaust Reaches Us All

"...Christianity had said in effect: You have no right to live among us as Jews.
The secular rulers ... proclaimed: You have no right to live among us.
The German Nazis at last decreed: You have no right to live."

~ Raul Hilberg (Holocaust Historian & Scholar)

By the middle of 1942, very little of the momentum of global conflict had shifted in favor of the Allies, and the ultimate outcome of the war was still in doubt. Everyone in the game knew the potential for victory was there because the United States of America had entered the war in full. Despite some early setbacks, especially in the Pacific, the full force of this industrial giant was already being felt. By this time, and due to the pure dynamics of logistical abrasion, Nazi German Army forces (aka the *Wehrmacht*) had hit a proverbial wall of ice on the Eastern Front.

The Soviet Army, even though it had won no particular individual victory, by standing its ground was nevertheless managing to wear the German juggernaut down in what amounted to a classic war of attrition. Stalin had gone overnight from being looked upon as an international villain to being regarded as the symbol of steely resistance against the Third Reich.

Stretched to the breaking point from its defense against Operation Barbarossa, the USSR was instantly bolstered by the formation of the Atlantic Charter and the oft alluded to Grand Alliance that included the Big Three

(USA, Great Britain and the Soviet Union) plus China. Since no one believed that China, under the shaky dictatorship of Generalissimo Chiang Kai-shek, would be able to make its influence felt in an all-out conflict against Japan, that left the Big Three to hold down the tenuous alliance signed onto by a handful of imperiled governments in war-torn Europe and nine countries of South America.

Even in amidst the ravages of World War II and the multifarious compromises often made simply if world democracy as we knew it was to survive, it is difficult to either fathom or comprehend the series of pragmatic compromises made by the British and Americans to accommodate Soviet Comrade General Joseph Stalin.

They did so, knowing fully that this was the same USSR that had signed the Molotov-Ribbentrop Pact with Nazi Germany in 1939. This pact allowed the Soviet Union to invade and gobble up half a dozen nations of Eastern Europe until it hit the winter wall of ice fighting Finland and got knocked back into a sense of reality. It was also the same Stalin/USSR that signed a Soviet-Japanese Neutrality Pact in 1941, giving Japan free reign to attack and invade China, Manchuria, Korea and eventually the USA without interference at any level from the Soviet Union.

(The commonly held theory was that Stalin knew all along that Japanese Prime Minister Hideki Tojo planned to invade the USA at the appropriate time in 1941, and signed the neutrality agreement with Nippon so Russia would not have to come to the aid of America and thus have to fight a war on two fronts. This was a canny and utterly ruthless strategic move on Stalin's part, and one that served him well in the war years to come.)

All these duplicitous moves by Stalin's were either disregarded or buried in the Western press on orders from Roosevelt and Churchill because the new alliance needed Russia to "hold serve" against the Nazis on the (German) Eastern front since the Soviets were at that time reputed to be the Bulwark against the full force of the *Wehrmacht*.

The (Not So) Grand Alliance. Keeping Stalin Happy.

Through Franklin D. Roosevelt's Lend-Lease Act that was given congressional mandate in 1941, the USA agreed to provide a perpetual string of war planes, tanks, heavy equipment, Naval support and raw materials, including aluminum, rubber, petroleum and especially steel to the British and Russian war machines.[7]

The Brits, already stretched paper-thin, tried to supply the USSR as well, but Stalin was hard pressed to look upon their aid—which he considered both inadequate and tardy—as anything but an insult. To Stalin's way of thinking, Russia deserved to be at the top of the list of considerations...and history doubtless proved him correct.

Stalin thought priority number-one among the Allies should be war machines, aircraft and raw materials for his factories. Both Great Britain and especially the United States needed to pump up the volume to meet his long laundry list of requirements if he was going to successfully fend off the Nazi hordes still ravaging his country.

This had also become a time in the world when nations fighting the Axis Powers formed a universal brotherhood of men, and the people of Russia and its Soviet Union were held in high esteem. These were those brave souls whose every need was to be taken into the Allied embrace—they were brothers (and sisters) now daily poised on the point of the Nazi spear, and were the heroes and heroines of daily broadcasts and newsreels everywhere.

Sending his Foreign Minister Vyacheslav Molotov to meet with his opposite numbers in the UK, Anthony Eden, and US Secretary of State Cordell Hull, Stalin was able to remain stiff-necked behind the scenes, while appearing to be both reasonable and congenial. Molotov, a seasoned negotiator, correctly gauged the vulnerability of Eden and the gullibility of Hull and successfully extracted every concession the USSR wanted for both during WWII and after the conflict was over. Hull, an almost egregious Stalin enabler, returned to Roosevelt with a hat full of compromises he felt were necessary to assure the

---

7   The *Lend-Lease Act* was the initiative Franklin D. Roosevelt introduced to Congress in early 1941, whereby the United States would loan a large amount of military equipment, weapons of war, and strategic raw materials to both Great Britain and the USSR for a specified amount of money to be paid back in two phases: 1) at the commencement of the loan, and 2) at the completion of the world war over a protracted period of years. Item 1 was generally "forgiven" at the outset, and repayment of Item 2 virtually never took place. So this turned out to be yet another unpaid marker added to the US national debt in the post-war years. Privately outraged, but publicly reticent, Stalin refused to hold formal meetings with Churchill or Roosevelt until his demands were met. (In Stalin's way of thinking, by petitioning to meet with him, both leaders were showing signs of weakness that he could later exploit.)

Soviet Union's loyalty in the months to come, many of which Stalin didn't even ask for.

Eden was a bit more reserved in his responses, as both he and Churchill had already been stung in the past by this "Devil they knew." Yet both men were caught in-between the reticent, demanding Stalin and Hull/Roosevelt, who were practically falling all over themselves to give Stalin everything he demanded—not only material, equipment and weapons of war but also territories previously obtained from the Ribbentrop-Molotov Pact in 1939. Prisoner exchanges and demands for strategic primacy and installation of Soviet troops in newly won areas of conflict were also approved. This would later include a partition of Germany and of the city of Berlin itself, if and when the war ended in an Allied Victory.

By this time, both Eden and Hull seemed willing to give the Soviet Premier anything he wanted. This act of affiliation was privately looked down upon as a despicable kind of appeasement by Stalin. From this point on, Stalin dismissed both the US and Great Britain as weak an easily manipulated... something he would later set about to prove.

Meanwhile, word of Hitler's atrocities against the Jews, his depredations in Eastern Europe, and his ethnic cleansings were being suppressed by the two most significant world leaders of that time—for two disparate sets of reasons that tended to define each: First had been the body of lies put out by journalists that exaggerated German atrocities during World War I, which were later denounced as pure myth and put a justifiable taint on the world press from which it had not fully recovered during the late 1930s. So, in his way, Hitler was virtually getting away with murder.

Second, and even more paradoxical, had been the fact that by as early as 1941 both British Prime Minister Winston Churchill and US President Franklin Delano Roosevelt had in-depth intelligence at their disposal detailing Hitler and Himmler's plans for Jewish extermination, and indicating they were already underway. Yet both leaders suppressed all press coverage regarding this. Churchill did so through the National Secrets Act, making it treason to reveal any government secrets in times of war. Originally, Roosevelt did it more as a means of personal fiat and for the most cynical of motives—to keep America out of the war.

Suppressing this information was not an easy thing for Churchill, who had especially close ties to the Jews, had expressed tremendous admiration for them, and had been a highly vocal advocate for a Jewish Homeland as far back as 1921. He knew about Hitler's planned ethnic cleansing of German Jews and it had even been witnessed by his cabinet as having shed tears over their fate. In July of 1944, Jewish leaders brought Churchill a horrific account of Auschwitz gas chambers which was smuggled out by two escapees. When asked by General Ira Eaker if he should bomb the camp, Churchill gave it full support, suggesting that it was something Americans could and should do. The US Air Force was in charge of daytime operations while the British were assigned to night bombing.

For reasons known only to him, Roosevelt was a complete contradiction in his treatment of the Jews. On one hand, he had so many Jewish advisors in his Cabinet that his New Deal economic recovery program was often labeled "The Jew Deal" by his political opponents. Yet Roosevelt was also reputed to be a notable closet Anti-Semite, especially where the Jews as a people were concerned. From 1934 to 1941, he lowered all quotas, making it even harder for European Jews fleeing Europe and trying to come to the USA. He denounced the tales of Jews fleeing Germany, Austria and Poland as a kind of typical Jewish whining. He even wanted to invoke professional quota-ceilings for the numbers of Jewish doctors, lawyers and bankers in the US to reflect their percentage of the population (an initiative that failed). So, when he finally had confirmation of the concentration camps in 1944, he ignored all pleas to bomb the train lines, essentially lumping the Jewish problem into the same category as all European refugees of war.

(In truth Roosevelt was caught between a power struggle inside the US Jewish community over the establishment of a Jewish homeland in Palestine… and simply had larger fish to fry—like saving the entire world.)

It is a twice-told tale and yet still has to gnaw at the conscience of any feeling human being when they realize that between 1941 and 1945, six million Jews perished at the hands of the German Nazis and their collaborators. As Elie Wiesel wrote: *"Proud as we are of the generosity that America showed in fighting against Nazi Germany, we are embarrassed and dismayed by its behavior toward Hitler's Jewish victims. Roosevelt's politics were only part of the problem; the rest had to do with the particular mood of the country at that time…"*

The unequivocal opposition to immigration by the US Congress, the near-silence of the Christian church and the burial of the death factories in the back pages by the press—made it painstakingly clear: this open generous country closed its doors and its heart to the European Jews of the ghettos. Even in 1945, after the victory, Roosevelt was overheard saying: "I still did not want to have anything to do with them."

(My own paternal grandfather, grandmother, aunts, uncles and nephews—74 in total—were among the six million who perished. I will come back to this tragedy later in the book.)

By the summer of 1942, the US and Great Britain had suffered massive setbacks against the Japanese in the Pacific. Great Britain, in particular, was logistically stretched paper-thin when it came to the war effort, and had been forced to abandon its troops in places like Bataan and Corregidor, leaving them to starve and die under brutal conditions in Japanese POW camps.

On the other side of the coin, despite General Douglas MacArthur's hasty abandonment of the Philippines and recovery to Australia, the US had used its Navy to rally its position in such places as the Battle of the Coral Sea in May of 1942 and Midway in June of the same year. Both Naval battles, despite heavy losses, did much to restore US confidence and reassert its naval primacy in the Pacific.

Meanwhile, the Soviet Union was beginning to receive massive resources, especially from the United States. From 1942 to 1944, America would send the Soviets more than 11,000 planes, over 6,000 tanks and tank destroyers, and 300,000 trucks, jeeps, amphibious vehicles and other means of military ground transport. Determined to obtain priority for his efforts against the *Wehrmacht*, Stalin received a surprising degree of materiel by mid-1942, much of which he would need for battles where Hitler had decided to make a major thrust at what he considered to be the most significant inflection points...the first being at Stalingrad.

Stalingrad was significant for two reasons. First, it was one of the Soviet Union's three major industrial centers with several factories churning out war machines for the Red Army. Second, it was considered a strategic floodgate to Western Russia that, once breached, would cause the rest of the country to open wide to easy capitulation.

Aware of the role weather played in any further incursions into the Soviet Union, Hitler launched Operation Uranus against Stalingrad and hit the strongest level of Red Army resistance yet. Under the command of Semyon Timoshenko and later Georgy Zhukov, the Russians retreated slowly across the Volga River while exacting heavy German casualties along the way, making sure that the *Wehrmacht* paid the price and that the war dragged on into the winter months where the weather would be the ultimate factor.

By slowly giving ground, the Soviet Army held off the remaining German troops, approximately 650,000 of them, while another 91,000 were surrounded by the Red Army and promptly shipped off to Russian POW camps where they were either executed or left to freeze and starve to death.

In the midst of this, Stalingrad became the USSR's symbol Russian bravery to the world. The Soviet Union, not the US or Great Britain, was now being looked upon as taking the brunt of Nazi brutality and coming out on top, creating a bulwark from which the Germans never recovered.

In truth, in late December of 1942, Stalin (for a change) allowed his generals to apply some innate tactical military genius and launch Operation Uranus, a clever counter-punch that worked to surround the German Sixth Army, rendering them unable to move. Out-manned and out-gunned, *Wehrmacht* commanding Colonel General Friedrich Paulus followed Hitler's suicidal directives to hold the line no matter what the cost. Promised reinforcements that never came, Paulus kept the entire division locked in place to be picked to pieces by Red Army artillery for several months in a row.

By the time the battle had reached its crescendo in February of 1943, Stalingrad became a synonym for bloody conflict. This battle is still on record as the bloodiest in the history of modern warfare. The Red Army lost 1.1 million men. The German Army lost nearly 500,000, with 91,000 taken prisoner, including Field Marshal Friedrich Paulus who refused Hitler's invitation to commit suicide. (Paulus later became an avid anti-Nazi, and taught in Moscow at the Air Force Academy. In 1953, he moved to East Germany.) There were also more than 80,000 civilian fatalities. This was beginning of the end of Nazi military domination.

Meanwhile, in 1942 and early 1943, the Allies appeared to be "nibbling around the edges" of real war with the Third Reich, despite Allied victories such as El Alamein in Libya and campaigns in Egypt and Morocco, cutting off the German access to needed petroleum supply lines. Also, despite the invasion of Sicily and the recapture of Italy and Greece, the Allied forces were still forced to deal with Stalin, who was now in high dudgeon over what he considered a failure to provide any plan to attack Germany directly.

Both Dwight D. Eisenhower, as head of Allied Command, and General Sir Arthur Tedder, as Deputy, knew any direct invasion of Germany in 1943 would be both premature and disastrous. At some point, everyone indulged Stalin's posturing to become the center of the show and he finally agreed to meet in person with Roosevelt and Churchill in Tehran, Iran, in 1943, where he conspired to gain further leverage once the war in Europe was won.

Tehran Conference, November, 1943.
The first of several between Stalin, Roosevelt and Churchill.

The Big Three came to several accords during the meeting in the Soviet Embassy in Tehran in November 1943. Stalin was apprised of the Allied intention to plan and conduct Operation Overlord, which involved a direct invasion of Nazi-held territories in France as a pathway to drive toward Berlin. They also agreed to many other accords, most of which favored Stalin, including Russian hegemony over all territories of Eastern Europe won prior to 1941. This included a partition of Germany that was highly favorable to the Soviets. Stalin's primary concession was to agree to break his neutrality pact with the Japanese once Germany was defeated and victory in Europe was assured. This ended up being something he never had to enact, since the insertion of nuclear warfare and the bombing of Hiroshima forced unconditional surrender by the Japanese and ended any agreed to obligations from the USSR.

Nonetheless, it is fair to note that Stalin held both Roosevelt and Churchill in low regard for their constant solicitations of alliance and willingness to bury Soviet atrocities as an "inconvenient" truth. Wartime decisions can be dicey, and compromises of both morality and conscience are often casualties to achieve desired results.

(It is common knowledge that Churchill had to permit the bombing and utter demolition of Coventry rather than reveal the fact that the Brits had broken the codes for Enigma, the encrypted Nazi language for all military operations. We also know that both Roosevelt and Churchill were aware of Hitler and Himmler's pogrom against all European Jews well in advance of 1943, and that they knew of the termination camps at Auschwitz, Dachau, Treblinka and others but did nothing. Perhaps most egregiously, they also did nothing to stop Stalin's war crimes, including the capture, torture and execution of military prisoners of the Red Army throughout the war.)[8]

The most notable among these war crimes was the infamous Katyn Massacre, where more than 22,000 Polish officers were brought under the liege of Russian overlords in 1940, an act of mass murder against an Atlantic Charter Ally that was revealed in 1945 and never once mentioned by either the US or British well into the 1950s. This was despite the discovery of mass graves filled with more than 5,000 bodies. (This was [conveniently and originally] blamed on the Germans.)

After a blind eye was turned to this, one can only imagine that Stalin must have felt emboldened to commit whatever crimes against humanity he deemed were within his province to act out. (On a personal note, I was a visitor to the site of the Katyn Massacre in 1970. I found it, as did every other visitor there, to still be a monument commemorating Nazi atrocities against the

---

8 The only two non-signatories to the Geneva Convention, dictating mandatory humane treatment of all military prisoners, were Japan and the Soviet Union, both for their own philosophical reasons. For the Japanese, the code of Bushido—death before dishonor—still prevailed, so all forms of surrender were looked upon as despicable. For the Soviets, it was a more cynical point of view. Stalin simply didn't feel it necessary to make any humanitarian concessions to military prisoners of war, since the terms of the Convention required treating them better than he often treated his own troops.

Poles, including the 3,500 Polish officers buried there, when nothing could have been further from the truth. This was yet another example of Stalin's perfect propaganda machine, collateral damage from a world at war and some very cynical *Realpolitk* still practiced by the West.

Later Stalin would find more resistance in the form of US President Harry S. Truman, who proved to be a much tougher negotiator than Roosevelt. It also didn't hurt that he had a new nuclear arsenal to back him up. It is often said that the real Cold War began with the animus between those two men at Potsdam in 1945, and was compounded by the return of Winston Churchill's backbone, demonstrated in a series of speeches that openly denounced Stalin and Soviet expansionism in 1946 as an imminent menace to world peace. This helped to summoned in the Iron Curtain era.

The Saga of David Dragunsky:
The Inception of the "Captive Mind"

In the midst of the brutal years of our Great Patriotic War, years that marked our struggle for survival, some heroes invariably rose to the occasion. They revealed themselves and received both fame and recognition for their courage. One such man was my uncle, David Abramovich Dragunsky: Twice-Hero of the Soviet Union. Yet he was a hero in the tradition of the "Captive Mind."

Famous Polish poet, Nobel Laureate and political philosopher Czeslaw Milosz perfectly described the mentality of a well-placed person in a Soviet Stalinist-type society, regardless his inner convictions in his 1956 book, *The Captive Mind*: "Since I find myself in circumstances over which I have no control, and since I have but one life and that is fleeting, I should strive to do my best. I am like a crab attached to a crag on the bottom of the sea. Over me storms rage and huge ships sail; but my entire effort is concentrated upon clinging to the rock, for otherwise I will be carried off by the waters and perish, leaving no trace behind."

This oddly adaptive mindset is not an easy thing to explain because it is not enacted consciously. According to Milosz, the "Captive Mind" is something that exists in several stages called Ketman: Nationalist Ketman, Ethical Ketman, Professional Ketman, Aesthetic Ketman...seven in all—with various plateaus of rationalization, all of which entail a kind of "double-think" necessary to survive in a totalitarian society.

In the beginning, the tenets of the "captive mind" did not necessarily infiltrate the consciousness of my father's only surviving brother, David. This is primarily because no ambitious young man feels himself to be a prisoner of circumstance.

Much like a tropical fish in an aquarium, the glass walls and floor became his known universe. As was the case for all in Stalin's Soviet Union, there was no other way. So, this was the sole reality he had been given. That in mind, in the beginning, David Dragunsky simply became the best Soviet he could be. As such, like any patriotic man of his generation, he pursued his career with both dedication and passion.

A rising star in the Russian military even from his early days, Uncle David soon became a decorated hero in World War II and a national military celebrity. Known for many accomplishments, my uncle has often been either misquoted or erroneously reported on in Russian journals and foreign publications. So, I think it is incumbent upon me to set the record straight—especially to correct some mistaken perceptions that persist even to this day.

My uncle David Abramovich Dragunsky was born on February 15, 1910 and after completing school in Novozybkov, the closest town to his native Svyatsk, he, following my father (his older brother, Zalman) also moved to Moscow. There, he worked in construction on building sites. His public activity began with joining the *Komsomol,* the Young Communist League, in 1928. This was a key to rising in the ranks as a Communist Party member. As a result of that affiliation, he was one of the *Komsomol* activists sent by the Soviet authorities to rural areas to carry out the brutal collectivization of the peasants known as *Dekulakization.* This misguided class-cleansing was instituted to eradicate all forms of meritocracy from the Soviet socialist horizon and expunge what remained of personal initiative from the collective consciousness of the average Russian.

As a point of reference, thanks to the experiments in private enterprise previously allowed during the New Economic Policy (NEP) instituted by Lenin to save the population from starvation after the 1919 farmland distribution, some peasants were permitted to apply profit-initiatives to their farming practices. This resulted in a significant number becoming, through their own efforts, rather well-to-do people and agrarian initiators known as *Kulaks.*

As an illustration of the innate power of capitalism, within the next 10 years, these *Kulaks* developed a unique class of their own. Unfortunately, they were unaware that their own success had made them targets.

In the mid-1930s, in a slow but relentless reverse of the NEP, Stalin re-established the centralization of government supervision over all farming in the Soviet Union. This entailed the expropriation of farmland, and a deliberate program of social and economic retribution for the mortal sin of making a profit that labeled as many as two million *Kulaks* as "Class Enemies" of the Soviet Union. Stalin somehow managed to make innovation a crime against the state, and ultimately saw to it that the mass of these people were loaded into cattle trains and sent to the work camp GULAGs in Siberia. There, as many as half-million died from cold, hunger, disease and executions within a matter of two years.

So it became part of my uncle's job to take these "fat cat" farmers and rehabilitate them in the only way the Stalinist model of Communism offered at the time: brutal repression and re-education in the most horrible ways imaginable. By any means of measurement, this was not a favorite chapter in David Dragunsky's life, but it was one he carried out with patriotic zeal. He was driven not only by a certain level of blind ambition but also his awareness of the consequences that awaited him if he did not perform his assignment.

While stationed in one of the villages he was helping to "reorganize," my very young uncle met a local woman, fell in love and got married. In an ironic turn of events, this woman happened to be the daughter of an Eastern Orthodox priest. Since, in the world of Stalin's Russia, Eastern Orthodox priests were often discredited as "enemies of the people," my uncle soon received a formal request to have his wife officially renounce her father as a "class enemy." This was something she simply would not do. Faced with this Hobson's Choice, the woman chose leaving my uncle over denouncing her own father and seeing him condemned to the GULAGs to freeze and die.

Shortly thereafter, David officially became a member of the Communist Party in 1931, was drafted into the Army in 1933, and graduated from tank school as a junior officer in 1936. While serving in the Trans-Baikal area in 1938, he participated in the Soviet-Japanese military conflict at Lake Khasan. During that conflict, he introduced a brilliant piece of innovation and technological achievement by ordering his unit tanks to be specially sealed and tightened at the seams, thereby making them waterproof. For the first time ever in the history of tank warfare, his tank battalion crossed the Tanbogatyi River underwater, remaining entirely undetected. This turned out to be the first of many innovative tactics my uncle introduced to the tank battalions under his command. For his role there, and for his remarkable sense of innovation, he received the first of many prestigious awards: The Order of the Red Banner.

From early 1939 until the German attack in June 1941, David studied at the Frunze Military Academy. He began the war as commander of a tank battalion, and then fought near Smolensk and at the battle of Kursk in the summer of 1943. In October of that year, with the rank of Lieutenant Colonel, he became commander of the 55th Tank Brigade. In that post, he participated in battles in Ukraine, including the liberation of Kiev. He was then recommended for the highest honor: Hero of the Soviet Union, but instead received his second Order of the Red Banner award. (The underlying reason for not receiving the higher award was later acknowledged to be because of his Jewish name.)

In December 1943, David was seriously wounded (one of fourteen such wounds he sustained during the course of the war) and, after a long period of recovery/rehabilitation, came to Moscow to visit my mother, Sonya, and me. While convalescing, he learned that both of his parents, his sister and all his other relatives who had remained in Svyatsk had perished at the hands of their Nazi captors. He also learned that his two younger brothers had fallen: one as tank commander and another in the trenches during the defense of Moscow. His older brother, my dad, was stationed on the Far East Front in Manchuria, facing an imminent Japanese invasion.[9]

After being released from hospital, Lieutenant Colonel David Dragunsky returned to his brigade and took part in the liberation of the rest of Ukraine. In September 1944, for bravery displayed at the crossing of the Vistula and in capturing and holding the Sandomir bridgehead, Colonel Dragunsky was awarded the first of his two decorations as a Hero of the Soviet Union.

---

9   Prior to the Soviet-Japanese Neutrality Pact of 1941, the two nations had been in a number of skirmishes and battles over territory in Manchuria, China and Japan from 1938 to 1940.

In the second half of April 1945, Colonel Dragunsky took part in the battle of Berlin, and then his brigade rushed on to help liberate Prague—a "last stand" by the *Wehrmacht* Panzer command in Czechoslovakia after VE Day had already been proclaimed. For his role in those two operations, he was honored a second time as Hero of the Soviet Union and took part in the Victory Parade in Red Square in Moscow on June 24, 1945.

Here comes an interesting and probably little-known page in World War II history: Ending the prolonged combat in Prague where German resistance continued even after the fall of Berlin, I grew up looking upon my uncle David as a Prague liberator. During my visit to Prague, while living already in Chicago, I was proudly showing my wife and our friends the monument of my uncle's tank sitting in the city center on a tall pedestal. Although a number of years earlier while still living in Moscow and being engaged in the risky business of reading contraband books, I came across several lines by Aleksandr Solzhenitsyn, describing the liberation of Prague from Nazis by the so-called Vlasov Army. Being seriously puzzled by this hard-to-believe version, the first chance I got, I quietly confronted my uncle with Solzhenitsyn's denunciatory passages as an obvious anti-Soviet lie.

Letting me finish, he responded with a somewhat self-conscious smile, saying, "The tank window provides a limited field view." ... So, some research after my own liberation reveals the real story, which in no way diminishes Uncle David's bravery, military acumen and hard-earned victories during his 1939-1945 battlefield career. This is just another example of Soviet duplicity, and the first indication that, even then, my uncle was engaging a bit of *Political Ketman*—overlooking the flaws of a Stalinist Russia to focus on his career.

The Russian Liberation Army (ROA), also known as the Vlasov Army, after its commander, Andrey Vlasov, was a collaborationist formation, primarily composed of Russians, that fought under German command during the early years of World War II. Vaslov himself was a Red Army general who had, in an early flash of revelation, become a Nazi collaborator. The first years of World War II he fought in the Battle of Moscow and later was captured attempting to lift the siege of Leningrad. While in captivity, he started to collaborate with the Nazis because he saw their mission of liberating the Soviet Union from the Stalin's dictatorship to be the lesser of two evils.[10]

As the war was ending, Vlasov changed sides again and ordered the first division of the ROA to come to the aid of the Czechs in the Prague uprising against the German occupation, which started on May 5, 1945.

The first division engaged in battle with *Waffen*-SS units that had been sent to level the city and afterwards continue moving on to surrender to the Western allies troops in an attempt to escape the capture by Soviets.

The ROA units, armed with heavy weaponry, fended off the relentless SS assault, and together with the Czech insurgents succeeded in preserving most of Prague from destruction and liberating the city itself.

When the Red Army (my uncle's brigade) finally reached the Czech capital, the city was essentially free of German troops. The Red Army appeared in Prague only once the war had ended, *de jour* and *de facto*.

Due to the predominance of Communists on the new city council, the Vlasov Division was ordered to leave the city. They tried to surrender to the US Third Army of General George Patton, and the majority of soldiers were initially taken into Allied custody by the 44th Infantry Division and other U.S. troops. However, as a part of a previous pact, and in a move that the Allied command kept secret for many years, they were then forcibly handed over to

---

10 *Mass Scale Collaboration* was a result of the German invasion of the Soviet Union in 1941 in the wake of Operation Barbarossa. Since it had already been established that as many as 1.3 million Red Army soldiers surrendered to the Germans rather than face the consequences of failure inveighed upon them by their own government, these two other main forms of mass collaboration in the Nazi-occupied territories were both military in nature. It is estimated that anywhere between 600,000 and 1.4 million Soviets (Russians and non-Russians) joined the *Wehrmacht* forces as Hiwis (or *Hilfswillige*) in the initial stages of Barbarossa, including 275,000–350,000 Muslim and Caucasian volunteers and conscripts ahead of the subsequent implementation of the more oppressive administrative methods by the *Waffen*-SS. As much as 20% of the German manpower in Soviet Russia was therefore composed of former Soviet citizens, about half of whom were ethnic Russians. Another estimated 180,000 volunteers were Ukrainian forces serving with units scattered all over Europe but primarily at the Eastern Front. The second type of mass collaboration included the indigenous security formations (the majority of ethnic Russians) running into hundreds of thousands and possibly more than 1 million (250,000 volunteers in the East Legions alone). "Military collaboration," wrote Alex Alexiev, "took place in truly unprecedented numbers suggesting that, more often than not, the Germans were perceived at first as the lesser of two evils by Soviet Non-Russians."

the Red Army due to a previous agreement between Churchill, Roosevelt and Stalin saying that all ROA soldiers would be returned to the USSR.

As a result, between May and September of 1945, approximately 33,000 men were returned to the Red Army forces, and it was commonly acknowledged that their fate was sealed. In the Stalinist tradition of retribution against dissident members of his own military, they were either summarily executed or sent to the GULAG Archipelago in Siberia, which was also tantamount to a death sentence.

Some Allied officers, who were sympathetic to the ROA soldiers, permitted them to escape in small groups into American-controlled zones in defiance. Later on, I met one of these men who happened to be my client while doing work at the Great Lakes Naval Station in Chicago's north suburbs. That's where it was confirmed to me that, not surprisingly, General Andrey Vlasov and several other leaders of the ROA were tried and hanged in Moscow on August 1, 1946.

Back to the story of my uncle David Dragunsky, and separating legend from reality. I remember that, at the war's end, his Army Commander, General Pavel Rybalko (who later became Marshal of all Soviet tank troops), frequently referred to David Dragunsky as his favorite tank commander. Rybalko, besides appreciating David's service, was a very decent man who also proved to be his protector from the all-too-frequent rants against Jews that went on inside the Russian military. His sponsorship eventually led to my uncle being commissioned to the rank of Major General in 1955. At that time, however, Rybalko's authority and personal prestige proved insufficient to overcome the growing anti-Semitic sentiments going on in Russia as they seemed to accelerate in both range and volume. Apparently, it had been upon Stalin's direct orders that all promotions of Jews in the Red Army be brought to a close, with no more rank advancements allowed.

Thus, it would appear that my uncle, despite being already twice named Hero of the Soviet Union (1944 and 1945) for combat exploits in the crossing of the Vistula and the capture of Berlin, would be granted no more rank advancement, with those advancements now being awarded to lesser men (this meant his promotion to General would be postponed for nearly 7 years). Altogether, Colonel David Abramovich Dragunsky had already won 13 awards during his military career. Despite early denial of his commission to

Major General (the Red Army equivalent of Brigadier), he was one of a very few high-ranking Jewish officers who were retained in the armed forces after the late 1940s.

In the fall of 1945, my uncle enrolled into the General Staff Military Academy and to my delight was housed in a Moscow apartment a short street car ride from where we lived. His arrival in Moscow created quite a buzz among the hero-worshiping youth of WWII Moscow, and came along with many perks for a seven-year-old boy like me.

Before arriving in Moscow, David, like all other senior officers, was given both access and connections to bring back trophies of German-owned properties. The volume and richness of these things was directly proportionate to the rank of the key officers involved. Among my uncle's "swag and plunder" I best remember a roomy gray four-door convertible Mercedes Benz with an additional separate seat in the back that had been plucked from the garage of none other than Nazi Propaganda Minister Joseph Goebbels.

One of my fondest memories as a young boy of seven or so was riding around town in that top-down beauty. This aroused a lot of shock and awe, especially when the battery located under back seat caught a fire in the middle of Moscow's main Gorky Street...

While in Moscow, my uncle received his first of many future public exposures that helped to bring him through the thorn bush of political scrutiny from that of a Jewish advocate and person of conscience to a more complex and controversial figure, rendering his life a continuum of both honor and celebrity.

My uncle's role in Soviet public life was perennially a complicated one. On the one hand, he was not ashamed of being a Jew, as indicated by the fact that he did not alter either his first name or his patronymic Abramovich to something more Russian-sounding. This alone, in the face of postwar Soviet anti-Semitism, was significant. For the Soviet Jewish population, which was constantly under scrutiny, he became one of the main symbols of national heroes. He was only the second Jewish Red Army officer ever twice-awarded the coveted decoration Hero of the Soviet Union,[11] which was comparable to

---

11   The first ever combat veteran twice-awarded, *The Hero of the Soviet Union,* was a Jewish Commander in the Soviet Air Force named Yakov Smushkevich. Originally awarded in 1940, he was later arrested, tried and executed in 1941 for being involved in, "A conspiracy against the Nation," charges later revealed to have been falsified and contrived—all too little too late.

Colonel David Abramovich Dragunsky, circa 1945.

the Congressional Medal of Honor in the United States. Only a total of 101 Red Armed Forces members had ever received it—including the entire leadership inside the Kremlin.

In 1944, David was appointed by the Soviet government to the Jewish Anti-Fascist Committee (JAFC) chaired by famous Soviet actor, Solomon Mikhoels, who was the artistic director of the Moscow Jewish Theater, a prominent actor and the best-ever (according to British sources) King Lear. Throughout WWII, Mikhoels was sent to the United States on fundraising missions, raising millions of US dollars for the Soviet Army. Shortly after the war's end, David proposed to his friend Mikhoels, who was often a guest in our home, that the Committee should concern itself with the mass burials of Nazi-murdered Jews around the country. This project couldn't gain traction with the Soviet authorities and was never realized, even as he revealed his own tragic family history for the first time.

In his letter to the Supreme Soviet he wrote:

> After four years of war, I had the opportunity to visit my native region—my home town Novozybkov and Svyatsk, the village where I was born. …For in my home town the German fascist monsters executed my entire family —74 members of the Dragunsky family in all. But what especially saddened me was that no graves were arranged.
>
> The little bones of my sisters and children are scattered about the fields. Cattle had trampled them. In places they had been plowed under. In a word, all human dignity had been lost. And in the village council there was no list of how many,

or when and who had been murdered…Nor was there even a mass grave to mark their vicious execution.

It's true that, at my insistence, the city fathers of Svyatsk are now taking action, but these facts induced me to write you a letter and raise the question of delegation to the Anti-Fascist Committee the work of setting up monuments for the executed children, old people and women. There are murdered victims of fascism in all cities, towns and villages. And yet there are no graves. Often cattle graze in the fields where human bones are scattered. This doesn't only refer to Jewish victims, but also many partisans, executed children, women, and old people who have neither graves nor their markings.

You will be doing a great and necessary service through such work. The humiliated victims and the fascists' unheard-of degradations will not be forgotten for centuries. It is difficult to forget this four-year nightmare. We must erect fences, monuments, and inscriptions everywhere and show the dates…

At the end of the 1940s, with little support from the local authorities, Colonel Dragunsky personally funded and organized the removal and transfer of the remains of his family members from the murder site in Svyatsk to Novozybkov for reburial at the Jewish cemetery there.

Not surprisingly, many Western intellectuals over the years have argued that assertions of Stalin's anti-Semitism rivaled Hitler's didn't square with the historical records. To prove their point, many of them were stating that, while Hitler never exhibited any sympathy toward Jews and banned them from serving in the German armed forces, Stalin had in fact shown such sympathies by recognizing Israel, allowing arms shipments from Czechoslovakia to the fledgling Jewish state in 1948 and had Jewish high-ranking officers like David Dragunsky in the Soviet army. Although all these facts are true, these intellectuals were missing the reasons underlying these historical records as they appear.

In simple truth, Stalin turned out to be the consummate political pragmatist. If anything, his opposition to Jewry was more based in his early struggles for primacy in the Politburo against the Jewish-Bolshevik cadre led by Leon Trotsky and other Jews to install a power structure inside the "inner circle."

After Lenin's death and Stalin's appointment to Secretary General, these military icons were gradually and systematically undercut, arrested, tried and executed for treason by Stalin's henchmen, including hundreds of Jewish soldiers who, under Trotsky, had been promoted to high-ranking officers. Over his career, another of Stalin's traits was that he was an equal-opportunity oppressor and would crush anyone and everyone—regardless of religious faith or cultural origins—who dared express even the slightest opposition to the party line.

The reason Joseph Stalin was the first state leader to recognize Israel and help her in her 1948 war for independence was not because of his sympathetic attitude toward Jews. Instead, it was because he saw it as an opportunity to get a foot in the door in a Middle East, which was fraught with anti-Soviet ideologies. He hoped to establish a satellite state there and expand the Soviet influence after WWII. Nothing, historically, had proven more inimical to these global ambitions than a Union of Soviet Socialist Republics based in an atheistic state. So, during World War II and especially thereafter, key Muslim nations such as Turkey, Syria and Iran expressed violent opposition to Stalin's Russia. This meant no Arab country in the late 1940s allowed even a scintilla of Soviet presence, no trade was established with the USSR and no Soviet ship was permitted to make any port of call in that region…even to refuel.

On paper, with its Kibbutz approach to building an economy, the original Socialist inclinations of a young Israel had probably facilitated such hopes. These hopes were quickly dashed in the early 1950s with the solidification of the State of Israel and its ties to the West and the USA.

The unexpected, and perhaps divine, serendipity of Stalin's death in March of 1953 saved millions of Soviet Jews, myself included, from what had been rumored to be Stalin's planned expulsion of Jews from Moscow and other major cities to Siberia, where there was meager chance of survival much less a decent life. Stalin's anti-Semitism did rival Hitler's perhaps with the difference of Stalin being credited with destroying 20-25 million lives of Gentiles and Jews alike. Anyone who wants to know more about Stalin's pathological anti-Semitism should read his daughter Svetlana's eponymous autobiography that is, unfortunately, now very hard to come by, but worth obtaining for a clearer portrait of what may prove to be history's most powerful paranoid schizophrenic and the monstrous police state he created. The best evidence I can offer of this would be inside my own family and the constant claw of uncertainty that held us in its grasp—and that included my illustrious uncle, despite his proximity to power.

Later, upon graduating from the Academy in 1949, David received the post of Commander of the 5ᵗʰ Tank Division in the furthest corner of the country, the *Chitana Oblast,* six time zones from Moscow. It was literally out in the middle of nowhere. In his own words: "I was sent as far away as it was possible." Yet, all things considered, this was a promotion.

So, we could easily note, without fear of contradiction, that there were a number of occasions where this Russian Jew, this twice decorated "Hero of the Soviet Socialist Republic," this boyhood hero of some renown, barely escaped the wrath of Stalin and the madness of his inner circle. It was only later, after Stalin's death, that there was a slight return to sanity, if only for a while. Still, life—even for my uncle, and for the rest of the Russian Jews—continued to be kept on a razor's edge. This was something that was never lost on me for a moment in my youth.

CHAPTER FIVE

Growing Up
in Stalin's Russia

"When there's a person, there's a problem.
When there is no person, there's no problem."

~ Joseph Stalin

Although, Germany signed the surrender pact on May 8, 1945, World War II officially ended on September 2, 1945. But in truth, as far as Stalin's USSR was concerned, it carried on virtually under the radar well into 1946 and beyond. Stalin's lust for territory in both Eastern Europe and his desire to extend his political influence over China was an ongoing and often bloody exercise, due to the fact the Red Army was so well-supplied with state-of-the art weapons and raw material provided by the Soviet war industry as well as what came from Lend-Lease Act, and fueled by American coffers, arrived in an endless supply.

By the end of World War II, the Red Army and armed forces in general had swelled to 11.6 million strong. Only the United States had a larger force at 12.5 million, but most of them would return to civilian life within the year.

As it was, the Red Army enjoyed a series of celebrations and most of its soldiers were greeted as heroes, including more than 1.8 million of them who had been prisoners of war. Their fate was a quite a bit different from the regular Russian combatant. Often honored in parades and even awarded hardship medals publicly, they were all either held prisoner or called in for questioning with unpredictable frequency. Many of them were later arrested or sent into the GULAG system where most would freeze, starve and die.

(Stalin was consistent in his lifelong paranoia regarding the Soviet Military, especially POWs. This was best evidenced by the fact that when his eldest son, Yakov, a Soviet Artillery officer, was captured by the Nazis in 1942, Stalin had Yakov's wife Yulia [a Georgian Jew] and their children placed under house arrest for more than a year. It didn't help that Yakov's German captors, once they learned his identity, used him for "photo ops" with the German high command—an issue that infuriated Stalin to such a degree that he refused offers of a prisoner-exchange and left his first born to languish in a German POW camp where he eventually died under mysterious circumstances in 1943.)

All of this was lost on us, especially on a boy like me—a young lad growing up in an atmosphere of victory and commemoration. There were parades in Red Square and celebrations everywhere for weeks in the summer of 1945. As far as we knew, and all that really mattered, was the Soviet Union was victorious, and all our Red Army soldiers were heroes, especially my Uncle David, who returned with the rank of Colonel, covered in medals and loaded with trophies lifted from Nazi households.

The same could not be said of my father Zalman who was drafted in the first days of the war and returned home after serving all four years on the Far Eastern front, purportedly fighting Japanese troops in Manchuria. In reality, the Soviet invasion of Manchuria did not take place until 1945, after the defeat of Germany and until the defeat of the Japanese was a foregone conclusion after Hiroshima and Nagasaki were bombed. Though the actual battles were intense but brief, the Red Army grunts had spent most of their time ramping up and conducting troop movements along the border. Still, my father had experienced his fair share of combat, and it was a vivid part of his consciousness by the time he returned home.

Almost immediately upon his return to Moscow, my father learned from his younger brother David that their mother, father, sister and her children plus more than seventy family members had perished in the Holocaust while they were serving in the Army.

The loss of their family was traumatic enough, but adding to its intensity was what my dad and his brother, David, learned about the specifics of the vicious and unconscionable way they had been dispatched by their Nazi captors. According to further eyewitness accounts—that all the men of the

Dragunsky family had been ordered to dig trenches, and were then lined up in front of those trenches and gunned down, while the women were coerced to stand back and watch. After that, the women were forced to shovel and close the trenches. Many of them were reported to have jumped into those same trenches, and were then shot and buried. All this had been witnessed by the children, who were the last to be executed. Their tiny bodies were later found scattered over the surrounding the woods.

Members of our perished family, except for my father and David (standing on the left). Next to them, two brothers killed in the war: one in a tank battle and another in the defense of Moscow. Sitting: my grandparents and aunt with her family—adults massacred and (some) buried alive by Nazis. Also on the front row: Twin brothers shot by next door neighbor after witnessing the agony of their parents.

We later learned that their executioners had in fact been German allies—mostly Lithuanians—along with active participation by locals, who had readily provided lists of Jews to the Nazis. My father's sister had six-year-old twin boys who witnessed their mother's execution, which left them hysterically crying and running away through the neighborhood. When they approached their home, a neighbor sitting on the stoops of his house next door pulled out his own gun, and with the words, "Don't cry, *kaiks!*" shot them both in the forehead.

While my uncle David had been able to direct his energy toward this tragedy in a constructive way and demand that their deaths be memorialized in the village of Svyatsk in every possible way, my father seemed to internalize his grief. So, his memories of the family had to have been more indelible and left even deeper scars.

I was sensitive, but in my youthful resilience I was able to shrug it off, and continued with my childhood in relatively normal ways. The $64,000 question then had to be, "What was a normal reaction to the horrors in Stalin's post WWII Russia in the late 1940s?"

Bombarded with party propaganda from *TASS, Pravda, Izvestiya* and omnipresent Moscow radio broadcasts, we were always told that there had been bumper crops on Soviet government farms and communes throughout the USSR's breadbasket in Ukraine and Western Russia. This always flew in the face of the realities in the Moscow shops and stores, where food lines were always long and shortages were a common fact of life. Moscow was ten times better than the outlying cities and villages whose residents were flocking to Moscow in search of food staples.

None of this seemed to affect any of the kids my age. We played futbol (soccer) in the fields and ice hockey in the winter, and went to elementary schools where we were bombarded 24/7 with Communist Party propaganda. This was the best of all possible worlds—at least that's what we were told—and would remain so as long as our "Genius Leader" Generalissimo Stalin stayed on as our national *Paterfamilias* and a hero to the world. Even then our dear Comrade General Stalin was the very air we breathed—solid, fearless and intrepid—even in the face of the Cold War that followed on the heels of the world war we had just fought.

Our former allies, the US and Great Britain, had now become the enemy in a serious struggle for world domination. Our expansion into Eastern Europe was explained as a protective measure, with territories assumed as Soviet Protectorates against the onslaught of Western expansion. Now Red China was the Soviet Union's newest and strongest ally. Mao ZeDong was fortified to the gills with Russian weapons and materiel to drive out the capitalist armies of Chiang Kai-Shek and send them off in headlong retreat to the shores of nearby Formosa.[12] This took place in 1949 and was heralded in the Moscow press as a glorious victory for world Communism.[13]

Virtually all of this flew over the heads of my primary school peer group, but not over mine. Even at an early age, I was obsessed with global politics and read, watched and listened to everything I could so that I could learn all there as about the world around me.

Little did I realize I was being spoon-fed (as we all were!) a total body of lies. From my altogether innocent point of view, the Soviet Union was the greatest place to be on the face of planet earth. Comrade Stalin, in our eyes, stood astride it all as a kind of Colossus. I was a died-in-the-wool patriot and would remain so for much of my childhood. However, convictions change in time, and soon enough there were chinks in the armor—little flaws I began to see, even with half-closed eyes.

Jumping ahead, one such crack set in my memory for a long time and it reveals a great deal about the Russian mentality, which I will address later, and stems from the long history of serfdom. While riding a subway train in the winter of 1953, I overheard a conversation between two slightly intoxicated men. One of them was asking the other if he heard of the letter the newly elected American President Eisenhower wrote to Stalin suggesting they meet, apparently to ease up the Cold War tensions. Continuing to show his political erudition, he made a statement with a certain degree of pride, "You see, he's afraid of Comrade Stalin and wants to talk." This was so typical of the Russian mentality—that you would only offer to talk because you're not strong enough and therefore are afraid. If you're strong, there is nothing to talk about because you have no need to affiliate.

Of all my family members, I came to be closest to my Uncle David—and I happened to be his favorite nephew. Even at an early age, when my uncle lived in Moscow attending the General Staff Academy, he would whisk me away

---

12 Formosa, meaning "Beautiful Island," officially became Taiwan in 1949.

13 The under-thread in all of this was that most of it had been funded, directly or indirectly by US Dollars, either channeled through the USSR by means of the Lend-Lease Act or, in the case of Chiang Kai-Shek, by direct US military and economic aid. What it did indicate was, for the next five years at least, China was a Soviet puppet and Mao's "Gang of Five" were all beholden to Comrade General Stalin. As such, China became the crown jewel in the Soviet hegemony…and remained as such as long as Premier Stalin was alive.

with him to enjoy the spoils of his trophies from WWII. Even though there were shortages everywhere, the senior and highly decorated military always had access to things others didn't without apparent recourse. Oftentimes, I was the only one who got to spend time with my famous uncle, and I relished those moments that, in retrospect, were some of the best of my young life.

Later on, while commanding the Tank Division in Transbaikal, which provided him a high privilege on his visits to Moscow, David would stay at the Moscow Hotel *(Hotel Moskva)*, a landmark so famous that its image is still on Russia's most famous vodka label: Stolichnaya.

Uncle David often managed to garner a roomy suite and invited his family and friends along to partake in some of the very generous portions of hard to get foods, libations and other spoils accessible to military heroes such as he.

We had a saying even then: "Success equals Access"—especially to the good life as others knew it. My uncle David and his high-ranking comrades certainly had it. All that time enjoying contraband goodies from all those other countries, I couldn't help but notice that—other than our world-famous vodka and caviar—all of the really delectable, classy, and comely things we ate, drank, took-in or wore came from "degenerate capitalist nations"—the ones that were supposed to be impoverished and struggling to survive.

Belgian chocolates, French wines and cheeses, furniture from Finland, autos, record players, and dazzling toys from the United States—all these wondrous products and more were something of a culture shock, especially since we were inculcated daily with propaganda that it was our own Soviet Union that had become the economic beacon to the world. And yet…and yet there we were enjoying this assortment of imported items while the general public stood in lines to get basic staples—from bread to vegetables to a decent pair of shoes.

Even our prized Telefunken radio had been made in Germany, and was, by design and function, clearly superior to any comparable piece of electronics made the Soviet Union.

Secured for us by my uncle, the shortwave Telefunken radio was my most cherished personal pride and joy. I found ways to listen to it every chance I got, much to the consternation of my parents. The *Voice of America* broadcast was jammed by Soviet networks, but the music from a dozen different nations managed to filter through the Russian media net, filling our heads with things like jazz and other forms of popular American music.

A Telefunken Shortwave Radio, circa 1948.

Modern music of all types was considered wastrel offshoots of Capitalistic societies in the Cold War-era Soviet Union. We were told that all forms of jazz, from Modern to Dixieland, ragtime, dance bands, even country swing were Capitalist tools meant to seduce the unwary into degenerate lifestyles and slovenly behavior, robbing us of initiative and virtually stealing our souls. Despite the fact that jazz was once an accepted art form in the Soviet Russia of the 1920s and '30s, it had taken a downturn and was now on the blacklist of items banned by the Soviet Ministry of Culture. Paradoxically, while the musicians from black ghettos such as Louis Armstrong, Ella Fitzgerald and Charlie Parker were considered to represent a bourgeois art form, aristocratic composers such as Mozart, Beethoven, Vivaldi and Tchaikovsky represented working class art.

The one exception that comes to mind was that of a black actor/singer/artist named Paul Robeson. Robeson, a Rhodes Scholar and All-American football player, was also a highly vocal supporter of Communism and the Soviet Party Line. Although never an official member of the American Communist

Party (CPUSA), Robeson made regular trips to Russia all the way into the late 1940s. He befriended many Soviet artists and directors, including cinema pioneer Sergei Eisenstein.

Noted for his performances of *Othello* and the lead, Porgy, in *Porgy and Bess*, Robeson openly declared his love of Russia, and often expressed his admiration for Joseph Stalin himself. "Here, I walk for the first time as a man and an equal," Robeson once proudly announced. "Something I have never had in my own country." In 1952, Robeson was even awarded The Stalin Peace Prize for his loyalty to the cause.[14]

Other art forms such as foreign movies were fed to us on a selective basis, and films like *The Grapes of Wrath*, depicting impoverished dust bowl farmers, were allowed to slip through the media restrictions. This was especially true of any that were penned by noted Communist screenwriters lauding the party line, such as *Song of Russia*, *Three Russian Girls* and *Mission to Moscow*, which was praised by FDR in 1943 because it showed bonds of cooperation between US and Russian forces. The only other films allowed were ones that showed the oppression of blacks or strikes and unhappy workers.

Nevertheless, there were those "gems" that revealed a different world—one filled with happy families, prosperity and open societies. Those were the ones that, even then, whittled away at the lie, the false narratives sold by *Pravda* and the party propaganda machine.

One of my favorite experiences with friends my age was watching Tarzan movies, starring Olympic Gold Medalist Johnny Weissmuller as Tarzan the Ape Man and Maureen O'Sullivan as his American princess, Jane. For some reason, Tarzan movies (over a dozen of them removed from the German archives with no need to pay royalties) were allowed by Soviet propaganda filters because, by some strange process of Communist party logic, they were

---

14 In late 1948, Paul Robeson got his first dose of reality during one of Stalin's purges of intellectual Russian Jews when he returned to Moscow to find that many of his "artist" friends had been arrested and imprisoned, and his dear friend Solomon Mikhoels had been "mysteriously run over by a truck on the streets of Minsk." Later, back in the USA, Paul Robeson himself was ordered "not to leave the country" by the House Un-American Activities Committee (HUAC) and held under virtual house arrest for nearly seven years—where he was not allowed to perform or travel outside his own city of Philadelphia. Even then, even in his later years when Nikita Khrushchev came out with his revelations about Stalin, Robeson refused to believe the stories, remaining a loyal Stalinist, all the way to the end.

considered to be degenerate depictions of Western Capitalist culture, where evil white hunters slaughtered animals and abused downtrodden African tribesmen. Tarzan, of no known nationality, appeared as the symbol of the underdog and as a kind of superhero and object of praise.

The logic of it still eludes me, because one of the most popular Tarzan movies I remembered was *Tarzan's New York Adventure*, where they traveled from Africa to visit his paramour Jane's family in opulent downtown Manhattan. Jane, the wealthy daughter of a New York plutocrat, brings her hubby Tarzan with her. He ends up chasing down the bad guys by leaping from skyscraper to penthouse roof-gardens to lavish hotel suites. These looked like lovely places to live, replete with servants, lavish furnishings and elegant meals—especially when compared to the typical dwellings in Moscow and other Russian cities that were stodgy, cramped communal apartments with clusters of families sharing a single bathroom.

Not surprisingly, having a shortwave radio and listening to foreign stations was considered seditious. Nonetheless the spare parts for such radios were common black market staples. Still, those clandestine radio shows were highly popular and practically everybody who could afford a radio was listening, despite the possible consequences. Somewhat stupidly fearless as a child, and stubborn by nature, I listened as often as possible, almost to the point of obsession. I was so infused with the joy of variety found in all the foreign programs that I heard that I couldn't help myself.

It particularly unnerved my parents that I was so drawn to such dangerous habits. Even then, on a daily basis, the adults spoke in hushed tones. This was especially true in Jewish families, where the elderly resorted to conversing in living Yiddish, so that the children, even if they overheard, could not understand. Everybody lived in dread of detection.

Children, by nature, possessed no filters and would repeat whatever fell upon their ears, out of innocence perhaps, but it was dangerous nonetheless. Without question, I was often admonished to never speak about my exploits or about our "treasured device." But the temptation was always there, and children loved to brag.

The WWII British Naval trope about "loose lips sinking ships" had taken on a deeper meaning in Stalin's Russia—all the way through and after World War II. It seemed to intensify even more once the Cold War had set in. Many a family had been punished or even disappeared due to a careless comment or two. Any whisper of dissent or social commentary or criticism of the status quo might net a visitation from the omnipresent NKVD.

This often prompted public expressions of adoration for our beloved *Iosif Vissarionovich Stalin* and rhapsodic satisfaction with the regime he'd created. So effusive were these moments of open praise that they became a matter of daily fare. It was also fodder for satire, and yet satire was a dangerous thing, indeed. Anyone who dared have a bit of fun at the government's expense might soon find themselves losing their jobs or worse—riding on a cattle train to a GULAG far-far away.

I remember a story that was widely circulated in Moscow relating to our famous Moscow Circus (*Tzirk*) and its very popular clown famously known to all as "The Pencil" (aka *Karandash*).

This short, tiny, funny fellow was adored by adults and especially us children and, as such, was a man of considerable fame. The Pencil once appeared before an always full house—half of whom were youngsters—sitting on a gigantic mound of potatoes. Seizing upon that moment when his assistant came out and asked why he happened to be sitting on potatoes, his answer was, "The entire city of Moscow is sitting on potatoes." Everybody understood exactly what he meant, because there was nothing to eat but potatoes. Since there were apocryphal reports by *TASS* of record crops from Soviet farmlands, but there were shortages in the stores, this blatant bit of misplaced satire infuriated the authorities.

This was especially dangerous since, from the time of the Bolshevik revolution, the Moscow *Tzirk* had always been a point of pride in the way of wholesome family entertainment. Special skills and high-wire acts of men on the flying trapeze from all corners of the country would gather at the *Tzirk* to provide a full afternoon of feats of skill, comedy and magic. This was supposed to be putting forth what was best about the Soviet social system.

In using this party propaganda forum for his personal political platform, The Pencil had risked all by openly defying the powers that be. Not surprisingly, within a matter of days he was placed under arrest, and only his national fame and the adoration of one of the Party bosses saved his life.

Despite all attempts to keep the news of The Pencil's disappearance out of the national press, a firestorm of gossip filtered down to the children of Moscow, where it traumatized us all. Yet I took it all in stride as long as I had my diversions. These included romps with my Uncle David whenever I had a chance to see him—riding around in his trophy cars that he kept stored in a small corrugated steel building next to our apartment in Moscow's outskirts.

This proximity to my hero uncle also covered me in some protective aura in my school, where Jews were often bullied and mocked for the sin of being Jewish. I was occasionally picked on as well, but not as much as the others. I was often paid the left-handed compliment, "You're not like other Jews." Still, it never escaped my notice that people were always reluctant to mention in public of the word *Yevrey* (Jew), since this word wasn't a part of the normal Russian vocabulary and was only used in a derogatory context.

Speaking of my uncle, in those years immediately after WWII, I saw him so proudly Jewish that, going against advice from others, he kept his middle name, Abramovich, clearly visible to the world, including military and political circles.

In 1947, as Israel struggled to have an independent nation in the Middle East, Colonel David Dragunsky wrote an open letter in which he described himself as a Jew who was happy about the USSR's support for the establishment of a Jewish state. He stressed the significance of the latter for the Jewish people, and very pointedly made a point to honor the many Jewish victims killed during the World War II.

As I mentioned before, David had, for years, been a close friend of Solomon Mikhoels, and several other actors of the Jewish theater. He occasionally brought them to our home on Monday evenings when all the theaters traditionally went dark. Dinners were always prepared by my mom, who was a passably accomplished cook. Special foods were often brought in *vis a vis* Uncle David's access to hard-to-get commodities.

Then, one cold snowy winter night, my uncle arrived at our home in Moscow and immediately pulled my parents to a side room for what seemed like a very long time. In a while, they emerged from their private cabal with expressions of grief and horror on their faces. What marred them from that moment on was the inside news that Uncle David had just learned— news he had chosen to share at his own peril: On January 13, 1948, Solomon Mikhoels had been struck down at high-speeds by an unidentified truck, and left to die in the snowy streets of Minsk. Solomon's only apparent "sin" had been his role as a highly-visible leader of the Jewish community—a community that Stalin had recently decided to dismantle and destroy.

Given the hit-and-run nature of the accident, there was absolutely no doubt that Solomon Mikhoels had been assassinated, apparently on Stalin's direct orders. This was something later revealed by his daughter, Svetlana, who remembered having entered the room just in time to hear the Great Leader on the telephone enthusiastically approving: "Yes, a truck accident…"

Typical of their hypocrisy, the Soviet authorities pretended their dismay and arranged a public funeral for the famous actor and patriot. Neither my uncle nor my parents believed the official version in *Pravda*. Worse, they were forced to face the prospect that something dangerous for them might well be on the way.

Within few a months, the only Jewish theatre ensemble in Russia per se was ordered closed. Three years later, during the *Doctors' Plot,* Solomon Mikhoels and his Committee were red-flagged in the state-controlled press as American, British and Zionist spies, who had plotted to overturn the Soviet system.[15]

With Mikhoels already dead, his associates were subsequently marked, arrested, interrogated and prosecuted over protracted periods of time. This all took place as a presaging of events—handwriting on the wall, if you will, predicting the chain of events to come. (Perhaps Stalin sensed in advance that his brief romance with Israel was headed for a breakup, and would officially be given its *coup de grace* once its charter was granted.)

Comrade Stalin's Dark Agenda Fails:
Turning Israel into a Soviet Satellite!

It can be said without fear of contradiction that very originally the Soviet Union was one of Israel's advocates in the Middle East, partly because the USSR's relationship with most of the Muslim nations there had hit rock bottom. Even more important was the fact that the original economic and political structure of the nascent Jewish state appeared to be highly Socialist—even communist in structure. Its system of kibbutz collectives and communal farms throughout the country appeared to Stalin to be cookie-cut carbon copies of

---

15   Doctors Plot. A fictionalized conspiracy, and pivotal point in the history of Stalin's Russia, which we will cover shortly.

those established by Lenin back in 1921. (Could it be, he had to wonder, that Israel was on a socialist economic trajectory that would somehow complement his own?)

To counteract an ongoing Arab boycott of the USSR, Stalin had shown such sympathies as recognizing Israel's autonomy, allowing arms shipments from Czechoslovakia to the fledgling Jewish state in 1948.

Let's start with recognizing Israel. All historians agree that Israel's creation is owed more to U.S. President Harry Truman than to any other leader. Truman declared himself to be like Cyrus the Great—the ancient Persian ruler who restored the Jews to Jerusalem from Babylonian exile. But truth be told—everything we say about the Israel's sponsorship by Truman we can also say about the contributions of Stalin, only his were done so earlier in the game… and for very different reasons.

Yes, the American delegation voted for the partition of Palestine, still under British mandate in November 1947, only to reverse itself in March 1948, declaring partition impossible and replacing it with the proposal of temporary UN trusteeship. Just days before the British withdrawal from Palestine ending their mandate, American top diplomats warned Jewish leaders against declaring independence. At the same time, Stalin ordered the Soviets to not only vote for partition, but also to be the first to recognize the state on May 14, 1948 *de jure*—all while Truman, as a matter of historical record, recognized it later on the same day.

Stalin's decision and the motives behind it still remain a mystery because it wasn't made out of any measure of sympathy toward the Jews, evidenced by the fact that, in their milestone summit meeting at Yalta in February 1945, Stalin pointedly described the Jews to President Roosevelt as: "middlemen, profiteers and parasites."

Leading Soviet expert George Kennan called the partition of Palestine "favorable to Soviet objectives of sowing dissension and discord in non-Communist countries." Even Shmuel Mikunis, Secretary of the Israeli Communist Party and later a friend of my uncle David, while staying Czechoslovakia in early 1948 received a call from Stalin's future successor Georgy Malenkov, authorizing him to continue mobilizing the Eastern European volunteers for the Jewish struggle in Palestine.

A truck with the face of our Beloved Comrade General Stalin at the Labor Day Parade held in Tel Aviv on May 1, 1949.

At the time, the Israeli insurgents were struggling, not only against the local Palestinians and other Arabs from Jordan, Yemen and Syria, but also against Great Britain, which was still the occupying power and, as such, vehemently opposed to an independent Jewish state.

With the Cold War already brewing, Stalin saw in this nascent struggling nation a potential lever to the Middle East, one that might politically align with him. So, while Israel struggled to establish an independent state, Stalin wanted to appear to the world to be their steadfast friend. One of the ways he did this was to send an ongoing supply of remnant German and Czechoslovakian weapons, ammunition and vehicles to the Israelis to aid in their long fight for freedom. Soviet Ambassador to the United Nations, Andrei Gromyko, was also one of the prime advocates for the State of Israel to be granted its charter.

Russia's sponsorship to the United Nations to establish a Nation of Israel created a "false spring" for every Russian Jew—in fact for every Jew in Europe— and made Stalin the man of the hour in the Soviet Jewish community.

Then a sudden, sinister paradigm shift occurred.

On October 4, 1948, Golda Meir, newly arrived in Moscow as Israel's first ambassador to the Soviet Union, showed up at the capital's Choral Synagogue on the first day of *Rosh HaShanah*. The State of Israel had been declared less than five months earlier.[16] As pointed out earlier, the government of Joseph Stalin had been the first country to officially recognize this new nation. This awareness triggered a phenomenal event right in the heart of Moscow—one that shook the USSR and Stalin to the core.

"Instead of the 2,000-odd Jews who usually came to synagogue on the high holidays, a crowd of close to 50,000 was waiting for us," Golda recalled in her memoirs. "For a minute I couldn't grasp what had happened or even who they were. And then it dawned on me: They had come—those good, brave Jews—in order to demonstrate their sense of kinship, and to celebrate the establishment of the State of Israel." Yet, local Jews had been warned to keep their distance from the Israeli delegation, and the Israelis were apprehensive about making contact even with their own personal relatives in the Soviet Union.

Israeli ambassador to the Soviet Union Golda Meir (circled) surrounded by crowd of 50,000 Jews near Moscow Choral Synagogue on the first day of Rosh HaShanah in 1948.

Out of fear for the Jewish community while being smart and politically savvy, famous Soviet writer (and Stalin's favorite) Ilya Ehrenburg tried to defuse

16 *Golda Meir* eventually became the third Prime Minister of Israel, serving from 1969-74.

This same 1948 event was commemorated on the "back side" of the 10,000 Shekels Note, issued in 1984.

the issue by writing in *Pravda* at the time, claiming, "The State of Israel has nothing to do with the Jews of the Soviet Union, where there is no Jewish problem, and therefore no need for Israel."

Shortly after her arrival to Moscow, the Ambassador of the reborn Jewish state invited the most outstanding Jew in the Red Army—my uncle—to meet her and then presented him with a gift from the newly formed Israeli government: a golden pocket watch. (The watch, if I remember correctly, was paid for by a Chicago Jew.) The records of Jerusalem's Yad Vashem show Colonel David Dragunsky's following words at the receiving ceremony: *"I smashed the Germans as a commander of the Red Army and as a Soviet citizen. Furthermore, they were beaten by the Jew who lives in me and who is fiercely taking revenge on them for torturing and abusing the Jewish people."*

It is so happened that this watch was left in his suit pocket when he asked my mom to give it to a local dry cleaner. To my uncle's utter dismay and my parents' chagrin, the watch was lost and eventually forgotten. But it turned out to be not so lost and forgotten in the records of the omnipresent secret police (MVD), which will appear later and haunt my uncle during the infamous Doctors Plot (see the next Chapter).

A few weeks later, Meir attended a diplomatic reception in honor of the Soviet Revolution, where she was greeted by Polina Molotov, wife of longtime Foreign Minister Vyacheslav Molotov. Mrs. Molotov urged Ms. Meir, in Yiddish, "to continue attending synagogue."

Behind the scenes, all these events sent Stalin off the rails, so much so that by the end of November, the Soviet Central Committee had labelled the 2.5 million Jews in the USSR to be a Fifth Column. The meaning here was implicit: that we were becoming a nation within a nation and a matter of possible threat and grave concern to Stalin.

From that point on, the paradigm shifted. Not a single Jew in the Soviet Union could consider themselves safe. Even my Uncle, the Twice-Hero of the Soviet Union, now came under scrutiny. He and all of our family had been advised that we were being "watched."

By then, Stalin's paranoia had become a form of national monomania. It only grew worse in the years that followed and created a kind of new normal to which we all had to adapt—but not without some serious side-effects and a danger to us all.

Stalin was not long in responding to the "threat" of revived Jewish nationalism. By early November 1948, the leaders of the previously influential Jewish Anti-Fascist Committee were arrested, and Jewish cultural institutions across the Soviet Union were shut down—particularly in Birobidzhan, which had been set up as an autonomous Jewish *oblast*. In December of that same year, Polina Molotov was arrested for treason, forced to divorce her husband, and sentenced to a labor camp for five years.

One can only imagine the impact that kind of event made on the Russian psyche. Molotov had been Stalin's foreign minister for more than 15 years—it would be comparable to Richard Nixon having his Secretary of State Henry Kissinger's wife Nancy arrested and tried, or Ronald Reagan throwing George Shulz's wife in jail. Perhaps the most egregious aspect in all of this was Molotov's public disavowal of his own wife, something he was forced to do with very public fervor.

Molotov wasn't alone among his upper echelon comrades seeing his wife off to Lubyanka dungeons and GULAG system. Mikhail Kalinin, the country's president, was also forced to stand by as his wife, Ekaterina, was held for questioning and then languished for a decade in a prison camp. Both Molotov and Kalinin, as well as many other Communist leaders, continued serving their boss, beloved Comrade Stalin, in fear of own demise on a minute's notice. (Molotov had in fact lost his job but managed to stay-on as an advisor, mostly due to the peculiarities of Joseph Stalin himself.)

Such was the Soviet Union in which we all lived. It was a place of obsequious patriotism, where even the slightest pause to reflect could cost a man his career, if not his life. No one, not even our highest officials, could feel exempt from Stalin's reprisals.

CHAPTER SIX

Coming of Age: The Death of Stalin

*"The Soviet experiment was an absurd horror film
stretching out over 70 years. With government orchestrated famine,
hideous show trials, brutal GULAGS, mass murder—
life in the Soviet Union made the plagues that fell on Egypt
seem like a week in the Catskills."*

~ Actor, Leonid Bronevoy, 2014

There was little doubt that the fallout from the purges of mostly Jewish intellectuals and dissemination of the remnants of Jewish cultural institutions in 1948 and 1949 meant no one would be safe, including my illustrious uncle—a decorated war hero and a role model to us all. Even though he was passed over for the rank of Brigadier General upon finishing his courses at GHQ (General Headquarters) Military Academy in 1949, Colonel David Dragunsky was awarded the post of Commander of the 5th Tank Division. His division was stationed in the furthest corner of the country: the Chitana Oblast, six time zones away from Moscow, out in the middle of nowhere.

(As far as others were concerned this was something of a feather in his cap, since this Command was a post reserved for the rank of a general. For those in the know, it had a deeper meaning: the post was meant to get my uncle out from under Stalin's nose. Given our beloved Comrade General Stalin's new blood-lust to make an example of Soviet Jews, high ranking military officers would certainly have made perfect fodder for his newfound Anti-Semitic obsessions. So, it was rumored that some of Uncle David's military mentors, like Marshals Konev and Rybalko, whisked him off to this new assignment to get him to a safe haven.)

Uncle David played all this down to the family and simply took his new remote assignment in stride. He boarded a train for the remote posting and we didn't see him for well over a year. My uncle's departure from Moscow hit the family hard for a number of reasons: His status had always been our shield and his high-level connections meant access to a better life and perks.

Although I was a died-in-the-wool 11-year-old patriot drinking the Communist Kool-Aid, I was prone to saying things that could be considered, under the Party microscope, as not sufficiently patriotic. This became a sticking point with my parents—to the point of obsession. They were constantly admonishing me to monitor my language and to be careful not to say anything "controversial" while out among my peers.

I felt their concerns were overblown, as life for me was a simpler matter and the stress the adults were feeling was just the cost of living in the most formidable country in the world. In fact, all the public effusions of patriotic fervor and adoration of Stalin seemed quite normal to me. Nevertheless…bit by bit, piece by piece, my perceptions began to change. Over the years, I came to realize that the Soviet Union was a nation of 180 million people obliquely frozen in time—with a case of collective Stockholm Syndrome that was both congenital and chronic.

The signs all came in drips and dabs but were indelible nonetheless. The first came with all my forays into the cultural underground. Even though I thought of myself as a patriot to the bone, I was always poking my nose into "contraband" media…such as radio broadcasts from America and other parts of the globe. Along the way, I couldn't help but notice that other nations, by their language and verbal exchanges, were much freer in their expression, including their opinions about their world and their politics in general. These were all things that might have gotten them arrested in Stalin's USSR.

My fixations with pop music and Jazz especially from America helped to open my eyes. I loved it all from my first exposure and couldn't get enough. Especially in Stalin's Russia after World War II, all forms of music from the West had been banned as symbols of "Degenerate Capitalist Culture," and yet here were the songs of Ella Fitzgerald, Duke Ellington, and Louis Armstrong (all from poor families and the grand-children of slaves) somehow being banned as degenerate. Meanwhile, the classical musings of aristocrats such as Mozart, Liszt and Chopin were constantly being performed and lavished with praise. This musical forbidden fruit drove me to the *Voice of America*, where the music would often leak through, and to contraband markets where we could get American music recorded on used X-ray films.

So here I was, "a patriot" doing illegal things, and virtually devouring words and music from far forbidden places, something that intensified as I galloped toward my teenage. My obsession managed to drive my mother crazy. She worried that I would risk such things and openly ask such questions that seemed both daring and seditious. Others who had family members that happened to speak out in public, saying anything that might possibly challenge the status quo, very often paid a dear price for their candor.

As for me, I was still awash in party propaganda—ever so much the "true believer," and a zealot to the core. Nothing exemplified this more than my longstanding desire to join a Young Communist League called the *Komsomol*. The Komsomol was something of an honor for any politically motivated youth inside the Soviet System. It dated back to the early days of the Bolshevik Revolution, and was often the way ambitious youths could rise quickly in the government ranks.

Although there are few parallels that might be drawn in other countries, and though, as Confucius once noted, "comparisons are odious," it was generally considered a stepping-stone to those who were looking for a career in politics or government and was mandatory if you wanted to go for a higher education. One had to reach 14-years of age to join the *Komsomol*, but I had conspired to jump the gun.[17]

Its emphasis was on youth, and all the clichés applied: strict locks on morality, temperance, moderation and morals. I have to admit, at that early age, I fancied myself as possibly having a career in international affairs. That was, until I learned quite later, that it also entailed the fine art of spying, informing on the activities of dissenters and reporting them when asked. Still

---

17 Keeping in mind that the *Komsomol* had also proven to be one of my famous uncle's stepping-stones to success.

in 1951, that was where I stayed fixated. I was so zealous in my patriotism that I pulled a few strings just so I could join at 13-1/2 years of age, hoping to rise far and fast as a patriotic youth. It was a passion that didn't last, because an upcoming cascade of events, however late in coming, shocked me into a new awareness.

A Series of Ominous Events...

One paradigm shift for me—from patriot to "push-back"—came shortly after I was 14 and, as I recall, nearly a year after my uncle's visit to Moscow. Even though he'd been sent as far away as one could imagine from the locus of power in Moscow, Uncle David was still a high-ranking officer in the Red Army...and a decorated hero. So, one of the perks that still remained for an officer in his position was an annual four-week vacation to a sanitarium in Kislovodsk in the Caucasus Mountains. It was what we would refer to in America as a health spa.

It was the perfect retreat designed for highly-placed Party officials and military officers. Replete with Turkish baths and saunas, frequent full body massages, therapeutic mineral baths and sumptuous healthy meals with a proper endless supply of decadent cultural indulgences from Capitalistic dens of iniquity—these were lavish perks in the extreme. Resorts such as this were well-known to be places where higher-ups could interact, hob-nob and enjoy the fruits of their labors. Not surprisingly, such retreats were often fraught with loosened-tongues and insider party gossip.

Mindful of the perils at hand, it was still surprising for my uncle to see just how careless men could be after a bit too much to drink. Often, indiscretion was an offshoot of the stay.

Upon his return to the East, he came back through Moscow in December 1952 for a visit. Uncle David appeared refreshed, suntanned and revived while spending a few days in his favorite Hotel Moskva. Boarding the train back to his post in Zabaykal, he gave me a wink with his customary intimation, "See you next year."

In retrospect the statement proved to be bone-chilling in its irony, as Stalin's paranoia had reached a fever pitch, especially when it came to anything involving all Soviet Jews.

On January 13, 1953, the newspapers *Pravda* and *Izvestiya* announced that a group of nine highly prominent physicians, ones who had previously attended major Soviet leaders, had been arrested. This was the beginning of the notorious *Doctors' Plot,* which was a highly publicized, but utterly trumped-up, conspiracy. The story was that prominent Soviet medical specialists planned to murder top government and party officials, with particular focus upon Stalin himself. Purportedly having been investigated by the MVD Secret Police for from 1951 to 1953, a clique of predominantly Jewish doctors from Moscow were accused of this secret plot to assassinate Soviet leaders, especially those in the Central Committee. The press proclaimed this plot had gone on for years.

To begin with, these notable physicians were specifically charged with having poisoned Andrey A. Zhdanov, Central Committee Secretary, who died in 1948; and Alexander S. Shcherbakov, who had been head of the Main Political Administration of the Soviet Army. There were also "confessed" attempts to murder several prominent members of the Red Army high command. These nine doctors—at least six of whom were Jewish—were also accused of being secret employees of U.S. and British intelligence services, as well as serving the interests of international Zionism and Israel in particular.

The Soviet press reported that all of the doctors had admitted their guilt. This exposed plot was later accompanied by publications of numerous anti-Semitic articles pointedly denouncing their Jewishness in the media—ones that talked about the threats of Zionism, accompanied by an open denunciation of all Russian people with Semitic surnames. In the wake of this, many Jewish doctors were dismissed from their jobs, arrested, and tortured to extract confessions and admissions of guilt.

The official January 13 announcement followed by the non-stop radio and press campaign of accusations, which basically painted all the Jews as traitors and poisoners, was a deliberate tool of terror used to intimidate everyone in the medical profession into a state of both frenzy and submission. Unfortunately, that ethnic stigma spilled over into the schools, so much so that just a short walk to and from my school often became a daily ordeal.

From that point on, the hours spent in school were torturous for Jews—as we were always on the defensive and made to feel guilty for just being ourselves. The only protection I felt I had was my heroic uncle and the family name I carried around as a badge of honor.

That is until that day in February 1953 when my Uncle showed up unannounced on our doorstep. He was no longer suntanned and self-assured but white as a sheet of paper. Subdued and shaken, Uncle David confided that, upon returning to his post, he had been ordered back to Moscow for an "interview" with Party officials on issues of state Security. The interview lasted a couple of days, and it was at that time that they presented my uncle with the full body of evidence they had against him as a dedicated Zionist and possible traitor to the cause of world Communism.

If you will recall, I earlier emphasized that the pocket watch left in my Uncle David's suit had been reported as lost at the cleaners. It was out of sight and out of mind for nearly five years, but it was in fact *never* lost, because photographs of it had been well-preserved and placed with care inside the MVD archives.[18] At this special interview, it was presented to the Colonel again, along with photos of him with "Top Zionist Agent" Golda Meir and all her minions from the Israeli delegation.

These were shown him, along with his damning letter penned and published in 1947—the open letter in which he described himself as, "A Jew who was happy about the USSR's support for the establishment of a Jewish state"…and where he had stressed the significance of the latter as a lifeline for the Jewish people, particularly for the many Jewish victims brutally mass-murdered as a part of Hitler's *Obstplan* during World War II. (This, even though Stalin was openly courting the nascent state of Israel at that time, so my uncle's letter had doubtless escaped scrutiny until now.) My uncle was "on the bubble" and was advised of as much.

His situation had doubtless been aggravated by persistent gossip that he had been sought out by the Israeli delegation during the time that Israeli Ambassador Golda Meir was stationed in Moscow. He also attended her social gatherings with other Soviet Jewish luminaries.

(It had even been rumored, though never confirmed, that my uncle had been offered the post of Defense Minister for the new State of Israel but had declined. Since even rumors in Stalin's USSR could get a person killed, this was dangerous word-of-mouth in the extreme.)

---

18 *MVD.* New Soviet Security Apparatus, "Secret Police," but not so secret reconfiguring and reconstruction of the NKVD (from 1946-1953) under Lavrenti Beria.

Why they didn't arrest my uncle on the spot is anybody's guess. They let him go back to his remote posting. My uncle left Moscow more haunted than I had ever seen the man.

While first published in January of 1953, the MVD investigations had been ongoing for some time and had been enough to throw Stalin into what had now become a characteristic frenzy against the Jews. So intense had his paranoia become that he ordered barracks to be built to house every Jew from all major cities in the USSR—a number mounting into the hundreds of thousands.

In her autobiography, Stalin's daughter, Svetlana, revealed that these new barrack camps had been secretly under construction since 1952 but had not been built-up fast enough to satisfy Stalin, who was reported to be furious about the slow pace and lack of progress. The momentum of all this monomania came to a screeching halt when, on March 5, 1953, Soviet Dictator Joseph Stalin suddenly died from a stroke.

It would be accurate to say at this point that my Uncle David had probably escaped arrest and execution by a matter of days. Only the timely death of Stalin saved him—further proof that, in this life, coincidence can be Divine. No one inside the inner circle of the Soviet High Command was in doubt that had Stalin lived a few more weeks, my uncle's life would have been forfeit, and the lives of hundreds of thousands of Jews from Moscow and other large Soviet cities would have changed drastically as those GULAG barracks were ready to be filled upon a few-days-notice.

The post-mortem on the dictator read: "Death by a cerebral hemorrhage of the left hemisphere." But it had actually been a bit more complicated than that. Although not confirmed for months, it was reported that Stalin had briefly rallied two days after the stroke, but then collapsed again. Though the specific details of his prolonged stroke and death were never reported, those inside the *Presidium* surmised that his death had been at least due in part to the fact that his own inner circle were too paralyzed to act on his care for fear of the consequences of their failure.

(In an ultimate point of irony, Stalin's manufactured *Doctors' Plot*, backfired on the man. When he had his unexpected stroke, there were so few qualified doctors left available to treat him that Comrade General Stalin did not receive the emergency medical measures required, and ultimately died from the untended side-effects of the stroke.)

A few weeks after Stalin's death in 1953, the new Soviet leadership decided that there was a lack of evidence regarding the *Doctors' Plot* and the persecution was dropped. After an appropriate length of time, it was declared that the plot had been a fabrication, and all of the physicians in Soviet prisons were released and allowed to practice again—except for those who had already died from torture while in custody.

Nevertheless, the death of Stalin hit us like a thunderbolt, striking us all dumb at first...then bringing about a state of national mourning that bordered on pandemonium. People poured out into the streets, vociferously weeping and moaning, "Oh, no! Not immortal Stalin!" in effusions of lamentation that were nothing short of hysterics.

I was still naïvely convinced that this was a leader unparalleled in the history of the world, which I suppose was true in a way. Though I was not yet 15 at the time, I thought the proverbial sky had fallen. I was heartbroken like so many others. This was our beloved teacher and captain *(Vozhd)*! There would never be another. (We didn't realize then just how lucky we were that this was true.)

I was stunned to see my schoolmates enjoying themselves, playing ice hockey in still-frozen courtyards and enjoying a few unexpected days of vacation while the nation mourned. All that time I was shocked and depressed, and these guys were consoling me in a somewhat cavalier fashion, saying things like, "Don't worry, another will show up." What's interesting is "those guys" later became ambassadors and generals in the Soviet military and post-Soviet Russia...even as I would soon become a dissident.

Still infused with patriotic zeal and dying to pay my respects, I contrived to see Stalin lying in state. My plan was prevented by my mother, who always had very good instincts when it came to the psychology of self-preservation and "the madness of crowds." This time in particular, it might well have saved my life.

Such was the character of the "captive mind" that Stalin's own state funeral was attended by a million or more mourners. Some 900-plus of them were crushed to death in the crowd's drive to view his body lying in state at the Column Hall in the House of Unions, just across the street from the Hotel Moscva.

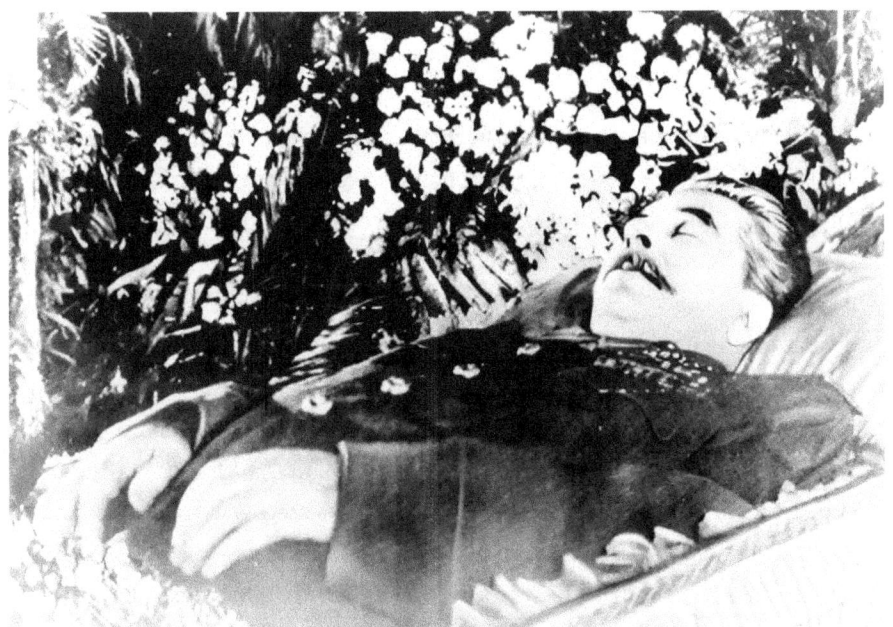

Stalin, "lying in state" at the Column Hall of the House of Unions (1953).

What happened in the aftermath was a jockeying for political position. Stalin's inner circle at that time included Georgy Malenkov, Stalin's likely successor and Deputy Premier; Lavrenti Beria, Stalin's influential Chief of Secret Police (the MVD) who was his self-proclaimed vicious hatchet man; Nikita Khrushchev, essentially governor of Ukraine and later Head of the Communist Party in Moscow, whom Stalin had summoned there to balance the power dynamics of Malenkov and Beria; along with that of Soviet Defense Minister, Nikolai Bulganin.

After a few months of sorting things out and a brief but relatively benign series of shake-ups, Nikita Khrushchev had risen from the number ten on the power list of the Presidium to becoming number two, essentially co-equal to Georgy Malenkov in what developed into a Khrushchev-Malenkov duumvirate. After a brief time, Vyacheslav Molotov, who'd previously been sacked by Stalin, would be reinstated as Foreign Minister. Meanwhile Molotov's wife, Polina, would be released from prison and reunited with her husband (who had some fence-mending to do). Rather uncharacteristically, this turned out to be one of Lavrenti Beria's very few benevolent acts before being arrested and shot by a firing squad in 1955. This all lasted for a couple of years, until Khrushchev forced Malenkov out and assumed the official title of Secretary General.

By 1954, I had learned quite well that there was life after Stalin. I was also forced to experience some pretty hard lessons. One of them happened to revolve around my Uncle David and his involvement in the Korean War in 1952. This originally occurred while I was listening to the *Voice of America,* where they had been describing the Korean War and entire armadas of tanks and weapons secretly delivered by the Soviet Union to the Chinese "volunteer" troops amassed at the border of North Korea.

According to the broadcast I heard, they'd been brought there in generous portions by the 5th Armored Division from the Chitana Oblast. All the ordinance the Chinese needed to carry on a sophisticated war had been carried there and left along with a handful of Russian advisers—all of them from Colonel David Dragunsky's Armored Soviet 5th. This underscored Russian complicity in a war in which the USSR had previously announced its complete neutrality.

Puzzled, I confronted my uncle about this during one of his visits to Moscow. What perhaps surprised me even more than this news was my uncle's response. It showed me a kind of twisted patriotism that I'd never quite realized before.

(It is here that I would have to revert back to Chapter Four and note as living evidence that Czeslaw Milosz's concept of the "Captive Mind" had really kicked-in for my uncle. He had now embraced a state of both political and ethical Ketman that would stick with him from that day forward. Ethical Ketman was the recognition that one was serving in a corrupt totalitarian environment but, by being diligent in one's duties, one could find opportunities to accomplish good things. Political Ketman was more cynical and is simply summarized as: "Success is survival." So…make the right pragmatic choices, regardless of circumstance.)

In truth (and it struck me then for the first time) Uncle David gave voice to his mission as a fulfillment of his duty to the Motherland, and to Comrade General Stalin, even knowing as he did this he was on "the bubble," and he was under scrutiny every day of his life. Meantime, tragic events were around the corner to shake my young life.

A week after my 16th birthday in April 1954, my mom passed away just few days short of her 40th birthday. Unfortunately, the birth of my brother Alexander in 1947 had come with some side effects for my mother that included complications and a non-stop spate of blinding headaches from which she could find no relief literally for the many years that followed. Whether it was migraine headaches or a brain tumor was something which the Moscow physicians at the time, even the best-known among them, were hard-pressed to find answers. There were no drugs then to effectively treat migraines or any type of brain trauma on a day-to-day basis. Often times, they sent my mother to bed where she would have to stay, often for days on end. This cycle went on and on, until her death in pain and agony, which happened in front of me. This was the end of my adolescence and made me my 7-year-old brother's keeper. Even with this responsibility, it took a long time for me to fully comprehend that my mom was gone.

One can never quite measure the value of one's mother…until they are no longer with us. I was devastated, and I also saw how much her loss affected our nuclear family. Here was my poor beleaguered father, missing his life mate and mourning, while struggling to get through each day and raise two sons who were 16 and 7 years old. This task would be daunting for anyone. So, he sought a solution…and found it in a way that impacted our family and me, personally, in ways I never imagined.

Knowing that my father was in desperate need of domestic help to tend to his growing sons and keep house while he was at his job daily, some neighbors told him about a homeless middle-aged Jewish woman who had just been released from a Siberian concentration camp and was looking for a place to live and work. Her name was Fanya Lvovna, and she turned out to be a godsend.

Shortly after she arrived, we again started having freshly cooked meals, clean clothes and made-up beds. At our first encounter, this woman looked much older than one would imagine a woman of 45-years should look. She told us she had a son, whom she was trying to locate. Her husband had been a Polish-born Communist (Jew) who was head of security at a large railroad line. She described him as a busy man so committed to the party line that—early-on in their relationship—he told her that Communist Party business would always come first and his own family second. To emphasize his patriotism, the man hung huge, life-sized portraits of Lenin and Stalin that took up half the main wall of their living room. Still, it did nothing to save him from what would come next.

One evening Fanya's husband didn't show up at home which, given his busy schedule, wasn't all that surprising. His absence on the second night, though, caused her some concern. When the young woman went to his work-place bringing along his favorite food, all she found was an empty desk and the downcast, frozen faces of all his nearby co-workers who were too afraid even to give a hint of what had happened. Finally, she learned from one or two reluctant staff members that her husband had been "invited" somewhere and had not returned. She knew he had been arrested like some of his comrades who, according to her husband, were found to be enemies and spies.

A few months after her husband's unexplained disappearance, two men in leather jackets stopped by her residence, saying they had a couple of questions to ask her and they wanted her to accompany them to the NKVD offices. Surprised by their sudden appearance, she remarked, "But I have a five-year-old son playing in the courtyard." They assured her she shouldn't worry, as she would be right back...

Yes, Fanya was back...18 years later, having spent all that time in a work camp, paying back society for violations she was unaware she had made. Once she was released, her mission was to find the son lost to her nearly two decades before.

As a postscript, she eventually did find her son. By that time, he was fully grown and working as a bus driver in Moscow. After her disappearance into the "GULAG Archipelago" he had been placed in an orphanage, where he was harassed and abused as the son of "an enemy of the people" (and a Jew to boot). Although he wasn't the only one branded as an "enemy" child there, this left emotional scars on him that lasted the rest of his life.

He used to come to our home to visit his mother from time to time. One could see that she clearly loved him and wanted to reach out to him. By that time, though, it was a one-way street. She was a stranger to him. They had become estranged in the most terrifying sense of the word. (Shadows of Orwell's *1984* and the fate of Winston Smith.)

A couple of years after her release from the camps and following Stalin's death, Fanya and her husband were "rehabilitated," and she received her own place to live along with a meager pension. She was also told that her husband had died in one of the Siberian labor camps.

The latter didn't surprise her much, as she witnessed thousands of deaths from exhaustion, hunger and frost. There were dozens of young, beautiful women taken in the middle of the night from the beds they shared with their husbands—many of whom had been high ranking government officials. These families had in-house maids, chauffeurs, and wives who had been strangers to dirty hands, and yet they ended up dying like flies once exposed to the nightly interrogations, cold jail chambers, starvation...and later to camp barracks with 14-hour hard labor in minus 40-degree weather conditions.

Fanya was a decent woman, so it was hard for any of us to imagine how anyone like her could pose a threat to the State. But the State lived in a bloody madness where imagined threats were posed by every soul whose only sin was being its citizen. That was Stalin's Russia, and this was another era! By this time, it was 1955 and things would be different now.

Or would they? Stalin was dead, but the long tail of Marxist/Leninist Communism still cracked its whip. Having forced Georgy Malenkov out after two years, in 1955 Nikita Khrushchev stood at the summit as de facto Soviet Premier...and immediately set about promising something like "peaceful coexistence" to the rest of the world. Not surprisingly, there was a wait and see attitude on the part of world leaders from the West. But Khrushchev worked hard to put a good face on it...for a year-and-a-half at least.

Things by then had softened a bit. But it was still the same Communist Dog (and dogma) with a different set of fleas. We were all still told what to do and where to move, and most items from the West were still unavailable or considered contraband. We still had to have personal passports to move across the country and couldn't do so without a dozen crosschecks and bureaucratic stamps. Travel to the outside world was closed off to us at all times.

What many people in the West, including so-called Kremlinologists, didn't understand (and still don't), is that the neither the post-Stalin Soviet Union nor post-Mao China had hawks or doves — we had ravens and vultures posing as hawks and doves, but they were quick to act as chickens when and if they faced a determined hunter.

The country where I was born and lived was 8.65 million square miles (by contrast the USA's 3.5 million), 11-time zones of land mass surrounded by a tightly guarded Arctic Ocean coastline along the north border and two rows of barbed wire and watch towers every 250 meters along the East, South and West borders. Any attempt to approach or cross the border led to a minimum 10-year prison term, and most often a death sentence by a firing squad.

After Stalin's death in 1953, very limited tourist groups made up of Communist Party members who were strictly vetted to ascertain their loyalty, were organized to visit Eastern Block (Socialist) countries. Rarely was the West, with its decadent dying Capitalism, a consideration. As it was for the rest of us, there was no chance of crossing the country borders. *(After all,* who *would ever think of leaving this working-class paradise?)* The rare exceptions were the Polish-born expatriates caught in the WWII German-Soviet division of their country who were allowed to leave with their spouses.

Indeed, nobody would dare to mention the thought of emigrating to the West out of the simple fear of free of charge transportation in the opposite direction.

Most of our information/entertainment was still blocked, and still no one trusted anyone.

By the time I'd reached my 17th birthday, I had come about 120° of 180° away from the robotic Communist Party Line. I found a way to secure my Komsomol file, and after checking the folder, took it to a nearby public privy and tossed it down the crap-hole, never to emerge again. Thus ended my illusions of party integrity, and then came the realization that there was no one—virtually no one—I could trust. Gone were my days of blind patriotism. I had begun to question everything. My cultural and political fascinations had all turned to the West, to the ugly specter of Capitalism epitomized by the nasty old USA, where everyone got to speak their minds any time they liked, where everyone could travel anywhere they wished and enjoy the fullness of life, every aspect of planet Earth so parsed out to us in segments—complete with copies of Communist indoctrination. These were all observations I'd made and I had reached that point in my life where I didn't worry about speaking my mind in the least—a fatal flaw in Stalin's Russia, but dangerous even in the wake of his demise…something I was very soon to discover.

CHAPTER SEVEN

A New Russia
"The Same Old Song and Dance!"

"We will bury you!"

~ Nikita Khrushchev's speech
to Western Ambassadors in Warsaw, 1956

Question: "What would happen if the Communists occupied the Sahara?
Answer: There would be shortage of sand."

~Whispered popular Soviet quip

For several months after Stalin died, there was a public softening of policy as well as a reprieve from the strangle-hold of terror that had gripped the Russian psyche for so long. Much of this was just for show, but it happened nonetheless.

The most evident one came almost immediately after Stalin's death in the summer of 1953 when an unofficial "amnesty" was declared, and Security Chief Lavrenti Beria released 500,000 prisoners, including political prisoners, from the GULAGs that spread from Smolensk to outer Siberia. This gesture of largess was mostly inspired by Georgy Malenkov who had no problem expressing his distaste for Stalin's longstanding brutal and repressive measures.

The youngest member of the Presidium and Stalin's heir apparent, Malenkov was to his core an intellectual who showed a penchant for lofty ideals and Eastern bloc literati. That caused him to come off as elitist with little or no sense of the Russian mind—something Nikita Khrushchev knew well and immediately started to mind. Setting forth a number of public works, he built up much of Moscow's residential area and restructured the *Kolkhozes* (collective farms), especially in Russia's wheat-belt from Ukraine to western Siberia. Severe or not, the restructuring worked, and the Soviet Union got better fed, something that hadn't happened in well over half a decade.

In truth, Khrushchev had already proved to have well-honed political instincts, which had helped him survive all of Stalin's purges since 1932. Much of this doubtless had to do with the fact that, when the occasion called for it, Khrushchev could be just as brutally pragmatic as Stalin, as evidenced by his enthusiastic role in Stalin's Great Purges of 1934 and 1937, where he personally presented the Inner Circle with a hit list of 2,000 wealthy *Kulaks* to be arrested and later executed for the sin of making a profit. As Governor of Ukraine for over 10 years, Nikita Khrushchev had, in Stalinistic fashion, eliminated all rivals to his authority by having virtually every member of the Ukrainian Central Committee arrested and tried for treason against the Soviet state.

Especially in Stalin's final years when he hated to be alone, it was always Nikita Khrushchev's role to act as the court jester, as it were, to keep Stalin laughing during those movie night drinking dinners that always included the Inner Circle and often lasted until dawn. So, even from the beginning, the smart money was on Nikita. It was just a matter of time before he would take over as Soviet Premier in fact.

Coming to power, Khrushchev inherited this huge country, suffering forever from two omnipresent chronic problems confronting the daily lives of the majority of her citizens: food shortages with long lines in grocery stores and primitive housing conditions.

Considering himself an agricultural expert, Khrushchev implemented countless reforms—all in vain. Nothing worked for one simple reason: socialist collective farms couldn't produce. While listening to Khrushchev constantly brag about record-setting crops, the people still found that the grocery store shelves remained empty. So, that left Khrushchev with one solution: purchase food staples like grain from the United States and Canada. This resulted in a widely circulated quip about Nikita being awarded the Nobel Prize for developing a new type of grain that was planted in Russia and harvested in Canada.

Khrushchev's new government also made the decision to improve the housing conditions of people cramped in communal city apartments—where as many as a dozen, families shared a community kitchen and single toilet (if the building had one at all), while confined to one room that was home to several generations. One large room shared with parents was the place comfortable enough to bring one's newly wedded spouse.

Back in January 1951, during an Architects' Convention supervised by Khrushchev (then Moscow Party Secretary), it was declared that a low-cost, expeditious technology of housing construction was to be set up as the main objective of Soviet architects and engineers.

From 1954, the Khrushchev housing program constituted a major turning point by implementing a mass-scale production of prefabricated (precast) buildings which began showing up throughout the country, beginning with Moscow. These buildings received the somewhat unflattering nickname of *Khrushchevka*, when they were in truth the beginning of mostly walk-up, five-story structures that, for the first time, at least provided private apartments. Although they may have been small and of poor quality, the lucky few who managed to acquire one could finally enjoy their own private places to cook, bathe, wash, poop and pee. Nevertheless, the new Party Program of 1961 promised that "during the first decade of the building of Communism (1961–70) the housing shortage will be eliminated ..." So, it began, but forever remained far from being realized. It was yet another casualty of the consistently shoddy Soviet bureaucracy.

A typical new construction block of precast concrete houses known as Khruschevkas.

Once Khrushchev concentrated the power in his hands, he immediately expressed that the Soviet model for World Communism would overcome Capitalism, which also meant he loosened the block on some forms of communication from the West. That is not to say it was removed entirely, but certain cultural "expositions" such as occasional Western movies and Western forms of music including jazz, pop and musical comedy were allowed to slip into the airwaves. Western broadcasts such as the *Voice of America* and others were still jammed in the big cities but had loosened oversight in surrounding areas, which became, for seekers like me, less and less of a challenge.

Although it was never trumpeted in *Pravda, Izvestiya* or *TASS,* the 2.5 million Soviet Jews had to feel the pressure lift in ways that could not be measured. Gone were Stalin's planned resettlement camps along with his anti-Semitic paranoia…at least to the degree that there was no longer an imminent threat. As a perhaps a subtle example, in 1955 my Uncle David Dragunsky was finally promoted to the rank of Major General.[19] He also lost the sense that he was constantly under surveillance.

Newly attired in his General's uniform, David Dragunsky poses with family, circa 1955.

---

19 The rank of *Major General* in the Soviet Army was equivalent to that of Brigadier General in the US and British forces.

Yet Khrushchev's attempts to "de-Stalinize" the Soviet Union were only subtle to a point. After waiting for nearly three years—until his seat as Secretary General was entirely secure—he finally delivered his famous Secret Speech to the closed session of the 20th Congress of Communist Party (a gathering of party elite from 26 different countries with only senior party members selected to hear the speech). The speech was titled "On the Cult of Personality and its Consequences." Although initially talked out of including the "juicy bits" about Stalin's atrocities and the murder of millions, Khrushchev eventually unloaded the "Full Monty," including a well-constructed four-hour harangue exposing of the myth of the magnificent visionary—Stalin—for the monstrous contrivance that it had become.

Such a propaganda masterpiece caught a great many in that Congress of 700 hand-picked delegates totally by surprise.[20] (In fact, surprise would be too mild a word since, upon being exposed to this run of condemnations, several delegates fainted, a number left the conference sunk into prolonged states of depression, and two even committed suicide within weeks.)

Beginning with record after record of his dismantling of a successful system of communes and ruthless repression of peasant rebellions in the 1920s and '30s, he cited chapter and verse Stalin's military purges, not one, but three times during his tenure—resulting in the execution of tens of thousands of officers and grunts simply for the sin of losing a battle or failing at the art of waging war. This was a precursor to Stalin's march of folly as he prepared for WWII, and the massive losses suffered during the German invasion and Russia's Great Patriotic War.

Although this seems out of context in the telling of the story, it isn't, because these atrocities and more were exactly what was detailed by Khrushchev during his exposition. This was what shocked the sensibilities not only of the CCP but also the Western world to whom the information was leaked within 72 hours (reputedly by Mossad).

During his nearly four-hour tirade, Khrushchev went a long way back and dug deeply into the Soviet Union's closet to bring out "piles of dirty laundry" that went back as far as the mid-1930s.

---

20   Plus another 100 handpicked "guests": Communist Party members recently released from Stalin's prisons and brought-in for moral support.

From 1935 to 1938, during what later came to be known as The Great Purge, at least nine Soviet nationalities—Poles, Germans, Finns, Estonians, Latvians, Koreans, Chinese, Kurds, Iranians—were subjected to what is now known as ethnic cleansing, most of which included torture, imprisonment, mass executions and/or banishment where they were left to freeze and die…all at the behest of Stalin, who personally signed the orders.

Also, by orders of the Supreme Soviet, from 1941 to 1944 the NKVD hunted down over 1.5 million ethnic Germans, Karachays, Kalmyks, Chechens, Ingush, Turks, Cossacks and Balkans throughout the expanse of the USSR and sent them to "special settlements." Stalin personally signed most of the orders to deport ethnic Germans from the Volga German Autonomous Republic outside of the European part of the USSR.

Policy failure after failure were cited in considerable detail, followed by a string of ruthless repressions and a gutting of the economy in a run of failed programs that lasted for nearly three decades—all these and more were itemized with such careful and quoted construction. It was said, "You could hear a pin drop," in this very large, cavernous room filled with people.

The speech included recommendations to establish a special commission to look into all the cases of people convicted on "anti-revolutionary activities" under Stalin. According to official Soviet estimates, more than 14 million people passed through the GULAG system from 1929 to 1953, with a further 7 to 8 million being deported and exiled to remote areas of the Soviet Union, and another almost 800,000 sham-tried and executed.[21] According to British historian Simon Sebag Montefiore, Stalin was ultimately responsible for the deaths of at least 20 million people through the executions, famine and incarceration.

After four hours, the closed gathering cleared in a virtual state of shock—not so much out of a sense of surprise, but because someone finally had dared to speak out against the heretofore "Icon of the Soviet Ideal."

In a surprise betrayal that was never very surprising, the Secret Speech followed Winston Churchill's adage, "Three people can keep a secret as long as you kill the other two." Within the week, Khrushchev's tirade appeared London's *Observer* and later in *The Guardian* and the *New York Times*.

---

21   *Robert Conquest, 1997. "Victims of Stalinism: A Comment."*

The irony in all of this was the American press—especially the *New York Times* and *The Washington Post*— sanitized much of Khrushchev's speech by editing out the laundry list of Stalin's crimes against his own people. Still, by then the news had spread in other world publications that, item by item, everything the new Soviet Premier had laid out against his predecessor. This seemed to be among the most important revelations of what the USSR was really like under Joseph Vissarionovich Stalin's reign of terror.[22]

This speech was by no means lost on me as it was played out fully and itemized in some detail on the *Voice of America* and other Western broadcasts. For me at least it put the final coffin-nail in the myth of Joseph Stalin—*pater-familias* of the Soviet Communist ideal. It was certainly a crushing blow, and yet as is always the case with truth: It may be painful, but it always sets you free.

The revealing part of Nikita Khrushchev's brash, bold—and in many ways self-sabotaging—speech was the profound push-back it received from many assembled there: not that they were uninformed as to the nature of it but that they were appalled that anyone—even a Soviet Secretary General—would dare to speak out in such a manner against such a "beloved" figure. It was very much a fulfillment of the Orwellian trope, "He who controls the past controls the future." Joseph Stalin, even in death, still held a 30-year lock on the Soviet political con-sciousness that was difficult to com-prehend, unless you were a Russian

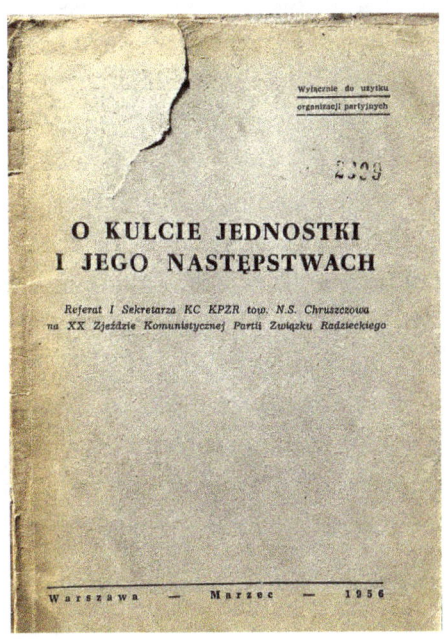

Numbered copy of the "secret speech" provided to Polish communist leadership.

---

22 This sanitization of Stalin's atrocities remained a staple of the US Media until 1963 when Svetlana Alliluyeva (Stalin) came out with her eponymous autobiography and blew the lid off the whole thing. By then, however, the whole world knew…and the "average American" was just the last to get the memo.

and understood the vestigial, cellular infusions of the "serf" mentality that went back a thousand years.

In his novel, *Everything Flows,* the famous Soviet writer Vasily (Iosif Solomonovich) Grossman wrote: "… I had the misfortune of being born in Russia, a country that, under the Czars as under Communist Commissars, had traditionally treated its people as if they were a conquered nation. There was only one thing Russia hadn't seen during these thousand years: 'freedom'."

Being treated as a conquered nation and having lived under a feudal system until the end of 19th century, during which the mostly peasant population were born tethered to the great estates of nobility, they no doubt did have a stamp of "serf" mentality ingrained as a part of their Russian soul. Russian Novelist Fyodor Dostoevsky once expressed it more profoundly and with an even deeper sense of dread when he wrote: "The Russian soul is a dark place."

One of the Russian soul aspects observers have noted over the years is a loose association with the truth. This is not the recent phenomenon of "fake news," which Russia excelled in, but something that has been noted for centuries by many, including such a writer as Gogol while describing surreal fibs. This mendacity, although omnipresent, still appeared to many visitors to Russia as blatant as in "no other place on earth." In his famous *Lettres de Russie,* the record of his trip in 1839, the Marquis de Custine had hoped to counteract the success of Alexis de Tocqueville's *Democracy in America* by applauding a benign Czarist autocracy. Instead, he was appalled by the shameless and sometimes pointless deceits he encountered wherever he went, as well as by the contrivances of the serfs in embracing their own slave-like condition.

Perhaps, political philosopher Joseph de Maistre had Russia in mind when he said: "Every nation has the government it deserves." The blind admiration for strength and the enjoyment of the humiliation of others (because of their apparent small size) were the Russian qualities that amazed me through all the years of my life. The basic Russian thought is: "If you are strong, you dominate and don't ask for negotiations." This thinking has persisted and even endures to this day.

While occupying and comfortably living in the emptied dwellings of the countries they conquered, like Baltic republics of Latvia, Lithuania and Estonia, the Russians never bothered to learn their language and culture but always looked down on the conquered population as too small to ever be noticed. Now, by means of Khrushchev's speech, these selfsame countries that were part of the Soviet hegemony were being informed that they'd been had for all these many years…and were now forced to face the fact that their fate was still being controlled by a political system born of the most ancient form of master/slave mentality as ancient as time itself. Though the monster of Stalin was gone, the ghost of his legacy still haunted them all.

My Career Quest meets with several disappointments… and a success!

As in my high school years, I was very interested in history, geography and world affairs, and was rather good in my studies at all three. So, my ultimate dream was to be accepted to Moscow Institute of International Relations (MGIMO) which was basically a training school for future diplomats. What 17-year old boy would ever listen to those who tell him that, as a Jew, he had practically no chance at all? For me, there would be no serious consideration—certainly not from the Communist Party elite. But you couldn't convince me of that while there was even a glimmer of hope. I went to the MGIMO Admissions Office, having been granted an interview through (some surprisingly received) recommendations from my high school, to get an application and an itinerary of entry exams. However, upon my arrival for my scheduled visit, I was advised that there were no application forms available on that day—and was further informed that there was no other recourse that could be afforded me at that time.

With all my dreams dashed, on my way out of the building, I stopped off in a washroom to attend to my urgent needs and clear my head. As I was standing in a stall, a gentleman walked-in, placing himself in the stall next to mine. After looking around to make sure we were alone, he collusively whispered in my direction, "Ask your uncle, the General, to get involved." After this timely appearance, he just as quickly disappeared out the door.

Buoyed up by a glimmer of hope, I thought to reach out to my uncle. But Uncle David was thousands of miles away, with letters and telegrams being the only means of reliable communication. No telephone calls were available to that remote military site.

As it was, I was too embarrassed even to approach him. I knew deep down that I was in a no-win situation with the entry exams fast approaching and gone. Fast forward: a few months later when we had a face-to-face meeting and I informed him of my dilemma, my uncle just shrugged his shoulders and told me with a self-effacing grin: "You understand the situation. Such is life."

So, I had to look into other possibilities, and a career in aviation certainly headed the list. As crazy as it sounds today, it was close to being insane at that time. The dream of escaping this Soviet paradise was born with the only possible way to do it—to become a pilot and fly the nest. Knowing that David's General friend was head of the Irkutsk Air-Force School, I asked him to help me, and he agreed. So, we both flew to Irkutsk (my uncle from the East and I from the West of this Siberian city) staying at the school Commander's rather sumptuous, roomy home. But all was in vain. I failed the vigorous air force physical exam—the reason being my somewhat mangled hand from infancy still impaired me.

Slightly daunted but not deterred, I took my option two: applying to the Moscow Medical Institute, where I experienced a similar outcome: my physical incapacity disqualified me from consideration…simply because, as I was informed, "some women might feel uncomfortable with my hand appearing handicapped!"

Talk about reverse sexism! Here, I questioned the real reasons, and yet in retrospect, it accurately reflected the time. The USSR under Khrushchev had done little to favor Jews, especially in the medical professions and most positions of power. Although there were still dozens of Jewish physicians returned to practice in the city of Moscow, the hangover from the *Doctors' Plot* in 1953 still gave the anti-Semites an excuse to be leery of granting more medical degrees to this community still looked upon as marginal at best.

As I may have already mentioned, there were some institutions of higher learning that were especially selective when it came to their criteria for admittance. Here I need to explain the hierarchy of higher education that existed that time. In the USSR, the institutions of higher learning were divided into two classifications that diverged slightly from those in the West: institutes and universities. Institutes were specialized colleges for skills such as medicine, engineering and the law, whereas universities were mostly liberal arts. To be admitted to the school, one needed a high school diploma, a grade transcript and to pass a series of entry exams—which normally included four different tests on specific subjects varying from one school to another and generally depending on the school's specialty (engineering, liberal arts, etc.)

Some institutes had stronger and some weaker filters for or against Jewish enrollment. They all had competitive entrance exams, with the ratios of applicants to vacancies ranging from 2 to 25—quotas having been set well in advance. Admittance was based on the exam grades and other factors, with ethnicity often being the most significant among them, though it was never stated. So, answering Jewish on the application, instantly blocked you from attaining certain societal roles.

Ethnicity was actually a line-item that they often listed upfront. As a result, we had to shop for the schools purportedly more receptive to our particular brand of social markers. Finally, after what seemed a last resort, I gained acceptance into The Institute of Construction Engineering. The current emphasis on massive precast construction created a great demand for professionals able to facilitate the progress of that kind of technology—making Admission Committees for construction-related schools less picky when it came to issues of Jewish ethnicity.

So, I was accepted…but not before something happened that amounted to a political wake-up call.

"The Scariest Day of My Life"

"You are invited to join us at the offices of the KGB."[23] That bone-chilling invitation happened to come on the eve of my 17th birthday. A few days before, a well-dressed gentleman showed up at the front of our home and handed me a piece of paper "inviting" me to appear as a witness at the infamous address of the KGB's Lubyanka (headquarters) building. Keeping the invitation to myself, but having a hard time keeping other things inside my head, I entered the KGB headquarters building, located in an infamous and utterly terrifying giant building in the center of Moscow. I remembered well the saying, "this is the tallest building in the world—because one can see Siberia even from its basement."

---

23 *KGB* the new Soviet Security Apparatus set up primarily by Nikita Khrushchev in 1954 to replace both Lavrenti Beria's MVD (assigned to internal policing) and the MGB (Secret Police set in place in 1953 after Stalin's death). The KGB became the new, more sophisticated face of Soviet Security until the official disbanding of the USSR in 1992. The changes were meant to indicate the diminished role of those organizations from the rank of Ministries (M) to those of Committees (K).

The most feared building in the USSR. KGB offices in Moscow,
often sarcastically nicknamed, "The Tallest Building in Russia...because you can
see all the way to Siberia from there."

Being met by another, even more stylish gentleman at the checkpoint, I asked why I was being called as a witness and to what? His answer was: "Some people enter here as a witnesses but leave as the accused." (Not exactly what one wants to hear a moment such as this.)

I followed him, ascending a wire-caged stairway (which I took to be a good sign)— thanking G-d for not being taken into the basement of this fortress, the bowels from which thousands upon thousands had visited, never to come out again. I was seated in front of two men who were elegantly dressed from head to toe in Western-tailored suits. I was presented with a series of my quotations published in a Norwegian newspaper where I had purportedly expressed criticism of the Soviet government, its legacy of intimidation, torture, imprisonment, its institutional lack of freedom, and so many other things.

Trying to keep my pants dry, I responded something like this: "Yes, I met a Norwegian tourist, had a brief exchange with him, but said nothing critical of my beloved country. How could I? Why would you believe a venal writer from a corrupt Capitalist newspaper more than a Soviet citizen raised in a socialist society?"

To my utter terror, I was counter-punched with the reply: "We have Soviet citizens—quite a few in fact—who can confirm your Anti-Soviet sentiments." Those were the head interrogator's words, and he had no problem speaking with emphasis, just to make sure I got the point. (Good heavens! Who would not?!)

The interrogation lasted perhaps another couple of hours or so, after which time I was let go—actually allowed to leave the gigantic building without benefit of escort! It is impossible to fully describe the sense of relief I felt along with a sense of wonder at seeing the beauty of a rundown street and smelling the welcome aroma of city air—simple things I'd taken for granted and never would again, once I found myself outside and able to breathe again.

I don't remember the sequence of events, but news of that afternoon rather quickly leaked out, getting almost immediately to my general family. Practically before I knew it, two of my uncles (my mother's sisters' husbands) paid me a little visit, descending upon me with furious warnings about the dangers I had brought—not only upon myself but also upon the entire family. Being almost brutal in their rage, they took great pains to warn me that I knew nothing about the destiny of the millions who had suffered and perished in the jaws of the GULAGs—and that I was endangering all our relatives as well, including my hero, Uncle David, who at that time was stationed in the East thousands of miles from Moscow.

That's when it struck me: Stalin was dead, but Communism was not. The number of firing squads may have diminished somewhat but the GULAGs were still fully functional—458 and counting by 1956. People like me were still being shipped off every single day...and for much less treasonous language than I had just been accused of uttering.

It was at that moment it struck me fully how endless the chasm that yawned before us all was. It also brought on the nagging question that now gnawed at me every day: How could anyone want to spend the rest of their lives in this place—this nation where fear was a way of life and peril a certain end, where personal merit was always at risk and pleasure was viewed as sedition?

At this point, you might ask how this kind of mass-mind thinking could prevail to such an extent and hold sway over so many people. I have to answer with the only reply that serves: this was the only universe we knew—one with no visible exit for the average man.

This was yet again an oblique manifestation of the "captive mind" that had seized not only my uncle but everyone around me as well; and by no means for the very first time. Here I was, despite myself, facing a grim reality where my last best hope was to educate myself out of this state of social paralysis and into a career that would give my life meaning and some freedom along the way.

There was a brief but welcome period of "humanity and rapprochement" that took place during the time after Stalin's death in 1953, but it didn't really kick-in until 1955 when Nikita Khrushchev officially took over as Secretary General of the Communist Party and de facto head of the Soviet State. Beginning in 1955, with his announced policy of "Peaceful Coexistence" to the Western world, Nikita Khrushchev found himself dealing with push-back from a Politburo preconditioned by a kind of "walking dead" Stalinist resistance to any mention of the "thaw" that he proposed.

Khrushchev was by no means a visionary, but he was politically savvy, and he knew when to loosen the leash on a USSR utterly caught in a Stockholm Syndrome that was both palpable and deep. So, he introduced these cultural measures that he proudly labeled, Khrushchev's Thaw (as in The Thaw in the Cold War). Although irregular and inconsistent, Thaw allowed a much freer flow of information in the media, arts and culture from the West. These included international festivals; carefully selected foreign films; uncensored books; and new forms of entertainment on our emerging national TV, ranging from massive parades and celebrations to popular music and variety shows, satire and comedies, and all-star shows like *Goluboy Ogonyok* (known as "The Little Blue Light") offering a surprising array of new ideas, satire, freedom of thought and artistic expression not displayed in decades. Such a cultural softening of Soviet policy had a salutary effect on the Soviet intellectual psyche and wielded significant influence on the public consciousness for my generation at least.

As for my family—even Uncle David, as wired into the "power structure" as he was—it was slower to sink-in, simply because they had been so inculcated with the paranoid politics of Joseph Stalin's terrorist state that their reactions to any freedom (of thought, ideas or movement) were accompanied by an almost Pavlovian sense of fatalism—thus a state of Ethical Ketman required just to survive.

But for a burgeoning student like me it couldn't have come at a better time. Still reeling from my little outing at the KGB, I was rather acutely aware that the screws, though loosened a bit, were very much in place and ready to be tightened back down at the least sign of my defection from the "Party Line." The only difference was in degrees. (Had I, during the reign of Stalin for example, been brought into the offices of Lavrenti Beria's MVD "to help them with inquiries," I never would have come out. As it was, I was given a warning that I was being "watched," which sent shockwaves through my family that were still being felt.) Flying in the face of all that, I was forever inquiring and looking West to do so— especially with broadcasts and literature from the USA.

As it was, Khrushchev was a paradox. He was liberal on certain things, while in other areas he was very much an advocate for World Communism as relentless as any other. That included his treatment of Soviet Jews. Whereas Stalin, in his highly paranoid final years, had declared the 2.5 million Soviet Jews in his charge to be a Fifth Column (a potentially seditious nation-within-a-nation), Nikita Khrushchev reversed the policy and refused to acknowledge that Soviet Jewry was ever an issue at all. Ironically, this visible denial of Anti-Semitism had the very same net result.

The issue of Khrushchev and Soviet Jewry and Israel in general came to a head in 1956 (not a good year as it turned out), when the British-French-Israeli forces came down on Egyptian President Gamal Abdul Nasser for initiating the Suez Canal Crisis in July of that year.[24]

In brief, the Suez Canal crisis started when Egypt chose to "nationalize" the canal and block it to outside use by sinking 40 ships, most British and French and trade vessels—an act that caused Great Britain and France to send their respective navies and ground forces down to descend upon Egypt for this sudden act of aggression. They were joined by Israel, whose very existence at the time was still dependent on access through the canal and its ports of call.

Surprised by the momentum of it, the outmatched Egyptian forces were quickly put into retreat when the USSR and other Warsaw Pact nations decided to intervene, with Khrushchev himself threatening the British-French-

---

24 *Suez Canal.* Along with the Panama Canal one the two most strategic waterways in the world where, by contract, sea-bearing cargo vessels are permitted to shortcut their deliveries of goods and services, fuel and personnel by weeks by slicing through the Sanai Peninsula to Red Sea ports in Sub-Sahara Africa, India and Asia. Owned by the Suez Canal Company—a British/French conglomerate since 1898—the contract with Egypt was in force in perpetuity, so seizure of the canal absolutely without warning was an "act of provocation" pure and simple.

Israeli alliance with shouts of "fire and fury," including threats of raining down nuclear missiles—and triggering World War III.

He was promptly backed off by the US President Dwight D. Eisenhower and his astute Secretary of State John Foster Dulles, who knew how to flex American muscle just where and when it was needed. In 1956, the USA was—by light years—the most powerful military industrial complex on planet Earth, and the whole world knew it. Eisenhower, the former Commander of all Allied Forces in World War II, still had a reputation as someone "not to be messed with." Eisenhower was also a vocal critic of what he saw as British colonialism and had expressed as much.

So, Ike (through Dulles) was able to make his presence known, clamp down on all parties involved, and talk some sense into them—bringing them all to the peace table and a negotiated truce. One of his first moves (as a peace initiative) was to promise Nasser US aid and monies to complete construction of the crucially-placed Aswan Dam, thereby granting Egypt further autonomy in its struggle for individuation...and freedom at last from French and English control.

Nasser blew it by his rapid-fire "nationalization" of the Canal, and the US withdrew its support, sending Egypt headlong into a coalition with other Arab Nations, including Syria and Yemen, forming a political hybrid known as the United Arab Republic (UAR). This in turn led to a Faustian pact with the USSR in 1958. Though it may have looked good for Khrushchev on paper, it proved to be a setback in the long run because in the court of world opinion, the lid was off his game.

The USA denounced the USSR to the UN General Assembly, underscoring the menace of world Communism and pointing to Nikita Khrushchev as an international threat equal to Stalin himself. (So much for "peaceful coexistence." The illusion of it lasted for about three years until, at the first given opportunity, Khrushchev showed his true colors.)

Back at home, the Presidium of the CPSU were still reeling from Nikita Khrushchev's 1956 Secret Speech. His denunciations of Stalin had led to so many aftershocks that it took a year or two for the USSR to fully regain its balance. In truth, it had so destabilized the Communist Block that it led to two political rebellions in both Hungary and Stalin's homeland of Georgia. These rose up with such dramatic outrage that Khrushchev had to put them down, not only with demonstrations of absolute power but also with draconian measures—ruthless, bloody repressions—to demonstrate to allies like Mao Zedong in China that Russia had not "gone soft." Hungary proved to be a particular problem because they actually overthrew the Communist regime there and flung themselves into armed open rebellion until Khrushchev brutally crushed them, while earning for himself the nauseating sobriquet The Butcher of Budapest.

By mid-1957, Nikita Khrushchev looked to be a man with a shaky hold on his power—so much so that he was met by a "palace revolt" engineered by Georgy Malenkov, Molotov and Deputy Premier Lazar Kaganovich. The intent of this rather poorly organized plot being a return to the old Communist Party traditions and a restoration (if you can imagine this!) of Stalinism. This *coup d'état* was clumsy at best and overlooked two things: First, the Marxist/ Leninist construct of dictatorship is so leader-friendly that—barring assassination—it is virtually impossible to "unseat" someone in a prime position of power. Second, no one can overthrow you with the army on your side. Siding with the Soviet Secretary General from the outset were Defense Minister Georgy Zhukov, and Field Marshals Vasilievsky, Konev and Rokossovsky—all of whom had been promoted and showered with so many honors and medals that their uniforms looked like fruit salad. Zhukov in particular (the only four-time Hero of the Soviet Union in history) had anticipated this clumsy cabal and shut it down virtually at the outset.

Though it was dangerous in places, it barely made the Soviet press—more closely posted in *Pravda* and *TASS* as an "overdue government shake-up" where Molotov (after decades of service) was finally retired…and both Malenkov and Kaganovich were summarily demoted to lesser government jobs and disappeared into obscurity forever. Khrushchev's threats to world peace during crisis periods like Suez and others were softened with compliments from Third World leaders like Egypt's Gamal Abdul Nasser, who embraced him with the oxymoronic compliment "a courageous warrior for peace."

That was the image Khrushchev was trying to peddle to the world: a "kinder, gentler USSR" that, even then, the West was finding difficult to swallow. *Even then* it was clear to see that Nikita Khrushchev was perhaps the "paradox" in Winston Churchill's definition of Russia when he called it: "A puzzle wrapped in a paradox and cloaked in an enigma."

Examples abounded, but there are a few: On one hand in 1955 and 1956 at the Everyman Opera, Inc., Khrushchev had his Minister of Culture restage George Gershwin's *Porgy and Bess* in both Leningrad and Moscow, starring a "reinstated" Paul Robeson, who had just been released from a five-year, land-bound house arrest inside his own country. Robeson performed before packed houses, while continuing to point to Russia as his Mother Country. Robeson, as famous as any Soviet celebrity had ever been, reveled in the adoration he felt from the standing room only crowds. Yet he—and only he—appeared to long for the days of Stalin where his performances had been constantly attended by the Comrade Generalissimo himself.

In 1957, the new Soviet Secretary General approved having Moscow host something called the 6th World Summer Festival of Youth and Students, instructing Komsomol officials to "smother foreign guests in our ideological embrace." So, they created a Socialist Carnival that involved over 3 million Muscovites, who were joined by 30,000 foreign visitors, ages 16 to 35, in events that ranged from discussion groups throughout the city and even seminars and concerts that took place at the Kremlin itself. According to Russian historian Vladislav Zubok, the festival, "shattered propagandist clichés" about Westerners by allowing young Soviet citizens to see them for themselves. What's more: It brought cross-cultural events—even Jazz concerts and small folk music festivals, including American artists like Pete Seeger. (Imagine that: Jazz concerts in the parks and venues in 1957. Jazz was a music form that had been forbidden to me for years, and it was now made available and at my fingertips.)

A reader raised in the Free World might have a hard time comprehending how any art forms or specific pieces of music, literature, paintings and sculptures can be controlled by a government. These acts of censorship are most often enacted by totalitarian leaders or their appointed toadies who lack even a basic education in art, music or literature. That is exactly what happened for decades in the USSR I grew up in.

My college years coincided with those years of the Soviet Union under full control of Nikita Khrushchev, who seemed to embrace the fact that he was a "living contradiction." A classic example of this would be the first-ever International Tchaikovsky Competition begun in Moscow in 1958. When a young American piano prodigy named Van Cliburn, from Fort Worth, Texas, USA, so utterly out-shined the competition that his genius could not be denied, the panel of judges, who were fearful of not awarding it to a Russian, called Khrushchev to consult him about their decision. He answered with one question: "Well...was he the best?"

"Far and away," the judges all agreed.

"Then give him the prize," Khrushchev replied, and hung up the phone.

At the same time Nikita Khrushchev openly loathed the works of Boris Pasternak, author of *Doctor Zhivago,* and banned them from readership in the USSR. He even pressured him to decline the Nobel Prize he was to be awarded in 1957. By the same token, he expressed a profound admiration for the writings of Aleksandr Solzhenitsyn and mandated that his previously banned works be published, starting with *A Day in the Life of Ivan Denisovich* in 1961 and *Cancer Ward* in '62, despite the fact that both works tore the cover off the hidden secrets of life in Stalin's GULAGs in the 1950s.

Suddenly a string of publications of formerly banned Soviet writers as well as Russian translations of books by foreign authors were permitted. I remember being lucky enough to acquire the one of them: A four-volume set of Ernest Hemingway's books, including the previously banned *For Whom the Bell Tolls* with a rather negative description of Spanish Communist Leader Dolores Ibarruri. To be able to subscribe to this upcoming publication we needed to get in line at a store, one which had been organized about two days in advance with the roll calls throughout the Moscow late fall or early Spring freezing nights.

The cultural liberation during the Khrushchev Thaw years also included visual arts, such as paintings and sculptures. As a sign of it, in 1962 the Moscow Union of Artists (MSKh) was authorized to open a show in the exhibition hall just outside Red Square titled "30 Years of MSKh". The night before the opening, Premier Khrushchev showed up to see it in person. Coming across one sculpture prepared just for the exhibit, he exploded in a rage: "Who is the author of this Western piece of shit?"

The sculptor, who was standing right there happened to be Ernst Neizvestny, a quite famous artist. The rage and screaming continued..."Go to the West and show them this crap, because it has no place in Socialist art. Why do you distort the faces of Soviet people?!"

To the surprise of many, and the delight of some, the artist did something that never happened before: He challenged the General Secretary of the Communist Party telling him, "I fought the Nazis for four years and spilled my blood for my country. And yet you want to send me out..."

In the end, the great art critic Khrushchev relented to some degree, while simultaneously issuing Neizvestny something of an ultimatum: "You're an interesting person. I like these kinds of people, but you have an angel and a devil in you at the same time. If the devil wins, we will destroy you. If the angel wins, we will help you."

SOURCE: VLADIMIR AKIMOV / RIA NOVOSTI

The gravesite and monument of Soviet leader Nikita Khrushchev's at the Novodevichy cemetery. Tombstone designed by Ernst Neizvestny.

In fact, Khrushchev's policy always vacillated between liberalization and the Stalinist tradition of total conformity, repeatedly upbraiding writers and artists who, encouraged by the new climate of tolerance, apparently exceeded the limits of permitted freedom. In March 1963 in a speech to about 500 writers, artists and other intellectuals, Khrushchev singled out among others Ilya Ehrenburg, Evgeny Evtushenko, Victor Nekrasov, and the same sculptor Ernst Neizvestny. He also spoke scornfully about, "intellectuals who forget their duty to the people and their Socialist fatherland ..." and become "lovers of decadent Western abstractionism ... and formalism." Ehrenburg was also separately attacked with particular severity for asserting that the Russians knew of Stalin's crimes but kept silent out of fear for their lives.

At the very end, in an ironic twist, it was Ernst Neizvestny who, at the request of Khrushchev's own family, sculpted the deceased premier's tombstone at the Novodevichy Cemetery in Moscow. In so doing, the artist masterfully reflected the controversial nature of the former Soviet Leader by making the monument black and white with the birthmark below Khrushchev's right eye transformed into a tear.

As both a repost and reward for his political and artistic courage early on, Ernest Neizvestny, like me, was finally allowed to emigrate from the USSR to the USA—and in the same year as I: 1977! This turned out to be a very good year for us both.

For me, this constant exposure to new ideas stoked the fires of my enthusiasm for the West to an even higher burn. A perfect example would be my frequent train rides to the Moscow outskirts where I carried my newly acquired portable shortwave radio just to indulge myself by listening the *Voice of America*, BBC, and whatever other broadcasts I could get through the jamming. This was oxygen to my body and soul. Luckily for us, the outskirts were usually outside the jamming range. While in the city, the two-hour program "Music USA" was luckily not jammed and became a routine devotedly observed by me and like-minded friends I'd made around our shared passion for jazz and America! America: the country where this magnificent music from the heart originated...and continued in free flow. What a great nation it became in our minds! How very much we longed to know more about all things USA!

One tradition I probably should have mentioned that started when I was about 18 years of age: Every year on the Fourth of July, I used to take long public transportation rides to the street where the American Embassy was located—just for the opportunity to walk under the American Flag flying from the building while being closely watched by the Soviet Secret Police.

About the same time, Khrushchev's continued confrontations with the West, especially the USA, grew to be so pronounced that he became the poster child for something called "Brinksmanship." This was a term coined in 1957 by US Secretary of State John Foster Dulles to describe what it took to keep someone like Khrushchev in check. The term came to define the relationship between the USA and the USSR for the next 20 years or so—the art of going right up to the edge of global conflict...without going over the top. A geopolitical "game of chicken" that nearly brought an end to us all, during what in the West was referred to as The Cuban Missile Crisis.

To top it off, in those days of contradiction, Khrushchev's animus toward Israel, though never fully publicized, took a sinister turn in 1958 that would affect me and every other Jew in the Soviet Union from that day forward. After 1956, Soviet-Israeli relations continued to deteriorate, not only because of Suez and Russia's subsequent endorsement of the UAR, but also because of growing Arab dependence upon the USSR for military equipment and logistical support.

As British Prime Minister Benjamin Disraeli once observed: "A *lie* can get halfway around the world before the *truth* has had a chance to get its pants on." There was no greater example than this. In 1958, a document was fed to the world that proved to be a stake in the heart to Israel from that day forward. It was a doctrine that didn't come out of the Kremlin, but was penned as a published paper along with several others that emerged from the Ukrainian Academy of Science.[25]

Claiming its authenticity while quoting apocryphal sources, it avowed that Israeli Prime Minister David Ben-Gurion had officially mandated the elimination of The Ten Commandments as a guideline for Jewish morality and had replaced them instead with a Zionist doctrine so zealous and racially charged that it compared in context and structure to Nazism. Despite vehement denials by then-retired PM and Minister of Defense Ben-Gurion, the Israelis had great difficulty convincing many intellectuals (even in the West) of the fallacy of such a document. Suddenly the cult of Zionism was hung around their necks and stayed for years to come, trotted out by Arabs in the Middle East (as well as the Supreme Soviet) on any occasion whenever the argument required.

The paper itself, though never embraced, was also never entirely denounced by Khrushchev or any member of the Central Committee at that time. Through sins of omission, the very absence of condemnation became a kind of endorsement. Of course, it was denounced in almost all publications in the West for being the "garbage" that it was.

Imagine the nauseating hypocrisy of such a body of work that would somehow conflate the struggle of the primary targets of the Holocaust who lost six million of its own people with the political philosophies of the very nation that had methodically slaughtered them! It is almost inconceivable and yet now a historical fact that this body of lies gained traction in some intellectual circles. Such preposterous and bigoted equating of Zionism and Nazi racism was made in the form of United Nations Resolution 3379 adopted by Arab and Soviet bloc countries in 1975. Later in the 1980s, Reagan's Ambassador Jean Kirkpatrick reacted to this resolution saying, "Zionism has as much rac-

---

25   This was reputedly based on the work of virulent Anti-Semitic "scholar," Dr. Trofim Kichko. Broadly denounced in the West as a hate monger, Kichko continued to publish volumes of his hate-filled Anti-Zionist fiction until the early 1960s and was granted a virtual pass by Khrushchev and his Minister of Culture who found "nothing outrageous" in the publications.

ism as the countries supporting this scurrilous document have democracy." These appallingly dishonest comparisons keep resurfacing even today with the support of many BDS intellectuals and extreme anti-Semitic political elements, even within the US.

CHAPTER EIGHT

Khrushchev Gets Fired.
Boris Gets Hired.
"And All that Jazz!"

"A righteous man falls down seven times and gets up."

~ Solomon, Proverbs 24:16

Throughout the first five years of his tenure, Nikita Khrushchev continued to both amaze his supporters and confound his critics with a bizarre blend of political *faux pas* and brilliant public relations coups that were always a constant surprise. In fact, it was Khrushchev who, from 1956 to 1961, slowly but steadily emptied out the GULAGs, decreasing the prison population, mostly political prisoners, from 13 million at the time of Stalin's death to less than 5 million. He did so incrementally but relentlessly nonetheless.

Meanwhile, Khrushchev's approach to the global spread of Communism continued to be a living contradiction. Openly competitive with the USA, he saw to it that the USSR beat them into space, first with Sputnik in 1957 and next with the first man into orbit—Cosmonaut Yuri Gagarin. Sputnik only beat the US satellites into space by a matter of a few weeks but accomplished a couple of things along the way: First, it won the PR battle in the world press, giving the illusion the Soviet Union was also ahead of the curve in other areas

117

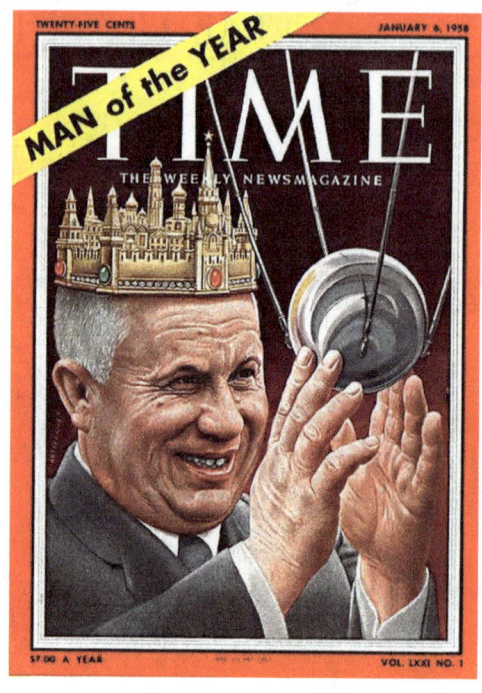

of space technology, and garnering for Khrushchev accolades as *Time* magazine's "Man of the Year," for 1958. Second, it falsely convinced the CIA and US Intelligence that the USSR was much farther ahead in its nuclear missile technology than it really was, causing CIA Director Allen Dulles, who was later fired by JFK, to invoke a frenzy of spy missions over the Soviet Union. This had the dual effect of the US intensifying its own ICBM program while giving the USSR a wider berth than it deserved.

Especially where Gagarin, the first man in space, was concerned, it was an international coup for the USSR. We had parades in Red Square (sans ticker-tape) and all kinds of celebrations. It was a timely morale builder and led to the Space Race that the American's eventually won. But at the time, it was a point of pride for the USSR, and a feather-in-the-cap for Khrushchev as its leader. Something to countervail the "Brinksmanship" that seemed to hang around all our necks like an albatross, during the late 1950s and early 1960s—ever present and waiting to erupt into something more serious.

At the same time, Khrushchev was ramping up the range and power of the KGB, spying on his home-grown city dwellers, infiltrating Third World Nations, and continuing selective bans on Western media, theatre, music and films—all while publicly proposing a period of "openness" that existed in his imagination only... His condemnation of all religion as an institution, resulted in mass closures of hundreds of churches, monasteries and Eastern Orthodox seminaries.

There was also little question that Khrushchev wanted to continue the traditional Communist Party line and phase out all religions, forbidding children under 10 to receive any further formal religious training, while at the same time permitting all faiths to practice as they wished.

Even more of a contradiction was Khrushchev's love/hate relationship with the USA during what came to be known as the Kennedy Era. Succeeding Eisenhower, for whom Nikita Khrushchev had a healthy respect, John F. Kennedy, upon their first meeting in Vienna in 1961, came across as naïve and very poorly informed.

(Clearly, Khrushchev underestimated Kennedy, who proved to be both a closet conservative and a very quick learner who was able to match the USSR, move for move, when it came to modernizing the military, initiating NASA to set up a state-of-the-art space program, and spreading the message of Democracy to a Third World now starved for developmental assistance.)

Still, first impressions being what they are, their Vienna encounter emboldened the Soviet Premier who saw JFK's inexperience as a chance to make both ideological and military inroads against what he viewed as this feckless new US administration. This initially led to the Berlin Blockade and later the Cuban Missile Crisis that nearly led to a World War III—despite the denials inside the USSR that this was ever an issue.

Career-wise for Khrushchev, both moves proved to be a PR disaster, especially at the United Nations, although he managed to spin it otherwise at the time. Particularly as it involved the Cuban Missile Crisis, known as the "13 Days", where the Soviet withdrawal of ICBMs from Cuba might have looked like a defeat. In military circles, though, it was a strategic success. In return for Russian withdrawal, Kennedy agreed to close down all US missile bases stored in the USA's NATO ally, Turkey, thus removing a tactical threat to the USSR that had long been its worst nightmare.

Nevertheless, to the rest of the word, to the Russian public and to me, JFK and his wife, Jackie, became symbols of all that was best about America. Young, innovative, exuberant and stylish, they epitomized the socio-political chic of the time. Also, thanks to brother Bobby and Secretary of State Dean Rusk, Kennedy grew to become sagacious in his command of foreign affairs, and a pioneer in Civil Rights at home.

Remembering JFK—
The Day the Whole World Mourned

US President John F. Kennedy—especially for us in the Soviet Union—came to be some-thing of a unifying force in that, over time, he grew to be a symbol of what was best about American democracy and, in that way, simply won us over.

When he defeated Richard Nixon to become America's 35th President, it was considered in the USSR to be something of a setback. After all, Nixon's "kitchen debate" with Khrushchev had become a world-famous event that showed us the kind of strength of which the USA was capable. So, when John Fitzgerald Kennedy defeated him in 1960, most of America's fans in Russia were disappointed in the extreme. (After all, who was this upstart and bootlegger's son who'd become the Chief of State?)

That bad first impression was soon put to rest by JFK and several things that characterized him: the swagger with which the man conducted himself, his utterly classy wife, and the fact that everything he did seemed to break new ground. Like the rest of the world, we Russians came to revere the man. For us, he became a symbol of hope that the West was to us all. This was why his assassination became such a tragedy to the entire world.

Even in the USSR, with Khrushchev in charge, the Soviet Premier thought it important to broadcast Kennedy's funeral on Soviet Central Television. I remember on that occasion in 1963 how devastated I was that since it would be during working hours and I'd probably miss the broadcast scheduled for the following day.

To my surprise my supervisor, a woman of some compassion, noted my fondness for Kennedy and threw me a lifeline that came as both a reprieve and a cause for gratitude.

CREDIT: NATIONAL PARK SERVICE

Meeting with Khrushchev in Vienna, June 1961. JFK soon proved to be a formidable adversary.

Without going into the reason for it (we both knew what *that* was) she simply told me: "Tomorrow you don't' come to work."

And so, the next day, my father and I watched the entire event—the parade down Pennsylvania Avenue, the mass at St. Matthews Cathedral, the solemn gathering of world leaders paying loving tribute to the man they all respected and to one another. This was a show of our humanity and the "angels of our better nature"—that in the end we are at our best when things are at their worst.

My College Years: Boris Dragunsky's Wake-up Call

My college years also were pivotal times, when I really started to develop my views on the society I lived in, the people I lived among and my constant quest for freedom that perpetually led to a perilous attraction to the West. I also learned how to play and make the most of my free time. The friends I started to make outside the college were the people of my age who I felt had the same inclinations. (Of course, we all kept it "under the radar," but there were social indicators that made it workable for people of the same mind.) Oftentimes, the first signs were attempts to wear something that was different from the dismal black-gray and grayish-black (Winston Smith) clothing sold and worn by ordinary people on the streets of Moscow.

With the trickle of Soviets visiting the West, athletes, ballerinas, dance and symphony artists were bringing back Western-made clothing, records and other items in almost open defiance of the dreck sold even in the prominent Moscow stores. Such rare commodities prompted the development of a black market where lucky travelers were selling Western-made goods in order to make a quick buck. Oh, what a buck they often made! A pair of real American blue jeans could be sold for what amounted to a month's salary for a teacher.

With banned currency exchange policies in place, Western tourists were selling their own, often used, belongings to get rubles to buy souvenirs or—for the more sophisticated among them—authentic Russian artwork. Eastern Orthodox Church icons were on the top of that list. Some goods made in the West ended up in several of Moscow's "commission" stores, where salespeople could make a good supplementary income by selling them under the table. So, some young people were going out of their way to stroll through venues like Gorky Street in Moscow, wearing button-down shirts, mohair scarves, wingtip shoes and even (never seen before) sunglasses, just so they appeared to be a western-looking chap rather than a drab soviet-looking comrade.

In the early 1960s, things loosened up enough to permit more open East-West exchanges. More Soviets—and now even strictly vetted tourists—traveled to faraway places. So more Western merchandise became available and more commonplace. My new friends and I united by one commodity: American music… especially Jazz! I was attracted to jazzy music even as a small child, and now I was sharing this affinity and developing even more interest and passion inside my new circle of friends. We devoted our nightly time slot from 10 pm to midnight to the program, "Music USA," by Willis Conover of *Voice of America.* We shared this, sometimes discretely, by having group listening sessions. With the majority of people still living in communal apartments, the jazz music coming from the rooms where we gathered could very often be overheard by some extremely unfriendly neighbors who were critical of our "treasonous" tastes. They had a penchant toward blowing the lid off everything we did.

Listening to the "Music USA" program made me sure that the team song used at the beginning and end of that program, "Take the A Train," was the USA's national anthem. When meeting, we had lively exchanges about the word-of-mouth things we'd heard, debating our preferences for the information to which we were privy. Not so inadvertently, we would also exchange our impressions about the selfsame country where the music came from. This would, for example, include arcane quizzes about American geography: cities like Chicago and Los Angeles, after listening to "Route 66" by Nat King Cole or San Francisco and the Golden Gate Bridge following "I Left My Heart in San Francisco" by Tony Bennett. Since we were being careful about sharing politically-related news, our verbal rhapsodies were usually restricted to such innocuous items as cars, skyscrapers, highways, music festivals, Macy's, Tiffany's, etc. Nevertheless, these were the endless streams of admiration we expressed for the political enemy we'd been told to "loathe and distrust." In our bones, every one of us knew better.

Our vocabulary was filled with such places and names as New York, New Orleans, Ella Fitzgerald, Duke Ellington, Count Basie, Louis Armstrong and Charlie Parker. As young Soviet patriots, we were supposed to discuss the achievements of the Soviet Socialist paradise, but we seldom, if ever, did. Instead we replaced this talk with some spirited exchanges that were invariably politically charged.

We also had new things to share as a result of our other acquaintances who had traveled to the West. They were bringing in vinyl records we could borrow and listen to! As it turned out, these records ended up traveling more extensively than their owners. This was the music of the "cultural underground" that was unavailable in our stores, was blocked from our hearing on Moscow radio, or listening to onstage. This was Jazz, the purest of pure American contributions to the world culture, born in "colored" slums and river bottoms and developed in the melting pot of the black ghetto blues, Jewish *shtetl klezmer* and European classics.

In the USSR, music fortunes were for decades dependent upon the political whims of unpredictable and culturally illiterate Communist leaders. This counter-cultural bipolar behavior wasn't just restricted to jazz music. Classical composers and artists could also incur the wrath of the so-called "cultural" powers that be: None more emphatically so than Soviet music prodigy Dimitri Shostakovich. Demeaned and belittled during the Stalin years of Soviet rule, Shostakovich, along with composers Sergei Prokofiev and Aram Khachaturian, was denounced for engaging in what *Pravda* described as a muddled kind of formalism. He was even called before the Soviet Culture Committee to make an official "apology." Later, he saw his music banned while Stalin was alive, only to be reinstated during Khrushchev's stewardship. Finally, he joined the Communist Party in 1960—an act of political capitulation, in which he had never before indulged during his more than 40 years as a leading figure in Russian music.

Similarly, the fate of jazz music was continuously changing between warm welcomes in Moscow on October 1, 1922, to censorship, prohibition and arrests of jazz musicians, especially during the Stalin years from 1928 to 1953, to its 100th anniversary celebration in the famous Bolshoi Theater on October 1st 2022. It treatment was all dependent upon the political climate in Russia at the time and its rocky relations with the West…mainly the United States.

As I mentioned earlier, shortly after Stalin's death in 1953 and with the arrival of the Khrushchev "Thaw Era," attempts at rapprochement, the claws of prohibition against music forms from the West were slowly but visibly retracted. So, from 1954 on, Moscow radio began occasionally playing tangos and foxtrot tunes. Jazz also received a new breath of fresh air in 1957, when the World Festival of Youth and Students was held in Moscow.

By that time, I took every opportunity to see the small jazz groups coming on tour from Sweden and Italy as well from Socialist countries such as Czechoslovakia, Yugoslavia and Poland. The latter was sarcastically called "the most cheerful barrack on our camp." Although run by Communists and a Socialist Camp, it managed most of the time to retain some signs of human freedom, even allowing the "church" to function and the jazz to play.

Gradually, limited jazz groups, jazz ensembles and jazz bands, mostly from Eastern Europe, started filtering in to perform in Moscow, giving me a chance to hear and feel real events such as Gershwin's classic opus to Americana, "A Rhapsody in Blue," performed by the Warsaw Radio Orchestra. But characteristic of Khrushchev's paradoxical relationship with his nemesis, the USA, jazz originals and American musicians weren't permitted to come to the USSR until the summer of 1962.

At the height of the Cold War, still presented to the Global Community as "The Thaw," Khrushchev came up with the novel idea to launch a cultural assault disguised as a competition with the West. This included sending troupes from the Bolshoi and Kirov ballets, Russian folk dancers and top Soviet classical musicians to the far corners of the world—all to showcase "Soviet superiority" in the performing arts. It so happened that some of these performers and their organizations were "forgetting" to return to their beloved Motherland. Defecting of the world-renowned ballet dancer Nureyev in 1961 was the most shocking to the Soviet mind. There was a joke, broadly circulated in the Whisper Network: Question: *What is the definition of a musical quartet?* The answer: *The Moscow Symphony Orchestra after touring the West.* In order for him to achieve this "broad-sweeping cultural adventure," there had to be some kind of reciprocity involved that included artists from the West, especially when the US Government sent the "King of Swing," Benny Goodman and his band of legendary jazz musicians over to tear holes in the Iron Curtain…and they sure did!

Getting tickets to concerts by Eastern European jazz groups was extremely difficult, often requiring days of standing in lines at the box office. This simply didn't apply to concerts by Benny Goodman, and nine years later the Duke Ellington Orchestra. Ticket distribution in Moscow for these events was tightly controlled by the Party Departments of Propaganda, which made sure ticket holders were vetted so they could face these Westerners and let them know their prestigious status in no uncertain terms and behave accordingly—there were pre-set limits for demonstrations of excessive enthusiasm. Full of their own importance, most of these "patrons" knew absolutely nothing about the music they were about to hear.

In a point of irony—and in a way supporting Khrushchev's bizarre sense of friendly cultural competition with the West—in 1962, two of the top 40 most popular albums sold in the US were *Benny Goodman in Moscow* and *The Soviet Army Chorus and Band,* playing to mixed reviews but brisk sales in America that surprised everyone. Purely in terms of musical artistry and cross-cultural breakthroughs, the Goodman album was amazing, featuring artists like saxophonists Zoot Sims, Phil Woods and pianist Teddy Wilson in the ensemble. (In 1936, the Benny Goodman Trio became the first interracial band to perform in public in the USA, with Benny Goodman, the son of Jewish immigrants, on the clarinet and African-American Teddy Wilson on piano). In 1962, Goodman's Moscow Concert was considered an artistry gem …and for a brief time was even permitted "under the table" sales in the USSR—for those who had access and could afford black market prices. If there is a will there is a way, albeit a tricky and expensive one, and sales were brisk.

Inside the USSR: Our Bumpy Love Affair with Jazz

After welcoming the jazz music in 1922 as the music of the oppressed American Negroes and other proletarians and letting it prosper till 1928 when a renowned Soviet writer Maxim Gorky authored (while living on Capri in Italy) a paper titling the new genre as the "Music Of The Fat Capitalists." With censorship growing in the 30's, the authorities were worried that jazz might move underground and actively pushed their own Soviet style jazz, featuring such band leaders as Alexander Tzfasman and Leonid Utesov who, in 1934, together with the most famous actress Lyubov Orlova, starred in the first Soviet musical comedy featuring a jazz musician as the main character and jazz compositions by Isaac Dunayevsky, even becoming Stalin's favourite movie.

The Great Terror years of 1935-1939 brought attacks on music associated with "freedom and improvisation," such as jazz. Not only jazz musicians (including the ones who introduced jazz in 1922) but also their many fans somehow managed to disappear into work camps. It was also publicly denounced as a "degenerate art form." One that involved such sins as travelling abroad and cultivating foreign contacts. What a cutting point of irony that these were the years when Nazi Germany had introduced a heavily enforced prohibition of jazz music, labelling it: "A Negro and Jewish art form." The first National-Socialist government in Thuringia passed a law in 1930, which equalled an indirect prohibition of jazz.

The WW II years, when the United States became ally in "the war," brought back a resurgence in the acceptance of jazz—with the "Soviet Army Chorus and Band" playing American jazz standards along with the very jazzed-up Russian folk songs (like "Volga Boatman, Dark Eyes," and later "Katusha"). After the end of WWII, as the Cold War picked-up, the Soviet authorities clamped down on any music or art form coming out of the West that they deemed corruptive—enacting bans and engendering a kind of cultural Xenophobia. The latter became a major tool of the soviet propaganda and it did work on a large portion of the Russian society—until jazz was proclaimed in the USSR to be a symbol of the hated Western world.

The late 1940s were the years of the vicious "anti-cosmopolitan" campaign, and jazz again suffered, as never before, physical and ideological oppression being labelled a "bourgeois art" and "an Anti-Soviet propaganda tool in enemy hands." Many bands were dissolved or renamed, removing the term, "jazz," from their names. Many prominent musicians who became popular on the radio, silver screen and stage during the war years were arrested for their sentiments. And this epidemic of "anti-cosmopolitism" proved to be nothing more than a thinly veiled form of Anti-Semitism, as the victims were predominately Jewish. The musicians who miraculously avoided arrests, became targets of other forms of repression, such as demotion or firing, stripping of prestigious titles, bans from filming, outlawed recordings and seizures of "contraband."

Valved trumpets, trumpet mutes and saxophones were considered perversions. Chords with diminished fifths, vibrato in the brass and the use of "blue notes" were prohibited. What became known as a time of the "unbending saxophones" brought in a propaganda phrase: "Today he is playing jazz. Tomorrow he will betray his Motherland." Party loyalists were ordered to patrol the places where music was played to make sure compliance with prohibitions were in force. However, with all the intimidation, love for jazz remained alive and brave faithful jazz musicians didn't allow it to die. In the 1950s, underground jazz publications and records made on X-ray films that were widely disseminated and something of the underground collector's prize possessions.

Fast forward to 1974 and a very costly lesson for me personally. The great jazz pianist Oscar Peterson was scheduled to perform in Moscow in the fall of 1974. One of the ticket box offices with which I had a long history of buying "hard to get" tickets had these available, so I leapt at the opportunity and happily paid a scalper's price— what amounted my weekly salary at the time—for two tickets.

What I wasn't aware of while I was going to all this trouble, was that the government official in charge of Mr. Peterson's concert accommodations apparently had no clue about who Oscar Peterson was and committed a string of unforgivable sins where his performance was concerned. First, he allowed, even though limited, a number of tickets to go through the regular box offices and not the usual tightly-controlled, ideology-proof channels of distribution. Second, this bureaucratic hack had relegated this world famous Canadian-born black musician to a remotely placed, second-tier hotel that featured inedible food, shoddy rooms and no transportation to the rehearsal. For Peterson—accustomed to regal amenities and royal receptions wherever he performed—this rude, dismissive treatment by his Russian hosts was (in his words) "untenable." As a result, he packed his bags and departed from Moscow for good.

Blithely unaware of this embarrassing chain of events, I arrived at the concert site proudly holding my tickets, only to learn of the cancellation…There was nothing resembling a refund available to me.

As a musical "happy ending" to this story: Many years later, I had the pleasure of seeing Oscar Peterson perform in a packed Chicago nightclub. When I reminded him of the Moscow misadventure, Oscar, out of sympathy for my boundless appreciation of his artistry, performed his third set—choosing an entire run of musical numbers at my request.

Indeed, for me and many others living in Soviet Russia, American Jazz offered something: a "freedom of movement" we'd never seen or heard before. The kind of unfettered energy this mélange of music—blues, Dixieland, and so-called "modern jazz"—creates was amazing to us. Up from the muddy bottoms of the Mississippi River, the mixed-race bars and marching bands of New Orleans, or the high-rises and jazz clubs of Manhattan—there was a kind of cross-cultural poetry, of riffs and runs and free-flowing expressions of self that depicted a country like no other. It is one that allowed the existence of bands like Benny Goodman's, made up of black and Jewish and Italian and Latino musicians who all gathered in the same place with no other thing in common but their music.

One would think that this kind of egalitarian expression would be perfect PR for the oft alluded to "Communist-collective-culture of equality," but nothing in the USSR could have been further from the truth. This so-called Marxist-Leninist system was not like something the airlines offered, with their designated first, business and coach classes, where you might be upgraded if you had enough "frequent flier" miles or downgraded due to a computer glitch or sudden changes in aircraft. One could move up the ladder only if one showed enough blind loyalty to party, country and cause.

Conversely, there was forever the imminent and unpredictable danger of falling down the ladder—as millions did—ending up losing jobs, homes and worse: being shunted off to GULAG labor camps and finally freezing to death, often for the slightest offense. Meantime, there was always someone just a little above you who could get into a better store, a "sweeter" vacation spot, a more prestigious place to work, or an assignment to a more "Western" country, where one could enjoy all the perks of a better life.

A classic example of the carefully layered "caste system" that prevailed would be the tale of my close acquaintance Tanya S.:

> Tanya was the daughter of a general, deputy commander of the Moscow Air Defense System, which was considered quite a prestigious position in the Soviet High Command, so she was easily accepted to the Moscow Institute of Foreign Languages, from which she successfully graduated with high grades and a specialty in English language. Following graduation an arrangement was made for her to meet the head of the Personnel Department of the Foreign Trade Ministry.
>
> Upon her arrival, Tanya was met by a very polite gentleman who, after a careful study of her credentials, asked her in which country she would like to be posted. Having specialized in English, Tanya promptly selected the United States or Great Britain as her first two choices. After pouring through her files, her interviewer looked her in the eyes and very politely said, "You see, Tanechka, with your father's position

I can offer you India or Egypt." What he meant in subtext was: *Your father is placed highly enough for you to study in that prestigious institute and be sent abroad, but not high enough to get you assigned to the US or UK.*

Indeed, this was true, because her friend and classmate, the granddaughter of a Politburo member, was placed half an hour later by the same gentleman with the Soviet Trade Mission in New York.

Boris beats a "rigged" system and gets his shot at a PhD

First of all, let me say—and I say this from my own experience—I think discrimination and depriving anybody of equal access and rights because of such factors as a race, religion, ethnicity or anything else related to the one's birth is *insulting to the individual.* By the same token, providing somebody privileges because of all those factors is *equally damaging to both the individual and the society* that induces contortions to "level the playing field." Lowering the bar will ultimately cause people to lose the ability to jump altogether.

No doubt, two thousand years of persecution has left some indelible imprints on the Jewish character and psyche. However, I think we Jews have learned from our sages, such as the greatest Jewish thinker and philosopher (also physician) of the medieval period, Maimonides, who codified Jewish law and revolutionized Jewish thinking...and conceived the idea of social justice as a series of activities *(mitzvahs)* to help others.

Maimonides ranked these activities as the rungs of a ladder, where the lowest rung is giving handouts, the middle is providing loans, and the top rung is helping people get jobs that will result in the recipient becoming self-sufficient instead of relying upon the charity of others. With that comes the ancient adage: *"Give a man a fish and you feed him for a day. Teach a man how to fish and you feed him for a lifetime."*

Among other effects on Jewish character in general is a tradition of learning through a debate and criticism rather than obedient memorization. Also, forced moving between countries and cultures while being prevented from owing land and barred from many professions, we had to adjust and develop mental flexibility.

The overall effect of this has proved to be somewhat Darwinian in its ultimate result, because Jews have not only survived every incident of discrimination, but have also risen to excel. Perhaps this is one of the reasons of winning 20 percent of all Nobel Prizes while comprising 0.2 percent—a hundred times our share—in world population. T

The Jews have never received anything in the form of selective privilege to compensate for past injustices or unfairness. Let me bring up one example from my personal life which is familiar to many thousands of my countrymen.

After a favorable interview with the Head of the Laboratory and potential PhD advisor, Dr. Valentine Leirich, I was directed to obtain the entry exams, requirements and program. Arriving at the office of the post-graduate administrator, I was told that all the forms I needed had been already handed out, and there was not a single copy left for me.

It was then that Dr. V. Leirich took it upon himself to make the effort to find an extra copy for me, which he discovered incidentally in another stack that had been "conveniently" salted away. At the same time, it was brought to my attention that there were at least three other applicants for that self-same PhD resident position—an Army Veteran, a woman who was an active Communist Party organizer, and a young man from Azerbaijan who qualified as an ethnic minority—all of whom apparently had better leverage than I, due to what might euphemistically be deemed more "desirable" profiles.

Nobody among my family and friends knew about my aspirations. I'd kept them secret as my protection from being embarrassed in case things went sideways for me. I knew that if I were to succeed, it wouldn't be enough to be as good as those three candidates—I had to be many times better.

Had that disadvantage made me weaker or stronger? The answer is an obvious one. For the record, and to be perhaps both politically correct and gender balanced, the powers that be at the Institute did later open one more PhD candidate slot—this one for the selfsame female Communist Party Organizer, who very pointedly turned me in a year later for the sin of being "candid." An apparent slip of the tongue brought me to the brink of being expelled from the residence.

The tipping point proved to be an intermediate exam on the philosophy of Marxism-Leninism, which happened to be the easiest thing for me, even without extensive studies. For the first time in my life, I received only a "satisfactory" grade (a 3 on the Soviet scale). Obviously upset, I returned to the laboratory and told my advisor about it, adding somewhat brazenly, "evidently Moshe Dayan wasn't shooting the Arabs only." Again, the comment was timely because I made it in August of 1967, shortly after The Six-Day War—which was an eyesore in Soviet circles.

Many months later, as I sat in a night train car with Dr. Leirich on our way to Minsk, he told me that it cost him several somewhat painful days in heated arguments with the administration to prevent my expulsion. By the way, Dr. Valentine Leirich (of blessed memory) was of German descent, but with an out-look toward the Soviet system that closely resembled my own. It was also much due to the efforts of Dr. Leirich that I was able to gain acceptance to PhD pro-gram and conduct research and development that was badly needed in the late 1960s.

In 1958, the Soviet Union had discovered vast stores of high-grade oil in Western and Northern Siberia in what would turn out to be the largest plot of hydrocarbon production in the world. This potentially made Russia one of the three largest oil and gas producers, and set into motion what would turn out to be its number-one cash industry, even today.

In order to deliver oil within the Soviet Union and a growing western European market, the Soviets designed a gigantic pipeline system that required large-diameter steel pipes. Considering the economic and strategic danger of the West being dependent of cheap soviet oil (sounds familiar today?), in 1961 NATO, under American pressure, imposed an embargo on export of the large-diameter pipes to the Soviet Union.

Unfortunately for the West, the politics of energy always prevail. Eventually (if not sooner) Russia's vast stores of petroleum placed it in a number-four ranking of the richest oil reserves in the world, making it extremely popu-lar inside the Warsaw Pact and as a trading partner with such energy-hun-gry nations as Japan, India and Brazil. Ultimately, the cheap prices at the gas pump that would come from this were simply too tempting for even the USA to resist…further evidence that in the end, all decisions become ones of eco-nomic reality.

In 1966, I began my work on my PhD dissertation at the National Institute of Pipeline Construction (VNIST), the task assigned to me was to find steel pipe alternatives.

A word about the Six-Day War and how it changed my life

In 1967, my dream country was still the United States of America. It was the bastion of Democracy, the Paragon of Freedom and the antithesis of the Soviet Union where I was born and raised. At that point, politically and culturally my Jewishness had been a secondary factor, but on the evening of June 5, 1967, the world began to change. Leaving the main Moscow (Lenin) library where I was doing research for my dissertation, I picked up a copy of the *Moscow Evening* newspaper.

As I finished reading the lines about successful actions of Egyptian, Syrian and Jordanian air forces in the first hours of their war against Israel, I wanted—instead of going down to the next-door subway station on my way home—to run to Israel, to fight for Israel, to be a part of its soul. Just the image in my head of thousands Soviet-made planes covering the skies above this tiny nation, and dropping bombs on my Jewish brothers and sisters—the Children of Zion, was simply too much to take. Here I was, a grandson of Holocaust victims, feeling desperate and helpless and beside myself with angst reading about the catastrophe of Jewish annihilation happening once again.

This infused me with a level of dread that I'd never quite known before. It heightened for several hours until sometime after midnight, I was able to break through the usual jamming and finally catch the *Voice of America* broadcast, where I would learn the truth about the real events of the first hours of The Six-Day War. There was some relief, as the initial celebratory tone of Soviet propaganda gradually became more somber.

My sense of relief turned to pride as the real picture of the war seeped through the densely jammed Western radio stations with the pieces of information we manage to catch. This welcome news was shared through the smiling faces, the expressions of relief and the whispers exchanged between my Jewish friends and colleagues who experienced the same awakening of their Jewish identity that I did.

These were six memorable days featuring a David vs Goliath battle, during which time Israel, with a population of 2.7 million, crushed the armies of three Arab countries populated by 40 million people and funded by billions of dollars in dark money—all of them seeking her destruction. Misled by the boasts of Egyptian President Gamal Abdul Nasser, proclaiming they were, "drowning the Jews in the Mediterranean Sea," the UAR-led coalition that included Egypt, Syria, Jordan, Iraq and Saudi Arabia completely came unraveled—leading to massive losses of more than 26,000 casualties versus less than 1,500 for the Israelis. This was followed quickly by Israel's capture of the Golan Heights in Syria, the West Bank of Jordan and the entire Sinai Peninsula in Egypt.

This demonstrative victory made Israel the preeminent military power in the Middle East, able to prove to the world that it meant what it said when it promised: "Never Again." This was its vow to defend the Jewish People in the land it returned to after 2,000 years of powerless diaspora. This overwhelming pride I felt for Israel's heroic achievements led to changing my mental direction—from the US to Israel. This was exactly what I read later in the book by Klein Halevi titled *Like Dreamers*.

Discovering this not only affected me, but also several other Jews I knew in Moscow. We experienced a kind of passionate patriotism for our historical homeland in Israel that we felt for no place else. There was an emotional trajectory that united the Jewish people in a way never seen since the revelation at Mount Sinai 3,500 years ago. And, it was happening to us in the country with a vicious pro-Arab, anti-Israel propaganda machine running 24/7…where any support for Israel was looked upon as a form of treason.

As often happens at times like this, energies converge at the very same place in time, some of which collide with one's prevailing state of mind. Such was the case in early 1968 when I met, wooed and wed a lovely young, Jewish woman named Natasha. Natasha was a spirited girl with just the right kind of saucy allure that could catch the attention of a confirmed bachelor such as myself.

At that point, I was nearly 30 and one of the few men I knew who had remained unmarried. In fact, the thought of matrimony had seldom if ever entered my mind—and yet here I was. Natasha's father also happened to be a Lieutenant Colonel in the Red Army, knew of my famous uncle and admired him, which doubtless contributed toward their approval of me as a prospective son-in-law. The rest of it had to do with my prospects, as by that time I was well on the way to achieving my PhD and after that, the sky could be the limit: an ironic notion in an Orwellian nation where there were "many limits…and very little sky."

So, in 1968, Jewish born Natasha and Boris married, with no signs of a traditional Jewish wedding ceremony…instead it was a rather a simple "civic" affair with family members in attendance. There I was, my life seemingly laid out before me: marriage to a nice Jewish girl, my PhD in the offing, destined to raise our own nuclear family while enjoying all the amenities of a tidy, mid-level Soviet lifestyle (so long as I kept my head down and did not openly defy the Party line). Who could ask for anything more?

To quote Woody Allen, who paraphrased the Jewish saying: "If you want to make G-d laugh, just tell him your plans."

Jews and Jazz: "Strike Up the Band"[26]

Shortly after we got married, Natasha asked me why almost all my friends were Jewish. Later on, even today, some Jewish people I know get riled up (or even peeved) when I emphasize my adherence to our Jewish traditions.

In the famous film *Exodus,* based on Leon Uris's bestselling novel, the lead character Ari, played by Paul Newman, states: "I'm a Jew," to which his gentile girlfriend replies "All these differences between people are made up. People are the same no matter what they are called." But Ari asserts his Jewish identification: "Don't ever believe it. People are different. They have a right to be different. They like to be different."

This is very true, and as the French say: *"Vivre la différence!"* Our world is enriched by different identities and the cultural heritages they all bring. It would be impoverishing for our civilization to lose Italian or French or Greek, or any other "ethnic" identities. For us Jews, it would mean losing our 3,500-year-old heritage with all the religious, civil and cultural traditions we have developed and retained, including the Hebrew language, while living thousands of years in exile before restoring our own country, Israel. It would also mean forgetting the suffering and losses our ancestors experienced throughout history by the hands of their hosts and their neighbors, while managing not only to survive and retain their own identity but also to make

---

26 *Strike up the Band.* A hit song, Broadway musical and feature film by "America's Favourite Composer," Irving Berlin. A Russian Jew, born in Tyumen in 1888, Berlin emigrated with his family to the USA at the age of 5 and soon became the most prolific composer in the history of modern American music. He composed more than 500 hit tunes, and won an Oscar, three Tonys and a Grammy Lifetime Achievement Award. He composed all the music for the *Jazz Singer, Alexander's Ragtime Band,* and two dozen other feature films, many of them highlighting Ragtime, jazz and other forms of "ethnic" music. Berlin also composed the USA's *other* national anthem, "G-d Bless America," and was considered by several Presidents from Woodrow Wilson to Dwight D. Eisenhower as the most patriotic American in entertainment.

major contributions to the world's ethics, laws, sciences, business and music. And, "Oh, what music they made!"

It is thought that the oldest known form of musical notation—notes—can be found in the Tanakh (Jewish Bible), where every phrase has a sign to show how it should be sung or chanted. Such notes (or tropes) are still sung several times a week in synagogues around the world.

Listening to the jazz and *Great American Songbook,* I was often hearing and reading Jewish surnames like George and Ira *Gershwin,* Benny *Goodman* and Leonard *Bernstein,* which made me wonder about the soul and substance of the contribution of Jewish Americans to this kind of music. Soon after, I came to learn that, just like in the Soviet Union, the popular American songbook of the 20th century, extensively converted to jazz, was dominated by the people of Jewish ancestry—Gershwin, Arlen, Kern, Berlin, and Richard Rogers. The latter was told by a young Cole Porter, who at the time was still unknown, but he had discovered how to write hit songs, saying: "I'll write Jewish tunes."

Later on, Rogers said the most enduring Jewish music was written by an Episcopalian millionaire born on a farm in Indiana. Indeed, the haunting minor-key melodies of "Night and Day," "My Heart Belongs to Daddy" or "I Love Paris" often come-off as Eastern Mediterranean. In return, there are eleven iconic Christmas songs written by Jewish composers, including such hits as, "White Christmas," "Let it Snow" and "The Christmas Song (Chestnuts Roasting on an Open Fire) by Irving Berlin, Sammy Cahn and Chicago jazz singer Mel Torme. As I had mentioned, the USA's other national anthem, "G-d Bless America!", was also composed by Irving Berlin, and has recently gotten many votes to replace the Star-Spangled Banner—something Berlin himself would have never approved of doing.

In terms of pure musical genealogy, Jewish involvement in this uniquely American music form goes back to jazz beginning when the Sicilians and Jews were overrepresented in the early New Orleans jazz scene. The most famous black son of the Big Easy, Louis Armstrong was noted for wearing a Star of David around his neck for the entirety of his adult life—as a gesture of gratitude to the Karnofsky family who bought him his first cornet and instilled in "Satchmo" a passion for singing from the heart with their Yiddish lullabies. These musical connections are often traced to the shared history of suffering, which can be heard from the blues to the wailing in traditional Jewish payers.

According to Ray Charles, "If somebody besides a black ever sings the real gut bucket blues, it will be a Jew..." Sure enough, some of the crossover blues and aching laments of immortal lyricists such as Leonard Cohen, Bob Dylan (aka Bobby Zimmerman) and Paul Simon (of Simon and Garfunkel) have their roots in the muddy banks of the mighty Mississippi and the ghettos of upper Harlem.

In the 1920s and 1930s, when 20th century Jews were still not fully accepted, so-called Tin Pan Alley composers like George Gershwin and Irving Berlin were writing musical versions of all-inclusive America, creating "melting pot" compositions that incorporated a multitude of American ethnic groups. According to Charles Hersh, they saw their music as an embodiment of the American, prejudice-free meritocracy.

Most white Americans of the 1920s thought of jazz as the work of whites, as they danced to bands like the Paul Whiteman Orchestra playing the music of Gershwin and Berlin and listened to the phonograph recordings of Al Jolson and Eddie Cantor. This led one critic to write in 1927: "A good part... of what we know as jazz is Jewish."

From the mid-1930s to the 1940s, Jewish jazz musicians and promoters such as

Irving Berlin and Al Jolson, composer and star of The Jazz Singer. *The first ever "talking picture" produced by Warner Brothers. They are pictured after a round of golf at Riviera Country Club in 1929.*

Benny Goodman, Artie Shaw, Woody Herman, Norman Granz and George Wein were the first to break the racial barriers and engage with black musicians at a time when such engagements were taboo. Goodman was the first to have a mixed-race quartet, hiring Teddy Wilson and Lionel Hampton when white band leaders did not employ black musicians.

Even though in 1938 segregation was in *full swing* (pun intended), the Benny Goodman Orchestra nonetheless managed to smash all racial barriers with both Wilson and Hampton appearing on the bandstand at the first-ever Jazz concert at Carnegie Hall...along with six other artists of color, including Count Basie himself, and key artists from both Basie's and Duke Ellington's band. Interestingly enough, at that ground-breaking concert, Goodman, far removed from his Jewishness and married into the WASP Vanderbilt family, featured a klezmer-like solo by Ziggy Elman of a Jewish dance (*freilach*) as well as the all-American favorite song *"Bei Mir Bist Du Schön"*, which was later made into a top ten hit by the Andrews Sisters in 1944.

Doubtless to a connoisseur of great music, the list of immortal Jewish jazz instrumentalists is long, including such past greats as Al Cohn, Stan Getz, Zoot Sims, Mel Torme, Lee Konitz, Herbie Mann, Buddy Rich, Artie Shaw, Woody Herman and George Shearing. Musicians living today and still "rocking the room" are: Eric Schneider, Ted Rosenthal, Emet Cohen, Anat Cohen, Bill Charlap, Tamir Hendelman, Marlene Rosenberg and many others.

Jews also dominate the business of presenting and promoting jazz and other music to the public as record producers, publishers, managers, concert promoters, critics, historians and jazz festival organizers. The most famous jazz festival of all—the Newport Jazz Festival—was founded by George Wein, and Jazz at the Philharmonic by Norman Granz. The Joe Segal Jazz Showcase in Chicago has been the leading venue for hosting the world's jazz greats since 1947. It remains my most cherished place to hear great music and is a kind of sanctuary unto itself. The annual Jazz Festival at Sea (Jazz Cruise) is organized and directed by Michael Lazaroff, one of the all-time impresarios of modern music.

The Jewish role in Hollywood, which was an integral part in the Jazz popularization and promotion, is well known. It also had roots in the long history of discrimination when the elite theaters, just like law firms and prestigious hospitals, chose not to employ Jews. So, many Jewish entrepreneurs turned to Hollywood and the nascent film industry. While there were many non-Jewish studios, such as Disney and Epoch (D.W. Griffith Studios) who were racist and produced the KKK-glorifying epic, *Birth of a Nation*, Jewish immigrants from Germany and Russia founded others that became the most powerful in the industry—MGM (Metro-Goldwyn-Mayer), Warner Brothers, Universal, and Columbia to name a few. And it was Warner Brothers and Universal in particular that embraced musicals featuring Jewish composers such as *The Jazz Singer, Rhapsody in Blue, Alexander's Ragtime Band* and *The Benny Goodman Story.*

However, not all the close jazz related interconnections were always harmonious. Famous jazz and classical trumpeter Wynton Marsalis, who is also acknowledged as one of America's leading educators and musicologists, has claimed that, for a number of years the music business is controlled by "people who read the Torah and stuff" … and that they try to oppress blacks to compensate for their own history of persecution.

Goodbye Nikita:
Hello Stodgy Shadow Bureaucracy

By mid-1964, Soviet Secretary General Nikita Khrushchev had enjoyed a 10-year run that, by any standard of measure, had to be called inconsistent. A political animal of proud extremes, he had achieved some major coups, including winning a race to space and—through Soviet eyes at least—outmaneuvered JFK and his minions during the Cuban Missile Crisis, a seeming bit of "Brinksmanship" that, behind the scenes, got Russia just what it wanted: US removal of missile bases from the Turkish frontier followed by the Comprehensive Nuclear-Test-Ban Treaty (CTBT) that benefitted the USSR that was years behind in technology.

Domestically, he "de-terrorized" a deeply damaged Soviet psyche by permitting some carefully calibrated expressions of freedom, while remaining equally suppressive of broadcasts and publications from the West. He emptied out the GULAGS, but didn't close them entirely, still leaving 5 million or more inside the Soviet penal system—while moving many to "less dire venues" away from the deadly Siberian Archipelagos that Stalin seemed to prize so much.

Still he remained a foreign policy "hip-shooter" with a reputation for being both reckless and something of a "one-man band." This applied in good ways, marked by his months-long trips abroad to mend fences with nations like the US, UK and Western Europe. This only served to antagonize Mao Zedong and a rising China that found his liberal policies an insult to their view of world Communism. Even though Khrushchev tripled the size of the KGB and used its operatives in two ways: as a subtler tool of repression for the average Soviet citizen, and as a recruitment tool in virtually every Third World nation across the globe, his disregard for Red China led to a bottoming out of Sino-Soviet relations to such an extent that Leonid Brezhnev and other members of the Presidium began to grow concerned.

Finally, it was Khrushchev's style of governance that did him in. Rather than consult the Politburo or key members of the Presidium, he would act arbitrarily with little or no advance warning. Under the terrorist regime of Stalin, this might have been understood and even condoned, but Khrushchev himself had modernized the government to such an extent that he had created a monster of expectation.

Weary of being overlooked and concerned that the Soviet Premier's bipolar political policies were damaging its status inside the Warsaw Pact, Leonid Brezhnev and Alexi Kosygin combined forces in 1964 to force Khrushchev out of office—not by any coup, show trials or epidemic of arrests. They simply asked the man to retire. Betrayed in the end by his own KGB, somewhat meekly he did.

Left with a pretty decent stipend, on the way out Khrushchev commented to his successors: "If Stalin had been in power, there wouldn't even be a wet spot left of the men who had tried to arrest him. I have left office without a single drop of blood being spilled! That has been my contribution to the Russia that we love…"

CHAPTER NINE

Lift Off:
The Great Escape

"Freedom lies in being bold!"

~ Robert Frost

May 18, 1977

Apersonal note to all the loved ones I've left behind: I'm doing this for you—for all of us, for anyone who's ever longed in their heart to be free. I do this to be an inspiration, a role model for what it takes, and an example proving that when you struggle to find the truth, that path will reveal itself. As I do so—as I risk all—I am exhilarated, terrified, giddy, anxious and hopeful beyond hope as my Aeroflot Flight 129 (Soviet Airline) from Moscow to Vienna slowly pulls out of the gate and taxis down the runway.

I'm finally being permitted to leave the place where I was born and lived for almost 40 years: Moscow, Capital City of the country called the Soviet Union, crown-jewel of the USSR, and site of a storied tradition that goes back 1200 years.

(For the majority of my countrymen, Moscow was the apex, the "Capital of the World," the status symbol of all success, the center of the Soviet mindset and the Bolshevik Revolution, the seat of culture, the locus of Communist power, the heart of the Central Committee. For me, it had become a penitentiary, and I was making a jail break.)

I was living in a world best described by Aleksandr Solzhenitsyn when he summarized his own work, *The First Circle*: "Moscow is a prison. Its inmates work in the First Circle of Hell—as prisoners in the KGB secret research institute, *Sharazhka*. They joke, laugh, love, make complex moral choices, and yet there is no escape from Moscow and from themselves."

At this point, I am on my own. I'm now divorced. I've given up a relatively lucrative position and living standard. I'm leaving behind my family: generations of Russian and Ukrainian-born Jews. Though it pains me to do so at times, and though I shall miss my loved-ones, I am not looking back. (I can't afford to. I must look forward.)

Even though this is the culmination of 39 years of my life, it has truly been the last almost 20 years—of obsession, focus and passionate desire—that have led me to this moment. It hasn't been easy. No life-changing decisions ever are. This one came at great expense and in the face of mountainous opposition. Still, I had no other choice. It was either leave or become yet another gray eminence in a nation that had long ago lost its soul, thus creating a new reality that no sane human being can survive. ...To the backstory...

The birth of a Refusenik: Boris gets his wings

It didn't happen overnight. And yes to the unasked question: It was a compilation of events that truly began in my early teenage years. Yet there had to be milestones, revelations, tipping points and aha! moments that finally propelled me into searching, preparing myself and plotting my course of action.

Beneath the face of it, it had been the accumulation of over 20 years of disillusionment, awakening, investigation, and passionate pursuits of the truth through a maze of misinformation and propaganda that got me to this point.

The ray of hope, for Boris Dragunsky at least, was a series of events in Riga in 1968 when I beheld a beam of sunlight that revealed itself to no one else but me. There I was, recently married—the Jewish equivalent of "Boris and Natasha" enjoying the "idyllic upper middle-class" Soviet lifestyle that seemed to satisfy everyone but yours truly.

While doing experimental work for my dissertation at the Physics Department of the Riga Polytechnic Institute, I heard a rumor that thrilled me to the core of my being. It was about 1,000 Jewish people living in the annexed parts of the Soviet Union, such as Western Ukraine and the Baltic

Republics—individuals and families that were being allowed to leave the Soviet Union.

Realizing that my short stay in Riga, the capital of Baltic Latvia, provided me with a potential window for our getting out of the Soviet Union, I saw it clearly as a gift from G-d unlike any I'd ever experienced before. (Was it the opportunity of a lifetime? I would know soon enough.)

Upon my return to Moscow, I suggested to my wife that we move to Riga as a permanent residence, at the same time not yet revealing my underlying motives. This suggestion was looked upon by Natasha and members of both our families as nothing short of madness. To abandon our Moscow residence (*propiska*)—the envy and life-long dream of 200 million Soviets—and move to the "boonies" and Latvia to boot was unbelievable!

At that point my dream—my real dream—had been born. From this time forward, it grew from a dream into a desire…and from a desire into an obsession that would last until those airborne moments.

Several months after returning from Riga, I came to learn that even in Moscow there were now people seeking emigration to Israel and clandestinely studying Hebrew. Just like after the Spanish Inquisition, they studied in secret, with the danger hanging over their heads. This was done so much in secret, that when I joined them later, I didn't even share this with my family. I told Natasha on an earlier occasion, but she was too terrified to join us, and discouraged me from doing so. At this point, however, I was not to be deterred.

Given my career course, it seemed a kind of cultured madness for me to pursue in secret this "subversive" alternative course of action of embracing a culture and religious tradition denied me from birth, and seriously examining ways to get out of the "glorious" Soviet Union, the apogee of world Communism, and the seat of enormous power.

For those who knew me, it wasn't much of a surprise, because by then I had become known for my loathing of the Soviet system. It had always been something I had spoken of with a mixture of both fascination and passion—to make a change, to jump the Soviet ship of State and get free.

Flashback to 1966 and a vacation trip I'd taken to Bulgaria. I'd been allowed to buy into a group tour to Bulgaria as kind of perk at my workplace. Not surprisingly, it was a part of policy, even while traveling to countries inside the Soviet hegemony, that Russian tourists vacation together in preassigned clusters…and always under the strict supervision and watchful eye of a government-appointed tour guide.

At the time, I was a bachelor and didn't have much of an inclination to have my every moment monitored and controlled. So, when we got to Bulgaria, I often bolted from my tour group, spending much of my time on the sunny summer Black Sea beaches, tripping through the sand, and discretely searching for an American among the sunbathers, looking for someone who could help me to get on the day-trip boat excursion to nearby Turkey that constantly advertised on the hotel walls. (I assumed that every American was somehow concerned about the unfortunate people behind the Iron Curtain)

What I needed was somebody to be brave enough and politically motivated enough to "loan" his passport to a devoted Soviet hater and help him to get into a NATO country and find a pass to freedom (aka the USA). My thinking was that the next day that hero of mine could declare his passport "lost," and there would be no further problems for him. As one can guess, my naïve-as-it-comes quest failed quite miserably, apparently due to the lack of vetting on the American side for political motivations and guts of foreign tourists traveling to Communist Bulgaria.

Unaware of the real reasons for my frequent disappearances, my tour guide was nonetheless quite dismayed and, taking note of my departures from the group, assured me of one thing for certain: "Boris, with this kind of behavior, I can promise you that you'll never get to travel outside our country."

Travel, hell! I was trying to get away from this nadir of brain-dead Communist complacency—this dull, gray Orwellian nightmare where every thought, word and deed required abject obedience to the State!

So, with that memory still burning in my brain, I found myself in 1969 with everything going my way. I was a comfortably situated middle-class Jew in the capital of Russia, looking to move into a condo after the birth of beautiful twin daughters, Sonya and Olga. Yet, I led a secret life where the preponderance of my thoughts—24/7/365—now teemed with finding a way to get out of the USSR by any means possible!

For a while, I kept my secret life—my Hebrew studies and renewed embrace of all things Israeli—away from my family and even away from my wife. Looking for signs of disaffection, I hoped and even prayed that Natasha would eventually come around—that she would finally come to see the truth and pierce the veil of the false reality she'd been so carefully programmed to accept.

Speaking of careful programming…An update on my uncle, as his life's vector had come to diverge from my own.

From My Adoration and Pride to My Condemnation and Shame
The transmogrification of David Dragunsky…from the bravest fighter and Twice-Hero of the Soviet Union to the court's footman and "token Jew."

The great move for my uncle came in 1965 when he became the Army Commander stationed in Erevan, Armenia's capital. He loved his new position and home in a vibrant city surrounded by Mount Ararat, believed to be the home of another famous family—Noah and his arc. He wanted to share it with me, which happened the first chance I got while preparing to enter post-graduate school. My trip to visit my uncle in Armenia began with a little excitement due to my Armenian-like appearance.

Settling in my airplane seat, I was welcomed by an elderly gentleman who spoke to me in Armenian. My response in Russian meant I was loudly confronted, first in Armenian, and then in heavily accented Russian and told I should be ashamed of myself for betraying my own language and culture. His rage was becoming more and more heated until I managed to explain that I was on my way to visit my uncle, General Dragunsky.

The man's jaw dropped and after nothing less than enthusiastic apologies he began telling me that Dragunsky was probably Armenian as well, and that the entirety of Armenia was proud of him and had dubbed him among the locals as, "David Sassounsky," after David of Sassoun—the main hero of Armenia's national epic *Daredevils of Sassoun*. Besides learning how proud the Armenians were of their heritage, this trip also provided me with a few other lessons about the country where I was born and lived.

One was the favorite entertainments of his circle, which included the heads of the Communist Party and government cabinet members, was getting together to watch the latest western movies that they had proudly acquired through their sources in Moscow. (This was often done in the old Stalin-born tradition of watching Hollywood movies in a closed circle of elites and carried on with gusto.) While seated among these viewers, enjoying a new Italian movie preceded by a real feast of hard- to-get foods and libations, I asked the First Secretary of the Armenian Communist Party why the public couldn't see such a great art. His response was: "You shouldn't ask such questions."

Another, and more profound experience was the visual picture of the Soviet Border—12,500-mile-long, multi-layered fence around the country (the virtual Iron-Curtain of Winston Churchill's infamous allusion). It made reality the idea that we were living in one great prison—some just got to live in more comfortable cells than others.

As a real treat, and as a means of showing off his power and influence, Uncle David offered me a trip to the Turkish border, which his Army was positioned to defend. For those who never had a chance to visit Armenia, the Ararat Mountain, while in Turkish territory, dominates Erevan's skyline. Ararat is the logo on the labels of many Armenian products, including its world-famous brandy.

Driving towards Ararat, several things caught my eye and struck me to the core: First there was a barbed-wire fence with armed watchtowers set about 250 feet apart, followed by over a mile-wide, finely plowed "no-man's-land" space, followed by another line of watchtowers set about 500 feet apart, before reaching another barbed-wire fence featuring well-camouflaged armed posts. After crossing all this and getting out of the car, I was able to see the highly curious expressions of a Turkish soldier standing about 100 feet from me, while my uncle gently held my waist. I guess he could feel my mind's passionate longing to make the 100-foot sprint. Up to that point, I had never been *this* close to the "free" world. (It took me another 12 years to cross this Rubicon.)

In June of 1965, Lieutenant General David Dragunsky became the First Deputy Commander of the Trans-Caucasus Military District with headquarters in Tbilisi, the Capitol of Georgia. His new residence was the former opulent home of Lavrenti Beria—Stalin's sadistic hatchet-man, head of the (MVD) Soviet Secret Services. (His life had ended in 1954 in identical fashion to that of hundreds of thousands of his victims: shot in a Lubyanka basement as a traitor.)

The Trans-Caucasus Military District was one of the largest in the Soviet Army and covered the territory of three Soviet Republics: Armenia, Azerbaijan and Georgia. The former District Commander had retired due to illness. My uncle held the position of the First Deputy Commander *de facto* for many years but never became the official Commander. In Uncle David's own words, his Jewishness was the reason for not receiving the official title of Commander, (a quirk of perception, but nonetheless typical of the prevailing party mentality). Whatever the official designation, his new position was lofty enough for him to enjoy all the perks and privileges of the Soviet elite. And enjoy them my uncle did…which made his acceptance of a transfer to Moscow all-the-more confusing to some.

While serving as an Army Commander in Erevan, Armenia and later in Tbilisi during the 1960s, David Dragunsky's status was certainly the envy of many. It was a position of great power and prestige and—to many of his peers—what might seem to have been the apogee of one's career. All the more reason why so many were utterly astounded when, in 1969, he accepted an appointment as a Head of the Vystrel Higher Officer Courses, headquartered in the Moscow suburbs.

To most of his peers, it seemed like a loss in social status. In fact, his Tbilisi comrades, including the Georgian Secretary of Communist Party and the Prime-Minister, couldn't understand why he would ever agree to it. It meant going from being a pivotal figure known to every person and the "Locus of Power" in the entire Caucasus to moving to Moscow, the one place where there was a perpetual avalanche of generals vying to be in the "inner circles" of the Soviet High Command. He was essentially going from being a big fish in small pond to a small fish in a big pond.

He was told as much by the local elites: "David you're making mistake. Here, you're famous, but in Moscow you will be lost and will become 'a minnow in the ocean.'"

Since nothing identifies one's status in Soviet society as much as the privileged access to goods and services unavailable to others, my uncle had shown to his left-behind comrades that they were dead wrong and Lieutenant General David Dragunsky was still a "big fish," even in the power-mad, political circles of Moscow.

Once settled in Moscow and with a holiday coming-up—The Day of October Revolution—he purchased several gifts and sent them to those skeptical Georgian elites. Among the gifts were Scotch whiskey, Marlboro cigarettes, Italian silk ties, and Chanel N° 5 perfume for the ladies, to mention a few. The list of luxuries was extensive and delivered to make a point: "Even here I'm a 'big' boy." Nothing illustrated this better than these rare, treasured, prestigious and very Western perks. When he told me about his thoughtfulness, I sarcastically responded that my gifts might well have been more like sending these people the just-issued latest editions of Karl Marx and Vladimir Lenin publications...which openly characterized our still-close relationship at that time.

Shortly after moving to Moscow, David Dragunsky was promoted to the rank Colonel General—three stars in the Soviet Army—the highest general rank awarded to any Tank Forces Commander (before Marshal). Whether by circumstance or necessity, it was also about the time that our family gatherings with my uncle became less frequent and often concluded in what might euphemistically be described as a difference of opinion...over many things.

I also recall this time as a kind of open wound for me personally. It was the beginning of a confluence of events—ones that would alter all our lives for the next decade. And it was the period when my uncle's path would diverge from my own.

Many events would influence that slow but inevitable rift between us, along with occasions when I felt alienated from my own Russian homeland. Two would stick our more than any others. Mind-boggling were my memories of the pride and boastfulness of Soviet military personnel over their decimation of "eye-glass wearing" students, daring to protest their invasions in Budapest. Turning a tank turret and firing into the window of the building from which the kids were throwing stones gave this soldier a great rush of pleasure as he saw the young students turning to ashes. This also gave them further reason to brag about it in front of me.

Another shock was at the time of my post-graduation work when the Soviet tanks crushed the Prague Spring of 1969. The reform-minded, newly "elected" leader, Alexander Dubcek, unexpectedly decided to liberalize his Communist bloc country by opening the sealed borders, allowing opposition opinions to be published and broadcast, and opening diplomatic relations with Israel. This was too much for his Moscow bosses, who were afraid that other eastern European countries, especially Poland and Hungary, might follow Czechoslovakia.

While staying in the dormitory of Kiev Polytechnic Institute, where I was conducting experiments in their Physics Department, the only access I had to the radio were speakers installed in each room with daily broadcasts in the

Ukrainian language. One morning I woke up to a string of announcements I didn't want to believe I was hearing, and hoped I was misunderstanding due to my very limited command of Ukrainian. Going outside, I had the unbelievable horror confirmed to me: the Soviet commandos had descended on Prague and ravaged the entire city. Furious and ashamed of my Russian Bear country ripping a much smaller nation apart, I soon returned to Moscow and searched for consolation among my narrow circle of trusted friends.

One friend was a scientist, older than I, who was a part of our larger team. Anxious to share with him my emotions, we met in a secluded open area. After my exasperated, "How could we do such a thing to a small country like the Czechoslovakia?" I received in return his response: "But we liberated them..." Stunned, I had nothing to add to this very inbred Russian logic—We liberated them, therefore we owed them.

In my middle and high school years, I had many ethnic Russian friends but always felt a deep-seated anti-Semitism and prejudice that, beneath the surface of the entire society, including the families of my own friends. The company of 200 million great Russians was making me, one of just 2 million Jews, feel small, insignificant and alienated from the nation of my birth. Now, looking back, I remember having reached the age of 39 feeling like a foreigner living in the land where I was born.

These years 1969 through 1973 could also be counted among those where there emerged the most vicious anti-Israeli, anti-Zionist campaigns in the Soviet press, TV and public at large. This was also the time when my twin daughters, Sonya and Olga, were born and I was finishing my post-graduate work and preparing to present my PhD dissertation.

So, it stuck out to me even more (and wounded me even more deeply) that what had been those cherished times spent with my uncle while my brother Alexander and I were growing up, had now become bones of contention, matters of heated debate and frequent altercations between us—with other family members often finding it necessary to intercede.

Nothing highlighted this new love/hate dynamic more than this one event in particular. It took place a few days prior to my twin daughters' first birthday celebration. The official organ of the Soviet Communist Party newspaper *Pravda* had published a two-page spread containing an article titled "The Criminal Handwriting of Zionism" and it was signed by David A. Dragunsky.

That article tagged Zionism with a common thread of neo-Nazism that likened it to the philosophies of Hitler's Third Reich.

Arriving at our apartment and bearing gifts for their birthday celebration, my uncle was confronted by some very angry guests and his closest relatives. I was equally angry and ashamed, but as a host had to try to calm everybody down. Uncle David left before the party was over, but not without some emotional fraying at the edges. Though seemingly a minor flap at the time, it was the beginning of a new, infamous turn of direction in my uncle's life…one that would affect us all.

From that point on, we realized he had somehow changed from a Twice-Hero of the Soviet Union and morphed into a "token Jew in the Kremlin's Court," the principal conduit for its venomous campaign of anti-Israel propaganda constructed to abort any rebirth of the "Jewish State of Mind," and to slaughter it in the womb before it could find new life.

In 1971, as an apparent appreciation of his political (anti-Israel and anti-emigration) activities, my uncle was appointed to the Revision Committee of the (CPSU) Communist Party of the Soviet Union. This was a highly symbolic but prestigious political posting, and one that required a Faustian pact from him.

For those of us who felt it, this new sense of patriotic zeal for the land of Israel had been dormant for several generations. (But one can never slaughter an ideal, however fragile, once it has been granted even the slightest breath of life.) Nonetheless the pressure was there, and my uncle was turned into a Quisling—the Kremlin's agent to stanch this natural desire to leave the Soviet "paradise" and emigrate to Israel or wherever in the West where Jewishness was freely expressed and practiced.

In the face of all this opposition, propaganda and harassment—some lucky few Jews had managed a successful *Aliyah* (return) to Israel. While trying to keep a lid on my own feelings, I continued to pray to become one of them. As I mentioned earlier with my Riga experience, the seed of freedom once planted had grown into a dream and the dream had become an obsession.

In the meantime, life was taking its own course, and I was finishing my PhD dissertation and getting ready to defend it.

By that time, with my uncle's help, we moved into a roomy apartment at a prestigious Moscow location, and were permitted a home telephone (an extremely rare commodity) and lived, by Soviet standards, a rather luxurious lifestyle. I knew from the experience of my friends and other post-graduates that as a rule the dissertations by Jewish candidates successfully defended to the Graduation Committee were then being sent for final review to an anonymous "black opponent," and from there the failure rate had been close to 90%.

At this point, I was a study in contradiction. While I had worked so hard to achieve my PhD, I also housed a secret hope for being denied the diploma that would serve me well as proof of the blatant Anti-Semitism within the Soviety system and further justify my decision to apply for emigration. Initially, that was exactly what took place, but I was lucky in spite of myself.

Flying in the face of the approval by the 22-member Minsk Polytechnic Institute, my work on a high strength, low gas and oil-permeability concrete was sent for a penultimate review to a "glass expert." (Something I managed to learn through a bribed official.)

Openly dismayed but secretly delighted, I shared this news with Uncle David, who was waiting to congratulate me. Once he faced the evidence of this apparent prejudice, he took it very seriously and immediately called the head of the Military Engineering Academy whose staff member was on the Government Board of PhD Attestation. In a very short time thereafter, I received my PhD, followed by a promotion to Senior Scientist in the First Rank Research Institute of Oil and Gas Ministry (aka *Gasprom* in the parlance of today's Russia). So, there I was, rewarded—even as my secret hopes were dashed. And in an ultimate point of irony—as a token for of my contributions—I was also rewarded with the opportunity to purchase a soviet-made Italian Fiat.

So I, along with two other "lucky" recipients, got to fly to a "lovely" Siberian city called Tyumen (the birthplace of composer Irving Berlin), where the cars assigned to the Ministry had been delivered. Upon our arrival carrying a very large wad of rubles in our pockets, we found the entire car lot deeply submerged by muddy waters. My choice—a navy blue station wagon—happened to be resting right in the middle. Acquiring an irresistible incentive in the form of a few strategically placed bottles of vodka, I induced the enthusiasm of a crane operator who pulled out my mud-drenched beauty from the sludge, dropping it in front of me on a little less muddy unpaved road...

This was the beginning of what turned out to be a 1,100-mile journey, mostly on unpaved, poorly marked, one-lane roads that I had to share with huge timber trucks operated by envious semi-sober drivers, who had little problem trying to force me off the road. Typical of the travel time in this immense, forgotten land with its pathetic excuse for an infrastructure, it took me four full, torturous days to reach Moscow's paved streets. I arrived haunted by more misadventures and close-calls than I could count.

My work after receiving PhD degree included occasional trips to construction sites throughout the country. None of these trips were as memorable as the one I was requested to make that was labeled "very important and extremely urgent!"

It was explained to me that the gas turbines purchased from Italy for the new gas pipeline were required to be installed using strictly controlled concrete foundations to avoid the potential vibrations of the turbines they supported. The manufacturer, who assigned three of its own engineers to be present at the site, specified special non-shrink cement to be used in construction.

To save money, the Soviet authorities decided that they had enough of their own cement and left it off the purchase list. Happy with the hard currency saved, they poured the concrete into the foundation's pedestals all day and proudly walked in the next morning to see the fruits of their hard labor was all cracked. To put it mildly, a panic ensued as the Italian engineers had instructed them to stop the project. This is when our Research Center received the SOS call for help that was immediately translated to: "Assignment for Dragunsky."

To add even more difficulty to the equation, this had all taken place at a remote site in the middle of *Kazak Qyzylqum* ("Red Sand") Desert of Uzbekistan. After taking a long flight to Uzbekistan's capital of Tashkent, I had to transfer to a small, single prop-engine plane that I shared with a loaded generator and a couple of workers. With an estimated 40-minute flight time, we ended up flying close to an hour in heavy turbulence only to be informed by a young Armenian pilot that we were lost and he could not find the location in question.

The only navigation equipment he had was a compass—neither radar nor radio connection were available. We were deep into the desert, and the temperature in that low flying fortress had reached a level of required-competence that was above the pilot's IQ. Fortunately, one of the by-that-time-effusively-vomiting passengers noticed a footprint of the pipeline he used to work on. That was good enough to set me down—into the embrace of the anxiously-waiting Italian engineering trio. With evening approaching, I was invited to their mobile home for dinner, which I obviously couldn't resist.

The one big relief for me was being able to spend the evening in an air-conditioned room—truly for the first time in my life. I had heard about such miracles of inner-climate technology, but here I finally saw and felt it! (It was a world apart!) Keep in mind that the outside temperatures were hovering around 100 degrees Fahrenheit.

Soon afterward, I figured out the following socio-political make up of my hosts: one Communist, one conservative, and one claiming to be an Independent. An animated conversation most certainly accompanied our dinner—along with a (seen-in-the-movies) Chianti wine. As the lively badinage began, I reminded myself that the A/C wasn't the only equipment generously supplied with this dwelling—some listening devices no doubt came along as a package deal.

The capitalistic host began with his admiration for Russian classical music, the Bolshoi ballet and the magnificent subway he managed to see in Moscow. He also indicated the high regard he held for Russian writers such as Tolstoy and Dostoevsky! (No argument from me on that.) The independent fellow joined the first one in complimenting the Russian ballet and great violin players. So far so good.

"You Russians don't even have an idea how lucky you are!" (This was coming from my new communist friend.)

"What makes you to believe that?" I asked, directing my voice at the ceiling where I strongly suspected the microphone location might be.

Turning decisively towards me, he continued: "I have worked all over the world—Asia, Africa, Latin America—and you are the luckiest people on Earth… You don't even suspect how miserable is your life!"

(Even less argument here! These had been my thoughts for years, and were now expressed with a smile…from a third, disinterested party at that.)

That period of promotion and "reward" was followed by an occasion of longing, followed by a tinge of jealousy when, in the spring of 1973, I was seeing off my close friend Felix—architect, artist and jazz connoisseur—as he, with his wife and little son, prepared to depart for Israel, having been granted a visa to leave the country.

It was also in October 1973 that the Arab countries, trying to recover the losses they had suffered in the Six-Day War, had attacked Israel on the holiest day of *Yom Kippur.* Israel was prevented this time from a preemptive strike by outside pressure from the USA and its own intelligence failures. So, it had to fight for three long weeks before decisively turning the tide and defeating Egypt and Syria…yet again. During that time, it was almost a daily ritual for us to be glued to our short-wave radios, desperate to learn all we could while remaining faithful in our belief in a victory. This war, known as a Yom Kippur War, however, came at a cost in terms of human losses—ones that were three times higher than the Six-Day War, with almost 2,700 Israelis killed and more than 7,000 wounded.

For a small country such as Israel these losses were gigantic, and would be proportionately equal to 180,000 killed and 475,000 wounded in a country the size of the USA. For the entire month, each piece of news learned through jamming was very carefully and discretely shared by whispering with my trusted friends and colleagues.

As more—although still very few—managed to emigrate, additional letters were finally starting to come back; each one passing through dozens of hands with their contents spread about even more broadly. My main source of information was my now-living-in-Jerusalem friend Felix. His wife, long suffering from asthma, turned out to be another collateral victim of the war. Living in temporary housing for new immigrants, there had been an unusual run of cold, wet fall weather, and she succumbed to her illness late in 1973, leaving my friend and his teen-aged son without a wife and mother. In the wake of that, Felix, excellent writer that he was, still regaled me well with his impressions of a burgeoning Israeli society.

Notwithstanding his tragic loss, he was happy to be in Israel and loved living in his adopted nation's eternal capital of Jerusalem. There was, however, one caveat that stood out for me in his writings, which was Israel's semi-socialist economic and bureaucratic system of government. Indeed, the left-leaning Israeli Labor Party *(HaAvoda)* had been basically running the country since the establishment of Israeli independence in 1948.

That didn't sit well with me at all. *Not a socialism again!* I thought. *Socialism, granted—but at least with no oppression, censorship or omnipresent KGB.*

Shortly thereafter, I managed to join a Hebrew learning group that gathered secretly in different apartments, but was invariably discovered by the KGB through their active network of informers. Naturally, the presence of a Dragunsky in Hebrew study groups and later meetings with the people actively fighting for emigration, was always looked upon with suspicion.

Not surprisingly, my Hebrew studies were undertaken much to my wife's dismay. By this very act, to Natasha's way of thinking, I was "putting our entire family at risk," not to mention my newfound status as a thriving senior scientist. Guilt in these circumstances is always a part of the equation, and I was admonished to "think of the children." But in a way that's what I was doing… praying that one day in the future they could be free of all this.

Soon enough, this was also the beginning of my road to emigration, which just as surely developed into an aversion with my wife. She didn't even want to entertain the thought of embracing such an "uncertain life"—one that would involve separating from her parents to whom she was totally devoted.

Her father, a former Lieutenant Colonel and Commander of an artillery battalion, was forced to leave his beloved army, as his career had at last arrived at a virtual dead end. He was only too well aware that he had been sidelined because his name was Kagan—a Jewish surname. Still, he remained a loyal Communist and Soviet patriot to the end…and, as such, blindly devoted to the Party Line.

Nothing pointed that out to me better than the milestone event that took place in 1971, when US Astronaut Neil Armstrong became the first human being to ever set foot on the moon. On the day of the Apollo landing, we happened to watch the evening TV news together. After about 30 minutes of reports of the record *kolkhoz* harvesting and steel workers' outputs, along with the glorious successes recorded through all the socialist countries, the last 20-second fragment of a half-hour Soviet Central Television program mentioned, "the Americans managed to land a man on the moon." As the program ended with this signature dismissal, I asked my father-in-law what bit of news he thought was more important: the record cow-milking or fulfilling mankind's dream of being on the moon. His unequivocal answer was, "For us it's the *kolkhoz* news."

Another was a fluke in the postal service. I was subscribed to a small political weekly news magazine delivered on Monday. Because that Monday fell on the May 1st, i.e. May Day, a national holiday, the magazine was delivered on the preceding Friday and contained the next Monday's news that Israel had conducted a military parade in Jerusalem in spite of the international protests of its, "illegal occupation of Arab Jerusalem." When I asked him how come Friday's print managed to inform us of next Monday's event, his response was: "But they've done it…and it was illegal!"

Soon enough thereafter, I came to realize that I would never be able to convince Natasha that Israel would be an option…and it wasn't long before our marriage started to deteriorate.

By then, I also had another obstacle to overcome. Having a living parent, I, by a strict government rule, needed my father's written, notarized consent to allow me to emigrate. The age of either party didn't matter as far as the rules were concerned, and served as an artificial and quite effective barrier created by the authorities to truncate all attempts to leave our "beloved" Mother Russia.

My father had no love for the Soviets but, as any parent would have, had concerns about the uncertain future that awaited us in a foreign country. The other of his concerns was the constant fear of jeopardizing his only brother, who seemed to be at the pinnacle of his public life. So, he was asked me to wait at least until he was no longer a Central Committee member.

Meanwhile my uncle, no stranger to bragging about his privileges in front of his own politically aware nephew, often took time to share with me a confidential news bulletin called, *The Blue Book*. Available only to "key party members," discreet copies of *The Blue Book* were regularly hand-delivered to his apartment in Moscow. So secure was this document, that it was carefully bound with an assigned number exclusive to the recipient. As a part of such sharing, a couple of months after the Yom Kippur War, my uncle sat in his library-den, proudly telling me that he was recently with a group of top generals invited to inspect Israeli American-made tanks captured by the Arabs in the first days of the war and handed over to their Soviet satraps. Beginning with those American-made tanks so clearly inferior to the Soviet ones, he finished his lively description of their armored bodies as still having blood stains both inside and out.

Feeling my blood boiling, I said: "Uncle, this is the blood of Jewish boys, just like your own younger brother, burned alive in his tank. How can you even describe this without any feelings?!"

His answer to me was as blood-curdling as it was terse: "They weren't punished enough!"

This was it for me, the moment that broke my heart. The one that emptied out all concerns I might have had about my uncle's "prestige." I left his place in disbelief with tears in my eyes every moment I remembered it. How could those words come from my own uncle, the man I remembered courageously declaring in his younger years that he was "a proud Jew"? This was the man who'd been a proud associate of Golda Meir, who'd miraculously escaped Stalin's wrath, often whispering "our Jewish luck" under his breath, knowing in every moment the real truth of our heritage—a heritage crushed beneath the wheel of the Soviet propaganda machine. And now he'd entirely reversed himself.

I mentioned earlier and emphasize again here, the term used by Polish political philosopher and dissident Czeslaw Milosz in his 1956 book *The Captive Mind,* and how this conditioned state of being infused and controlled the mindset of well-placed individuals inside a Soviet-type totalitarian society:

Regardless of his inner convictions, warped by his own ambition, sooner or later descends into an evacuation of both courage and conscience as he announces to the world: "Since I find myself in circumstances over which I have no control, and since I have but one life and that is fleeting, I should strive to do my best. I am like a crab attached to a crag on the bottom of the sea. Over me storms rage and huge ships sail; but my entire effort is concentrated upon clinging to the rock, for otherwise I will be carried off by the waters and perish, leaving no trace behind." By now it had become a mantra that constantly echoed in my ears. I had pointed to this earlier but it bears repeating, because…this was the collective mindset that had so overwhelmed my uncle that he had now surrendered to the pathology of a Soviet Socialist state. And our "conversion," and his response had completely taken me down.[27]

When I told my father about my uncle's words, he was devastated but was still unwilling to compromise his brother in any way. Yet for the first time, he also welcomed my suggestion that I would ask David directly whether he thought it would be harmful to his standing if I were to apply for emigration. So, I requested a few minutes with my uncle to tell him about my plans and go over any possible complications this might cause for him. His reaction was

---

27 In retrospect, it is here that I realize that my Uncle had entirely gone down the rabbit hole of *Political Ketman*—that his party pragmatism had at last entirely subsumed his conscious.

surprising but freeing: "Do whatever you want. I don't care." (At least, that's what he said.)

For me, it was the permission I'd needed! *I can do it!* I thought. But my celebration was short-lived because my uncle had engaged in what had to be a bit of "cognitive dissonance," and had second thoughts on the matter. In fact, that same evening, David called both my father and my in-laws and asked to meet with them the next day at my apartment. With all of us seated around the table, he started questioning each person, asking, "Are you planning to emigrate?" In the presence of Natasha and her parents, my father responded by saying that his position was that the children should have the right to decide for themselves, an act of both courage and loyalty on his part that netted a terrifying response.

My uncle rose and stated: "Listen to me carefully. I don't give a damn what each of you decides. Here is my veto: Boris will never be allowed to leave the country. Should he try, he will end up either in prison or a mental institution, whatever the authorities determine."

But then came the surprise of the night, and one of the most revealing in my life... As David finished this tirade, my father Zalman, David's elder brother by a year, got up and said the following words: "David you are a Nazi. How dare you harass them?! This is their life and it is for them to decide!" (Here I must add that the word Nazi to my father's generation that went through the hell of war and lost entire families, carried much more weight and meaning for them than to those today who so frequently and nonchalantly throw this word onto people whom they simply don't like and disagree with.)

The next day my dad brought me his signed consent—notarized and official as any document could be. I had my father's consent, while my uncle had his close friend and neighbor, KGB Boss Comrade Chebrikov, have the *last word* as to my future.

My gathering of voluminous papers needed to apply for emigration (the only official course—family reunification in Israel) finally reached my place of work, specifically the so-called, "Special Department," a KGB affiliated security center headed by retired Air-Force Colonel Nikolai Tereshenko. A couple of years prior, while receiving a permit to make a Xerox copy (a routine requirement for using the only copy machine in our huge organization) the Colonel looked at my last name and carefully asked if I was related to General David Dragunsky.

Learning of our relationship, Nikolai Tereshenko got very excited, recollecting their friendship as junior officers serving in Manchuria before WWII. After getting my uncle's phone number, he contacted David, who was delighted to reunite. Later, they met and resumed some sort of communication and I got the Colonel's appreciation for my role in "reigniting" their friendship.

As a token of this appreciation, Tereshenko, the mention of whose name struck fear in the hearts of others, shared with me how he ended up in this civilian position after an illustrious career in the Soviet Air Force. Earlier in his career, he had been a Commander of the Soviet Air Defense Division when U2 pilot Gary Powers had penetrated Soviet air space on May 1st 1960, flying at a nosebleed ceiling of 70,000 feet—almost double the elevation capability of his Suchoi, with interceptors being airborne to shut down Power's U-2.

The Soviet planes never reached their target but a surface-to-air missile fired while the planes were still in the air made a direct hit on one of the scrambled aircraft and blew it up, causing a tremendous air shock that disintegrated the flimsy, lightweight U-2.[28]

As for Colonel Tereshenko, in a backlash from the "U2 Incident" he was called onto the carpet and reprimanded for his failure to protect the skies above his beloved USSR (even though he had precisely done his job). At that moment, he was humiliated by being forced to take off his military garb on the spot, and was never allowed to don his Air Force uniform again. To the surprise of no one, this made him a bitter man, who obviously held a grudge against the authorities who had so clearly misrepresented his efficiency and courage...due to a confluence of unfortunate events, which ironically ended up playing some role in my own personal Odyssey.

At first, I managed to continue in my job without obtaining a security clearance, which was mandatory if I were to be allowed to continue working in the Siberian oil and gas fields. Everything had a secret stamp, including the soil analysis, and the Colonel chose to close his eyes and didn't request his approval. Second, as soon as he received information about my moves, he pulled me aside in the corridor and quietly asked to meet him at an "open" sub-

---

28 By the way, as a matter of coincidence, the perished Soviet pilot is buried in close proximity to my uncle's grave.

urban rail station platform. Once we met there walking and talking through a loud crowd, he asked to confirm my intentions.

Hearing my affirmation, and the passion in my voice, he quietly asked if my uncle knew, and what his intentions were towards me. Learning about my uncle's outburst, the Colonel reassured me that I was not a traitor—and that I was well within my rights to seek a better life. To my surprise, he also emphasized that my uncle was dead wrong and that he was going to convince him not to stand in my way. *G-d bless your soul and rest in peace, Colonel Tereshenko! Wherever you are, my prayers will always be with you!*

Within next month or so I finally had all the papers needed and my petition for emigration had been officially submitted. That was the beginning, but by no means the end.

By Any Means Necessary...

My next phase was the waiting-period for the OVIR decision to come through. By that time, my lifecycle and circle of associations had altered considerably—as I often found myself keeping the company of many applicants, some of whom had been refused, and other lucky ones who had received permits within a couple of months. Knowing all the while that we were being watched by KGB agents 24/7, I still continued to attend Hebrew classes run by other either applicants or "refuseniks." I met many brilliant brave men and women there—people such as a professor Lerner, Felix Kandel, Natan Sharansky, Ida Nudel, Vladimir Polsky, *et al.*

As much as I valued their company, I also had an uneasy feeling that my presence was creating a certain tension in the air, and with it an atmosphere of political paranoia. After all, here I was the nephew of the now-infamous General David Dragunsky, whose TV appearances as a leading voice of the Soviet anti-Israel campaign had come to be broadcast in virtual perpetuity.

It was really challenging—having so much trouble because of both fighting a war of wills with my uncle on the one hand, and being suspected of being his agent on the other. Indeed, the KGB often succeeded in its attempts to compromise the Jewish community, especially by infiltrating applicants and *refuseniks.* Not surprisingly, these suspicions were tied to my name for years to come, even when I was already living in the United States.

This surfaced again not long ago when the intrepid and famous fighter for Jewish emigration, Pamela Cohen, confirmed as much in her recently published book, *Hidden Heroes*. It was unfair and, for me, a character assassination, but I was hard-pressed to stop it. Any attempt to protest would have merely proven a study in futility.

Unlike many other applicants waiting long months to learn of their fate, my "rejection" arrived within a couple of weeks. This decision was exactly what my father was afraid of. So, for a time at least, I thought it best to keep it from him, answering whenever he asked: "Still waiting, no response yet."

Soon enough however, he learned about my new *Refusenik* status from a friend who happened to listen to the *Voice of America* broadcast, which was reporting about sit-down demonstrations of Jewish *refuseniks* in the Supreme Soviet Offices, with the nephew of General David Dragunsky among them.

I also had to keep from him something else that had taken place about two weeks later. It happened when, upon returning from a lunch, I was confronted by the security guards who took away my pass, thus denying me access to the offices where I worked. I had been fired without so much as an interview, and became just like every other *Refusenik*, starting my new career, looking for a job—knocking on doors and waiting in lines at government offices where officials had "zero power," while the real decisions were made behind the scenes at the KGB.

These "government" offices, to be sure, put on a good front. They provided us with very official-looking documents and there were loudspeakers announcing the last names of the hopeless hopefuls. I was never called in by my last name—by the first and patronymic only, which appeared very respectful (but was done to avoid pronouncing the infamous name Dragunsky in front of other *refuseniks* in public). Once I managed to get an appointment with the head of the Moscow Police Department. A short, friendly general was reading my file as I entered. He looked at me and made an uncharacteristic offer for me to sit down so that I might feel more comfortable. His first words after raising his eyes from the file were: "Why do you want to leave this country when all your family and children are here?"

"Comrade General," I answered, "you want my children to grow up as Soviet citizens in the spirit of Socialism and Communism. But I am who I am sitting in front of you, and will only assert a corruptive effect upon them. I will just be a bad influence and nothing of what you'd like them to be."

To my surprise and delight, the General cracked up laughing, telling me that he was an old man and I should not try to change him. With this, he put his hand on my shoulder while very quietly saying that all these things were beyond his control and wishing me a good luck. "Be strong," he said as a parting reminder; not that I needed one. But every bit of encouragement was, at this point, quite a blessing, especially coming from the MVD General.

Facing many people of the authority and propagators of the Soviet system was further proof that many of them were fascinated by all images of the West. All the seekers of expatriation shared their personal stories: about the local police officers and even KGB agents coming to their apartments and spending an excruciatingly long time in their kitchens, just looking at them and asking questions, while listening with fascination about what these people knew of life outside the USSR.

I, myself, had two such encounters: one with the manager of our apartment complex and another with two young KGB agents who showed up in the middle of the day. The former had closed the door of his large office where I came to collect one of the papers needed—ones that indicated no financial obligations—and quietly asked, "Are you sure you can get a job over there?" The young KGB guys asked why was I refused, to which my answer was—either a mistake or a "miscarriage of justice"—whatever choice they preferred.

Along the way, I was also forced to run a gamut of angry Anti-Semites during my ongoing, and seemingly endless, emigration process, many of them determined to make life as difficult as possible for me.

Being fired from my prestigious job while being denied employment everywhere else caught me in a vicious circle, and caused something of an endless dilemma: "You don't work because you're fired. You cannot find a job because you are an undesirable element, and a possible traitor. The person who doesn't work is a parasite, which is punishable by law, and you're not allowed to live closer than 101 km to Moscow." (That was *The Catch 22* I was experiencing—the very definition of a conundrum.)

The other major change at the time involved a change in direction I had decided to make as to my country of choice. Although I remained passionate about Israel and supported the Zionist cause at all levels, I knew that any future attempts to be joined by my family would have a better chance to succeed in the more peaceful and prosperous USA than in the belligerent and socialist-bent state of Israel. For me, for us all, America was still the bastion of

Democracy, protecting the world from a Soviet takeover, standing strong as the safe haven of capitalism, and the place where all things were possible. "The Shining City on the Hill" was a reality in fact. So, it was a paradigm shift, the only one that made sense. I could still be a part of the Jewish people, a supporter of Israel, and always make *Aliyah,* while also possibly united with my children and securing their future.

Almost before I knew it, it was late 1975 or early 1976. My marriage had been on the rocks and finally ended in divorce. I was on my own, renting a room rather close to my daughters, doing what I could and earning my living "by any means necessary." The few jazz records in my collection were sold on the black market to feed me for a while, but was I was inevitably doomed to extinction. I had to know what to do next. Soon enough, my prayers were answered and I seized the moment when it came.

Fortunately, I found a way out, as I was blessed enough to find a part-time job as a technical translator actually working under somebody's else name. I managed to slip through the cracks of the highly draconian Soviet employment authorities.

It was also during this time that I'd become a thorn in the side of Soviet authorities, the KGB in particular, to the point that my last name was never announced through the speakers of the front organizations which were supposed to hear our complains and provide responses. By this time, the names of *Refuseniks* were heralded in the West and monitored by Jewish organizations under the umbrella of the National Conference for Soviet Jewry. My progress was personally monitored by the British group of women called The 35s.

I wasn't passive in my appeals, and my last name, Dragunsky, was becoming a sticking point. And so—at long, long last—I, Boris Dragunsky, was included in the group of *refuseniks* that the Supreme Soviet decided to release as proof of its compliance with the Helsinki Declaration of Human Rights. It was a timely gesture, just before the next Belgrade Conference scheduled for October of 1977, and a moment of political largess from which, for once, I was a beneficiary.

So, on May 18, 1977, I arrived at Moscow's Sheremetievo Airport, still not believing I was actually getting out of the Soviet Russia. After saying farewell to my father, brother, aunts, cousins and other gathered well-wishers—and just before going through the border and custom controls—I nervously went to a dangling pay-phone and dialed the number I hadn't called for a very long

*Colonel General David Dragunsky,
circa 1976.*

time. It was mid-morning and the phone was answered not by Uncle David, but by his wife, who asked why I was calling? When I told her I was leaving the country and wanted to say goodbye to Uncle David, she replied that he wasn't available, and promptly hung up with a click that resounded in my ear. *Had I made fateful mistake? What if…?* That was the unanswered question.

He needed just to pick up the phone but had chosen not to answer, filling me with a fear that was with me for another two hours as I waited, and even stayed with me as I was sitting in my seat on the plane, watching the green KGB uniforms passing by just outside the plane's open doors. I knew, even in that moment—as the doors finally closed and the plane started down the runway—that even though I was leaving Russia, it would still be a very long time before Russia left me.

Arriving in Vienna: A footnote

A pleasant female voice coming through the airplane intercom said: "Prepare for landing. We will be arriving in Vienna, Austria, in 20 minutes." That statement left me gasping for air. I hardly heard the continuing announcement—the words were coming from afar and I was running out of breath. I was finally out of the Soviet Union and out of their reach. For the first time in my life I would be free—my lifelong dream was coming true! I had closed the book on part one of my almost 40-year-long life.

Soon I'd be debarking into a wondrous new world where I would finally be free to choose…everything! My life would now be my own, to make decisions and follow the path that I wished. Mine to rise or fall in a world that would embrace the choices I made.

I'd sacrificed all to be here. I was virtually penniless, as well as homeless and jobless. Yet I would have done it all again...I only wish it had happened sooner! Of all the things I'd left behind, there was one I would never regret—that beast of fear that was present every moment of every day during my previous chapter of life. I knew that once that fear fled from my body, it would never return again.

CHAPTER TEN

Free at Last: "Rocky" Rome Adventure

"You may ask: 'How did this tradition get started?'
I'll tell you! I don't know. But it's a tradition.
And because of our traditions, every one of us knows who he is
and what G-d expects him to do."

~ Tevye
Fiddler on the Roof

I'm leaving you with this brief memorandum. I'm doing this so that you can read and gain some perspective about what it was like to change my life from Soviet oppression to breathing the rarefied air of freedom and so many of the little things that go along with it. I call them "little" though none of them were, because none should be taken for granted. Yet we do. We in the "free" world do, more than we know...

Summer, 1977

Rome. The eternal city, seat of Western civilization, birthplace of the Republican form of government, and for me, the greatest study in contrast I had known to that point in my life. My first weeks of freedom after being permitted to leave the Soviet Union, and after spending a few days in Vienna, are as follows: I was processed by the US Embassy here for admittance to the United States, and waited for my refugee papers. My days were filled with all kinds of paperwork, interviews and medical examinations, so my evenings were left for sightseeing. With practically no discretionary income at my disposal, this involved mostly window shopping. Still, the city is what Ernest Hemingway once described as a "movable feast." There is so much to do, so much to see—the richness and fullness of life, celebrated with a sense of joy and a loss of inhibition.

What matters most, and will for the rest of my life, is the realization that at last I'm finally a man unchained, someone who can see things and experience things, especially American things—without fear of oversight, spying or dire consequences for my actions. There would be no more Big Brother, no more KGB, no more worrying about my family or wringing my hands over every expression of my own individuality.

What can be more a moment of self-expression than seeing an American movie? The one I chose was a US/English co-production produced by United Artists and filmed mostly at Shepperton Studios in London. I went to an afternoon matinee—to see a "red-hot" film based on the smash-hit Broadway show, *Fiddler on the Roof*. I went to a movie on a whim, and it was in English!

For you, your friends and even your parents, and to millions of others young and old throughout the world, *Fiddler on the Roof* is a classic—an extremely successful 1971 movie preceded by the 1964 Tony Award-winning stage play and production. The backstory goes that even superstar Frank Sinatra asked, through his agent, to be considered for the lead in the film version. The Studio turned down his pitch for a number of reasons: First, Sinatra was asking too much money for the role; second, he had already garnered a reputation for being difficult to work with; third the producer/director Norman Jewison was convinced he needed a Jew to play the leading man, and he was right. So, they gave the role instead to Topol! (Chaim) Topol, the "Israeli Marlon Brando," who had also garnered a Golden Globe for the film and a Tony nomination while he immortalized the character of Tevye on Broadway.[29]

Without any idea that the movie I'm about to see is a story based on a Sholem Aleichem book, I've nestled down in a comfortable seat in a large theater—this one is filled to capacity by an Italian audience primarily made-up of women. Here comes the SHOCK! It is all about the Jews and the Jewish culture, and the open embrace of Jewish roots denied to me all my life. What's more, all the people on the silver screen are Jewish! The stories they are telling and songs they are singing and dances they are dancing are all Jewish!

By this time, I'm cautiously glancing around and cannot help but notice that the people surrounding me—regular everyday Italian people—are completely immersed in this alternate reality. They're captivated by the story, involved with the characters on the screen, and are both laughing and shedding tears. I can see you saying: "So what? This is normal. Right?"

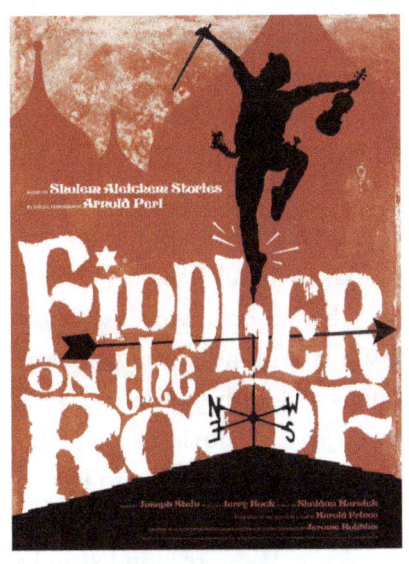

For me, in Rome in the Summer of '77, this is—the first time in my life that I've *ever* seen and heard that we, the Jews, are looked upon and received just like other people. What's more, we were being openly engaged with humanity, empathy and warmth.

Commemorative Fiddler poster, circa 1979.

---

29 After seeing *Fiddler on the Roof* several times on screen and stage over the years, I took my wife to see it again—this time in New York, played in Yiddish, the language in which it had been originally written in the novella by Sholem Aleichem. It was an enjoyable afternoon experience for the 500 people in the audience, and it was well done, providing a feeling of the religious traditions in which those people lived. There are numerous critics who wrote wonderful reviews of all the productions, including this one. For me, *Fiddler on the Roof* is much more than a moving story. With all the emotions and teary eyes, it infuses us with, it also carries with it a sense of loss—the loss I'll feel for never being lucky enough to see my own two daughters under the *chuppah*. Still, it happened to be one of the bookmarks in my travel to freedom.

To add a final point of irony to this cultural soup, *Fiddler* takes place in Russia. Not the Russia of my youth—not Joseph Stalin's Russia, or Leonid Brezhnev's Russia—but 1905 Tsarist Russia. The antiquarian Russia that was overthrown; where, with all its faults, they still allowed Jews to have their own identity, religion and traditions. (Who doesn't feel chills whenever they hear Tevye shout the theme of "freedom" to the winds as he sings: "Tradition!" and the entire cast joins in?)

At the moment of first seeing this, I said to myself: *this feeling alone paid off my long struggle for freedom.* I fully realize that it is difficult for a person born and raised in a normal society to comprehend the sublime novelty of this feeling. Here is the thing: In the Stalin's Russia where I was born—and even in the years after his death—the mention of the word Jew (*evrei* in Russian) was still considered risky. It was something that wasn't brought up publicly in a normal context. One could walk the streets of Moscow using the most profane language out loud without fear of being noticed or paid attention to, but once you uttered the word *Evrei,* a paranoia set in. People would start looking back at you as if they'd heard a shot fired, as if something sinister or dangerous had just taken place.

This wasn't a word used casually. You heard it spoken most often as an insult or in a negative, dismissive, antipathetic context. There were no such things as Jewish books or calendars connoting Jewish holidays—no Kosher food, Jewish schools, or anything of the sort. (I know I'd mentioned this earlier, but imagine having to live with this kind of stigma every day. It was our own invisible version of wearing a yellow armband with a Star of David on the sleeve. We were branded and always waiting for the other shoe to drop.)

I had developed an impulse which led me, even when I arrived in the United States, to lower my voice while uttering the word Jewish, even in a casual conversation. (It was that way for all Jews who had made the same trip to freedom.) This was a natural consequence of growing up and living in the anti-Semitic virulence that prevailed in the Soviet Union. The negative connotation attached to the word, Jew or Jewish, intensified there after World War II, with the concocted, preposterous persecutions and trials, especially after the formation of the state of Israel, and Stalin's paranoia over the 2.5 million ethnic Jews living in the Soviet Union. Prominent Jews and "cosmopolitans," i.e. Soviet writers, composers and other intellectuals, were all accused of having their work influenced by "Capitalist" ideologies from the West.

Recalling my first days in freedom, I was like the proverbial "kid in a candy store." As I processed my papers and jumped through the hoops of emigration, I came to enjoy, in limited ways, the life of a free man in Rome. There was so much to see and do there, even without a great deal of money. (Other than our passage out of the USSR, we were limited to exchange only a maximum of $100.)

Italians—even those in Rome—were open, lively and friendly. Gone were the suspicious glances, the aura of paranoia, the sense of being monitored that had plagued every day of my life. Novel experiences abounded—there were espresso bars and sidewalk cafés, and the streets were filled with wide-eyed tourists, all of them experiencing the city with awe, wonder and a sense of infinite joy. With little money provided by Jewish Organizations, I had to envy the Italians enjoying their cup or two of espresso shared in outdoor coffee bars. They looked like people who could pass the time without a worry over what comes next. There were also the theaters, nightclubs and movie houses—to have the opportunity to see yet another American movie in Rome was amazing!

As an unintended counterpoint, I have to recall that seeing *Fiddler* was not my only filmic experience at the time. I had a bit of a misadventure that was both comical and sad. Since I had studied English and was rather proficient in technical translations of the language, I proudly spent some of my very limited budget and went to see the recently released Oscar-winning film, *Rocky*. Entering the movie theater, hoping my skills in language would be rewarded, I walked out through the exit two hours later, my illusions of proficiency in English utterly shattered. I felt I'd lost a valuable commodity—I failed to understand a single word coming out of Rocky Balboa's mouth. How was I to know that Sylvester Stallone's thick South Philly accent was in no way representative of anything resembling actual American English and that people only spoke that way in one small borough in one very large city on the East Coast?

Poor as one can be—but with a priceless sense of personal freedom—I went out window shopping. While roaming through this wondrous world along the streets of Rome and marveling at the bounty available to so many, I came across a sign that read, American Restaurant Piccadilly. There I was approached by a gentlemen who had been apparently "sizing me up" for quite some time.

After learning I was a Soviet emigrant on my way to the USA, to a city called Houston, he offered me $500 (in 1977 money!) to carry precious stones (diamonds) and deliver them to some of his colleagues in New Orleans. The reason he was asking, he explained, was that I was a Jewish emigrant—therefore deemed trustworthy, since I was neither Italian nor American. Because of this, I was assured that customs would not check me. That $500 was an unimaginable amount of cash to me, especially since I had no more than around $35 in my pocket. This kind of money seemed like a fortune: manna from Heaven. Or was it?

Remembering the adage: "If something seems too good to be true, it usually is," I balked. There could be consequences for doing this, not the least of which I would be trying to slip contraband into the very country I'd strived to adopt as my own for all these years.

Dismayed by my reluctance, this fellow asked me to take one day to think it over. He requested that I meet him the following afternoon at the same place to give him my answer. Facing the dilemma of choosing between an enormous amount of money and cheating the authorities as my first step into the country of my dreams, I spent a restless night and morning thinking, *How could I start my new, although unknown life, as a smuggler and a cheat?* So, I really didn't ponder for long. My answer was an unequivocal, "NO!"

There is a saying in the Old South of the United States: "The Devil most often comes for you at the same time you get to Heaven's gate." Perhaps it wasn't Heaven, but it *was* America. A place called Houston, Texas, was close enough for me.

America the Beautiful...
and a "Garage Sale?"

*"My father described this tall lady who stands in the middle of the
New York Harbor, holding high a torch to welcome people seeking
freedom in America. I instantly fell in love... What a country!"*

~ Yakov Smirnoff

Yakov Smirnoff, a renowned comedian, and I came to this country the
same year and with the same longing for the United States of America,
and we had the same reaction once we arrived here, "What a country!"

So here I was on the way from Rome to my own American Port of Entry: a city called Houston, Texas. According to the HIAS representatives in charge of the Jewish refugee resettlement it was the fastest growing, fourth largest city in the USA, with the best opportunities, a melting pot of immigration, and… the one place I never had in mind while dreaming of America.

After all, Texas was the state where my idol John Fitzgerald Kennedy had been assassinated, his bloodied, brain-exploded head pitching forward onto the lap of beautiful First Lady Jacqueline Bouvier Kennedy. (Who can forget that dreadful day—the fated motorcade at Dealey Plaza in Dallas, the "pop-pop-pop" of rifle fire from an unknown source? It truly was the day the dream died.)

Even now, sixteen years later, another image is indelibly imprinted in my mind: the picture of that elegant couple standing at the Vienna Summit next to "Mr. and Mrs. Piggy," aka Nikita and Nina Khrushchev. There they were: the picture of youth and class and energy, the magical couple from Camelot, bringing America into a new Age of Enlightenment, openness and a Democracy revived.

After a night's stopover in a hotel near JFK Airport and seeing in the morning my only suitcase still standing in the driveway (apparently with nobody, even in NYC, sufficiently seduced to grab that "attractive," Soviet-constructed box), I'm hurried by a Jewish Agency rep over to an early morning Braniff International Airways flight to Houston. I find myself sitting among business-attired, well-groomed and mostly gentlemen passengers. While serving breakfast, the classy and chatty flight attendants quickly figured out that I was not a Chase Manhattan banker on my way to finance an oil deal.

After learning about my roots and happily telling me about her own grandparents who were born in Kiev, one of these attendants reached for a microphone and announced a "warm welcome" to a newcomer to this country on his first flight in the US.

This was followed by several people coming to my seat just to shake hands with a certain unmistakable warmth, and then smile broadly and wish me good luck. A pilot came by later, handing me souvenirs with a "red hot" Braniff insignia. (In 1977, this was the heyday of this Dallas-based airline that specialized in glamour flights, wild colors and ultra-attractive, very friendly, and well-paid flight attendants.)[30] This was my second emotional mid-air experience in the last three months and it was much less stressful than that first one—the one when I had been Vienna bound.

After walking through the impressive carpeted halls of the Houston International Airport (now George H.W. Bush) and being greeted by a representative on behalf of the local Jewish Family Services, I found myself on a huge, almost empty bus that was supposed to deliver me to a transport terminal.

This well air-conditioned bus provided a quiet ride, which allowed me to eavesdrop on a couple of men sitting immediately behind me. So, there I was on American soil, riding down a real American highway in my first-ever air-conditioned vehicle, and I was curious about the things people discuss here. The 45-minute episode of "overhearing" this conversation yielded not a single familiar word of spoken English. Zero! By this time, I had almost convinced myself that I landed in the wrong, non-English-speaking country. I knew I had to be mistaken though, because the signs outside were all in English.

(It comes to my mind that around the time of Kennedy assassination I was asked by some of my friends why I loved America so much since "they kill their Presidents." In answer to that comment, I said, "JFK wasn't killed in America. He was shot in Texas," exhibiting a bit of dark humor common in America.)

Later on, the Jewish Family Services representative, Barbara, who met me at the bus terminal and drove to my new residence, helped me to understand that those two gentlemen were real Texans and probably spoke like real Texans do, which would present some problems in the future but would also help to train my ear to understand the rich variations of American and British accents.

Keep in mind: My relative knowledge of written English and $27 US in my pocket were my only real possessions. Walking away dumbfounded in Rome, after seeing the movie, *Rocky,* and listening to busy passengers in their Texas accents caused me nothing short of anxiety about my future prospects here. To add to my feelings of inadequacy...during the first days after my arrival in Houston and meeting with a few other recent Soviet immigrants, I was asked by one of them, who was already employed and busy during the day, to check on the repair status of his car at a nearby gas station.

---

30 *Braniff International Airways,* the fastest growing airline in America from 1968 to 1978, went bankrupt in 1982. It was a victim of airline deregulation, and making big losing bets on fliers preferring glamour and service to cheaper rates.

I went with one simple question: "Is it ready?" I expected a simple reply, like yes or no. Instead, I walked away without a clue of what that mechanic had just told me.

After the Braniff experience, I naturally expected my adopted country to give a Red Square type celebration marking my arrival. However, my "ticker-tape parade" was overshadowed the next day by the death of Elvis Presley—Elvis "The King" of rock-and-roll. Elvis, the man who'd altered the course of American music. A man for whom I still had mixed feelings. On one hand, I liked his blues singing and admired his open embrace of the "black roots" Beale Street genesis of his music. On the other, Elvis, the Rolling Stones and the Beatles took shark-sized bites out of the fan bases formerly reserved for my beloved jazz icons such as Duke Ellington, Count Basie, Louis Armstrong and so many more. Nevertheless, there I was, Boris Dragunsky émigré, arriving in Houston on what amounted to a day of national mourning, like those reserved for "legends" and heads of state.

The next day, I was invited to lunch at a local restaurant by one of the volunteers. After living in Italy for close to three months, my palate had developed a certain coffee standard, one that thought the taste should be like a kiss: strong and sweet, and it should be served in small cups. Shortly after being seated in the crowded place with a white tablecloths covering the tables, an almost Russian-looking plus-sized plopped some sort of oversized ceramic vessel in front of me into which she generously poured some brownish liquid, while at the same time barking, "Hot and black!" without waiting for a reply.

Assuming this must be my coffee, I sipped it…and almost spewed it out. The first thought that entered my mind, *Someone failed to finish washing the coffee pot and served me its residual contents.* After asking for, and receiving a second cup of what was basically the same dark brown liquid, I realized this was American coffee. (This was 1977, mind you, and Starbucks was waiting to be born. So, no one around me knew the meaning of espresso or any of its wonderfully potent derivatives like cappuccino.)

Speaking of cultural surprises, the other came with observing the table manners of this restaurant's patrons, and later those of the majority of Americans. (I grant you this was not exactly a Michelin 3-star restaurant, but still it seemed to me that dining amenities had gone straight down the drain…which was also where the coffee surely belonged.)

For all its other wonderful qualities, dining habits in America are definitely very different from the rest of the world. With a very few exceptions, those being the people who'd experienced living abroad or learning etiquette on their own, rare is the occasion where one can see an American, regardless of their education, properly holding and using a fork and knife. It was quite surprising to learn that basic table manners are not taught in school while, according to our European friends, it is a part of their upbringing, with the expectation that all children have learned it by the time they are 5 to 7 years old.

There are many differences between other countries and America. One of them, as I learned later, is that unlike in most other countries, Americans have the unique habit of taking daily showers and not wearing the same shirt, suit or dress as the day before.

With the coming weekend, my caseworker suggested that I attend the Friday night services at the nearby synagogue where I could possibly meet people. My friend, Barbara, had no idea that her client, Boris Dragunsky, a 39-year old Jewish boy from Moscow, had never before set foot in a Synagogue. Sure, I had been outside the Moscow Choral Synagogue as a part of crowds traditionally gathered there in the early '70s on the Jewish holiday of *Simchat Torah*.

As anyone who had ever visited Moscow would know, the synagogue building was located on a secluded street that was practically dead after 8 p.m. On the days of those gatherings, the surrounding streets were blocked for "construction" and all the traffic from the center of Moscow was directed through the usually empty Archipova Street, and playground across the way—replete with basketball and volleyball courts—was suddenly becoming the place for competitive games between MVD soldiers. Hundreds of us pushed onto the narrow sidewalks, since we obviously couldn't be contained within their boundaries and were thus accused of obstructing traffic.

With these still-vivid memories I walked to the local synagogue. I found the doors wide-open, and myself completely lost. I guess my hopeless state was too obvious and soon I was surrounded by strangers asking if they could help me. Sure, they could... and *should!!!*

Looking into the prayer books handed to me, but even more so at my environs, I noticed a lot of young men and women but none of the elderly, bearded men I expected to see. After the services and following *kiddush* with wine and cookies, I was invited to someone's home where the host and guests were all newcomers, "transplants" as they called themselves. They had all moved to

Houston for the opportunities. It was one of very few prospering places in the USA in 1977 during the Jimmy Carter era. So, I guess the people in Rome were right to have sent me here. Also, I learned it was a Reform synagogue, or a Temple as it was called. This was the form of a house of prayer that I was to attend for the next 20 years.

Before my other cultural experiences, I went through my own transformations. Being born in a secular society, I had been deprived of complying with one of the most important Jewish laws: circumcision, which is the physical act of G-d's covenant with Abraham, and is supposed to be performed on the 8th day after a male's birth. Today the most of the world celebrates the New Year on January 1st: the day of Jesus' circumcision eight days after (birth) Christmas.

Fully realizing upon my arrival in Houston that I was somewhat running late, I still wanted to make up for the time that passed between the 8th day of my first birth (in captivity) and make it as close as possible to my birth as a FREE man. So, I did it. The arrangements were made and paid for by the local Jewish community. Instead of following the custom of giving sweet kosher wine to an eight-day-old infant to help overcome the pain, I was put to sleep by a very attractive female anesthesiologist and woke up a real Jew! I was given a robe to use as my only clothing for the next 10 days. I had developed a real feeling for, and attachment to, our Patriarch Abraham *(Avinu)* who was the first to have the same experience at the age of 99, but without being able to use the super-modern facilities of the Houston Memorial Hospital.

Meeting people on my first Shabbat marked the beginning of making myself comfortable and appreciative for this "port of entry" into my new American life. Within a very short time (after being able to put my pants on) I met and became friends with people who made me feel like a part of their own great families. One man, his wife and their children, are the ones to whom I owe the most…and to whom I will be grateful for the rest of my days.

Perhaps at this point, I should respectfully ask the reader to imagine a lonely person, almost middle-aged, a professional who has neither job nor family, nor home, nor native language, nor friends, nor accustomed surroundings and habits. If the reader does this, he or she will get—more or less—the picture of this writer's life during that early fall in 1977.

In the midst of this, as if by pure accident, I met the late Dr. Jack Alpert, *z"l* and his family. Jack, who was my age, was at the pinnacle of his life and career. He was a renowned neurologist, head of a successful medical practice, loving husband of Ruth, attentive father of three (later four) children, popular with many friends, and owner of a spacious house with swimming pool surrounded by a picturesque garden and palm trees. He was the very opposite of Boris Dragunsky, who had arrived in a beat-up Maverick for their Shabbat dinner. As it happened, we soon struck-up a lifelong friendship.

Besides spoiling me with constant access to an opulent doctor's club, Jack, along with his well-established friends and colleagues, constantly provided me with special guidance, lifesaving encouragement and warmth, which was especially needed during those "emotional lows" that I wasn't short on having. This, as well as numerous weekend trips, parties, dining out and just gatherings with their extended families made me feel at home and like I was an American as well. I was quickly losing that "poor immigrant" feeling that doubtless beset so many in my situation.

These were the most memorable times in my new life—and crucial beyond measure. They in no small way helped and guided me for many years to come. Being in the company of a happy, flourishing family only made me miss my twin daughters more. Knowing they were left behind the Iron Curtain and that I could do nothing for them at the time made me feel lonely and very much longing for my family when I came home to the condo I had acquired some months later. Was I jealous of Jack? Sure I was, and how! Yet his prosperity served to inspire me as well.

Jack was a man of many talents. Aside from being an outstanding practitioner and Professor of Medicine, he was a great writer, musician, athlete, naturalist and had a boundless sense of humor. He also had an unparalleled expertise in getting lost. And he was an artist at falling down whenever, wherever and from whatever, but has an incredible capacity for bouncing right back up. Our joint ski, bicycle and walking trips provided me and our companions with many extra gray hairs and irregular heartbeats because of this. We also never asked him to drive us for longer than 21 minutes—as this was his absolute limit for alertness behind the wheel—after that, it was usually "lullaby land," which is not the best place for a driver to go!

Upon my arrival in Houston, I had been warned by some of the Soviet immigrants to avoid one of the caseworkers from the Jewish Federation assigned to the resettlement program. Her name was Edis Parkans, and she was "a real tough Texan lady" who was notorious for "not giving anyone any slack."

At the time, I guessed she wanted them to be active in looking for jobs and studying English, thus getting off that small Federation's dole. For whatever reason, Edis and her husband, Sidney, became my greatest friends, and remained so until the last days of their interesting and charitable lives. My first-ever American Passover was experienced in their home, followed by many enjoyable days involving our mutual visits. I learned a lot from both of these Jewish American patriots and their active lives. Soon enough, I discovered Edis was the head of the Texas Hadassah branch and Sid was a self-employed and highly sought-after oil exploration geologist. Let their memories be blessed.

Another indelible friendship in my life was with a young Englishwoman named Marion Rifkind. As there are no coincidences, Marion had been sent to Houston by her London technical translation company to open its Houston branch and develop business with the major oil companies headquartered there and their pending contracts within Soviet oil-related industries. She was actively looking for Russian-speaking translators, and was referred to me by my friend Edis. The project never came through; however, the late Marion ended up opening her own multi-national translation company and became a sister I never had.

As it turned out, I ended up spending a lot of time with her and her husband—this included a lot of celebrations together in Houston, Chicago and London, where she left behind a very lovely and prominent family, including a former British Foreign Minister under Great Britain's longest serving PM, the "Iron Lady" Margaret Thatcher.

My American life: The beginning…

At this point, I was making Houston, Texas, my home; although I was not sure for how long. The city had its pluses and minuses. The pluses were the people—warm, friendly, open, helpful and very seldom judgmental. The drawbacks were the location and the climate: It was in something called a Bayou, lowlands noted for marshy waterways. It had extremely hot and humid weather—and the mosquitoes in summer were the size of hummingbirds! It was also a place, like so many in America, where you had to have a car to get around.

Some didn't have vehicles, I surmised, because being driven on the weekend and the next, I repeatedly saw signs that read: **Garage Sale!** "Why would they do that?" I wondered out loud. "Why would people have to sell their garages, and where would they put their cars once they were sold?! They apparently need the money badly."

That is when it was explained to me that it was common vernacular used when people wanted to sell things they no longer wanted with a sale at their house. I was told, "A Garage Sale is kind of a fun way to spend a weekend and make a little money. One man's trash is another man's treasure. It's kind of a tradition...an American flea market, if you will. It's a form of social glue unique to the USA."

It so happened that I was earning my first American dollars within several days after arrival in Houston. One of the Soviet emigres had opened a translation company and received a contract for technical translations that the oil companies often needed. Looking for help, he offered, and I grabbed the $5 per hour job. I was working 12-hour overnight shifts at Shell Oil's headquarters. A couple of months later, I found my first full-time job as a field technician (a great step up from that of a Senior Scientist for a Moscow institution) at a relatively small construction testing company.

I celebrated my first weekly paycheck by going to a coffee shop across the street for lunch. What a celebration it was, indeed! There I was, sitting at the counter just like everybody else, ordering my own "grilled" cheese sandwich (one of the few items I was able to distinguish on the menu), feeling like "one of the boys," and paying with my own green bucks! This was, and remains to this very day, my most memorable American meal...and a sort of rite of passage. I was feeling like I was a part of this country—America!!!

Working in a small company enabled me to have frequent contact with the owner, a Mexican American gentleman named Joe Murillo. Personal contact with him was not an uncommon event; however, two such contacts stand out.

The first happened to be just after my first week or so with the company. Mr. Joe Murillo came over to my desk and told me that one of our projects had a concrete related problem and he wanted me, the "concrete expert," to meet the project's architect.

Oh boy! I thought at the time...*This is a scary proposition.* This would be the "acid test." This would be my first face-to-face meeting with an American client requiring me to solve an American problem in English using my knowledge acquired on another continent, in a different country (and taught in Russian at that).

The night before, I drove my newly-acquired and very old Ford Maverick to the site of a high-rise bank building that was under construction, to make sure I knew my way around and that I would make it to the meeting on time. Arriving early at the meeting site, I was visibly nervous and perspiring all the while (or as the Americans tend to say, "sweating bullets"). Not quite knowing what to expect, I met the client, a relatively young man, who immediately asked me to come up to the top floor. Putting his arm on my shoulder, he led me to the edge of open floor slab. Stopping at the ledge, he turned to me, and drolly dropped a query on me that went something like this: "Boris, I have a question for you."

Now it's coming, I thought, feeling a queasiness in my stomach.

"You are from Russia. Right?"

"Yes," was the answer that came from my unstable voice.

"Tell me: Do Russians eat pussy?"

So, this was the first question in my professional American life, and I flunked the test due to my still-limited vocabulary in the field (of eating). The only thing I could determine as to how I should answer was that he said it with a grin. Apparently, this was a rather bawdy Texan way of taking the edge off the moment. He went on to tell me all about his affinity for this type of eating. (A bit more information than I needed at the time.)

A second, even more memorable meeting, was an unexpected encounter with my company's very Catholic boss when he stopped by my desk on the first day of the Jewish holiday of *Passover* with a question:

"Boris, what the hell are you doing here?"

"Working," I answered, waiting for the other shoe to drop…

That prompted him to scowl at me, and say in a very loud voice, "All my Jewish friends are in synagogues." Adding in a voice raised to an even higher in volume, "Get the f--k out of here and go where you belong!"

Clearly only his last words had landed inside the room. So, everybody within earshot was certain I was being fired, especially as I quickly made it out the door.

No, I was not fired, but I was made prouder of my new country and her people. Because here we were, an American Catholic boss sending his Jewish employee to join his People in the celebration of their Exodus from slavery. Here I was, 3,500 years later, encouraged to celebrate my own EXODUS!

Despite my warm feelings for everyone there, in time I came to realize that I'd reached my limits with this firm. Shortly thereafter, I was presented with an offer to move to a growing nationwide company and act as a Technical Director for their new Houston branch.

I had lived almost 40 years of my life in the capital city of Moscow with eight million people, with four seasons and many cultural venues. Houston to me was a fast-growing place where the air provided two choices: "You can breathe it or you can drink it." All the culture was on wheels...it arrived in the evening, left the next morning. And it only had two seasons: monsoons and stifling heat. All I could think was: "Thank heaven for something called air-conditioning—that purely splendid American innovation."

It didn't take me all that long to figure out that, for all its wonderful dynamism and charm, Houston was probably not going to be my final destination. That's when Destiny extended her hand to me once again.

While still in Rome, I had mailed a letter and resumé to a company in Chicago. It was a world-leading research institution in concrete technology. (Actually, they had responded, but their letter got lost in the notoriously inefficient Italian mail. Still, I knew Chicago was a mecca of construction technology...So I thought, why not give it another try?)

After all, Chicago was the third largest American city, historically known for being her biggest labor town, and the birthplace of such things (for better or worse) as skyscrapers, May Day (Soviet holiday), the 8-hour work day, the American Communist Party (CPUSA), McDonalds, Weber BBQ, Windy City politics and last (but not least for me) the number-two Jazz birthplace of Jazz after New Orleans. As *Chicago Magazine* claimed in 1953, "Subtract what Chicago has given to it, and you wouldn't recognize America."

Longing to better recognize my adopted country as well for having a "normal" climate, I obtained a copy of the Chicago *Yellow Pages* and sent my letters to several firms I thought might be foolish enough to offer me refuge. As a result, my employment and "real city" residence began just two short years after arriving on the shores of this country.

The position of Senior Consultant with a nationwide firm was professionally challenging but rewarding. As a plus, this was a city with all four seasons: spring, summer, fall and winter (the latter being something I had taken for granted but would never do so again).

It was also a reminder that I needed to respect my new environs, read the rules, and understand that "Citizenship 2.0" was something I needed to learn. A classic example: One sunny, crisp winter Sunday on the way to my new friend's home for brunch, I found my car gone…as in, it had apparently been towed away! *Welcome to Chicago! And you don't dare park on the streets with a maximum two-inch snow ordinance!*

CHAPTER TWELVE

A Litmus Test in the Midwest

> *"You cannot build courage and character by taking away people's initiative and independence."*
>
> ~ Abraham Lincoln

Prior to receiving and accepting the Chicago offer, I had several interviews throughout the country with no success, mostly because we both, the interviewer and I, didn't develop "love at first sight" feelings and didn't, at any level, feel that we belonged together. There was one interview in particular—a defense-oriented institution located in Columbus, Ohio—when I was made to feel "refused" again.

I found it both exhausting and eye-opening when, in the course of three days of professional questions and answers, I was invited to lunch and asked personal things about my family (my uncle) and my previous work in Russia, which was known to only a few people. Questioning myself about whether I wanted to spend my days in a secretive place with strict security clearances and limited doors I could open, I flew back to Houston and waited for the results with some very mixed feelings.

While still torn between a rather prestigious, well-paying job and what was certain to be a highly restrictive environment (I came for freedom!) it took six weeks for me to receive their letter of "thank you, you're great… but no thank you."…As was later explained, I was rejected on security grounds—the main reason being that I still had family in a hostile country like the Soviet Union, where there still existed the risk of having them used as hostages. The mixed feelings I had about being rejected combined with relief about not working in such a closed institution remained with me through the next month or so. But in retrospect I was soon able to remove all doubt.

With all this behind me, I was moving to Chicago and driving my Firebird while all my other belongings had been packed and shipped by moving van, courtesy of my new employer. Crossing the Mississippi River Bridge and seeing that great body of water for the first time, I reminded myself of a popular children's story written by my distant relative and beloved Soviet children's writer Victor Dragunsky about a lazy pupil called to a blackboard in geography class and asked to name the largest American river. With no clue but hearing the helping whispers from his classmates he spat out—"Missi-pissi!"

Soon after, I was seeing at a distance the world's tallest building at the time—the Sears Tower. Yes, it was 1979 and the US was still the home of the world's grandest skyscrapers, at least until 1998. Even now, today's world's tallest edifice, the 163 story *Burj Khalifa* in Dubai (as well as many others), were designed by Chicago architects and engineers.

Getting ready for my new job on the following Monday, I realized that my first day was also going to be the first day of *Yom Kippur.* As lax in observance as I still was at that time, I felt hard-pressed about going to work on that holiest of days. So, with great trepidation, I called the company VP whose name was on the offering letter, and told him about my issue and inquired as to the possibility of starting a day later. Not only did he insist that I not show up for work, he also saw to it that I was paid for that day. Even two years later, it was mind-boggling to contemplate the American welcome of my Jewishness. As comedian Yakov Smirnoff used to say: "What a country!" (Or at least it used to be...)

(Sadly, the same company, later on, under somewhat different management, no longer permitted leave for Jewish holidays to its employees, not to mention any paid days.)

Nevertheless, working for a company with many branches nationwide provided me with a great chance to see America; and most important, to interact with a great number of professionals of different backgrounds, many of them educated in, and having worked in, foreign countries.

Because the company founder and owner had graduated from MIT, he was giving priority to hiring graduates from that institution. So, for starters, I was a long-shot to even get a job there. Why in the world he hired me (even though he was asked to hold off by some at the table during a lunch conversation) is beyond me. Nevertheless, he did so, and for that I was truly grateful.

Interacting with the company staff as well as with our clients, I came to admire the practicality of American-educated professionals in my field. They appeared as always looking for, and coming up with, the most rational solutions.

I happily took on the provided opportunities to participate in conventions, conferences and seminars around the country, meeting and striking up long-lasting friendships with many colleagues, who later would be instrumental in the direction and success of my own firm. I also became active in various professional organizations and was elected to leading positions in chapters and on committees. While making presentations, I tried to follow the advice by Winston Churchill "A good speech should be as a woman's skirt — long enough to cover the subject and short enough to create interest."

Mostly fulfilled by my challenging work, I didn't have much excitement… until February 22, 1980. Being invited to watch the semi-final ice-hockey game at the Winter Olympics in Lake Placid, I arrived with an uneasy expectation of the inevitable win by the experienced Soviet ice hockey "Armada" when they played Team USA, a rookie crew of amateur hockey players, none over age 23, and entirely made up of college kids from Minnesota, Wisconsin, Boston U., and Bowling Green. They had been a team for less than four months and their only prior experience had been at the collegiate level. What else could one expect?

The Soviets looked upon their professional (though presented as "amateur") players as political propaganda tools, providing them with "no money asked" facilities, trainers, stipends and perks—everything they needed to be the best representatives of the Soviet system. How one could compare that to a group of US college kids, 100% of whom were in their first Olympics? Even though Team USA had surprised the crowds at Lake Placid with a 4-0-1 record—even beating East Germany to advance to the Medal Round—this was still looked upon as a terrible mismatch against the USSR's ice hockey juggernaut that had, up to now, gone 66-0-1 over the previous two years. They had also beaten the NHL All-Stars 7-2 just a few weeks earlier. So, going in, I

"The Miracle on Ice." Team USA defeats the USSR 4-3 in the Olympic Semifinal. (They went on to win Olympic Gold by beating Finland in the final: 3-2.)

really felt anxious for the "Yanks," and almost reluctantly took a seat in front of the TV set in my friend's basement.

And yet, surprise of surprises! All of sudden I was witness to the unbelievable taking place. Our American kids were outplaying the undefeated Soviets, and outscoring them as well! It was still early in the game, and I was afraid that the physically superior, well-conditioned Soviet hockey machine would relentlessly grind-down these "courageous kids" and simply overrun them.

Sure enough, in the middle of the third period, the Soviets pulled even at 3-3, and it looked like just matter of time before they wore out the youngsters and took over at the end. But, to everyone's surprise, the "Yanks" came back two minutes later and seized the lead again: 4-3…then held on for a full 10 minutes while the "Men in Red" took shot after shot at the US goal, only to find them all blocked.

Then came the final countdown chanted by the crowd of 8,500 electrified fans that sounded like 85,000: "…5-4-3-2-1-0!" After which, upon the buzzer, ABC sportscaster Al Michaels shouted, "Do you believe in miracles?!!" And so, the game came to be known as, "The Miracle on Ice," and was arguably the most stunning upset in the history of sport.

Team USA had won, and what a pleasure it was watching the devastated faces of the Russian players, their coaches and, above all, the Soviet officials as they sank back in their chairs! I was overwhelmed by happiness for many days to come at this amazing win! Driving home, I had to control the wheel in a state of elated dizziness that the impossible had happened. Then again, this was America, where all things could be achieved.

In a short time, my social and cultural life began greatly improving. After all, I was in Chicago, the city with its beautiful Lake Shore Drive along Lake Michigan, the Chicago Symphony, the Art Institute and some of the best jazz clubs anywhere, featuring the world-renowned jazz artists. It also had free Grant Park Summer Festivals of blues and jazz in the heart of the city. I learned about all these places rather soon and on my own. But it took almost two years to discover the real treasure located relatively close to my company's office. One summer evening I was invited to the Ravinia Festival. Walking to and from that great outdoor music venue with the pavilion stage surrounded by vast picnic areas, I also saw houses located just outside Ravinia Park. "Do the people living in these homes realize they live in paradise?" I asked my companion.

After living in a rental apartment in the city on the shores of Lake Michigan, commuting to our suburban office and absorbing the complaints of neighbors who didn't share my affinity for late evening jazz broadcasts by Chicago's own Dick Buckley, I managed to rent with an option to buy (on a great advice of some smart friends) a small house. Guess where? Just next door to Ravinia!

I was also soon receiving great news of my ex-wife apparently changing her mind about rejecting the idea of emigration and finally allowing my letters to reach our twin girls, whom I'd come to miss so much. This was potentially life-changing and cheering-up news!

I moved into my new house in anticipation of the kids' arrival, and was happy that it was located in an area noted for having very good schools. The move happened to be timed well, as I received the news that, after a long wait, the family of my beloved Aunt Maria had received permission to leave Moscow and would be coming to the US.

So, my newly-acquired house temporarily became a home for my aunt, her husband, my cousin Tanya, her husband and their two boys. At long last, I was surrounded by relatives and had homemade meals waiting for me, all of which contributed to my rapidly expanding waistline— complements of my aunt's carbs/fat-rich excellent Russian-Jewish cooking.

To meet this size family and later transport them around for shopping and showing off Chicago's many landmarks, I had to borrow a van or bigger cars from my office mates or just hand my Firebird over to my cousin's husband so he could run errands for his immediate family.

One day, I noticed my silver beauty standing alone on the highway shoulder while I was driving a borrowed car in the opposite direction. My cousin's husband—a man known for his technical skills—had apparently decided to show his appreciation for my hospitality by saving me some money on car service expenses, and had done so by changing my car's oil.

Proudly overcoming the difficulties presented by lack of lifting equipment in my driveway, he managed to drain and replace the oil just before taking the car for an appointment at the Social Security offices. Unfortunately, there had been an apparent missing step in his successful oil change operation—he forgot to put back and close the oil drain cap. Thus, the freely escaping four quarts of oil lasted for about five miles before seizing-up the engine.

These were also the times when I was getting involved in Chicago Jewish life, joining the Jewish Federation's activities on behalf of Soviet Jews stuck in the USSR and trying to leave it. As a part of the Federation, I went to Israel to take part in the World Conference for Soviet Jewry in Jerusalem and had a chance to meet the first Post-Labor Israeli Prime Minister Menachem Begin. The Conference was originally scheduled to take place in Paris but was canceled due to security considerations after an Arab terrorist attack on the Chez Jo Goldberg restaurant on August 9, 1982.

As it was, my trip to Jerusalem began with an adventure. At the request of my Israeli relative I purchased for him a video camera—a very expensive commodity in Israel. Though still costly, it was much less expensive in the States. With no direct flights to Israel, I decided to take advantage of being in Europe and bought the least expensive tickets from Chicago to Paris, and from there, Amsterdam to Tel Aviv. I planned to spend a couple of days in the City of Lights, take a night train from Paris to Amsterdam and indulge in some sightseeing before flying to Israel.

Boarding the train in Paris, I found myself surrounded by a rowdy group of young soldiers with uniforms changed for a much-anticipated vacation, most of which would be spent in Amsterdam's infamous Red-Light District. With the train half-empty, I moved to a much quieter car where I was able to watch the passing French and Belgian landscape until it dawned on me that I had left behind my expensive bag with the camera inside. Rushing back to my old compartment, I found it emptied-out—no soldiers and no camera anywhere in sight.

In a cold-sweat and ready to write the whole thing off as a loss, I found the conductor a couple of cars away who, after digesting my words, said, "Follow me," where after he stormed into every compartment of every car until we came across the sleeping soldiers. Confirming with me that those were the same people, he woke them all up and spoke to them in very persuasive and loud French that somehow managed to accomplish the impossible and have my camera delivered into my hands, followed by the cash still nestled in the bag's side pocket—all in a fairly short time.

Wow! was the first thought that came to my mind. *There is no way an American conductor could invade the privacy and roust out these soldiers or anyone else for that reason.*

Coming back from that memorable and invigorating trip, I was faced with the reality of the restructuring taking place in the company I had enjoyed working for. My status as a Corporate Senior Consultant was being subordinated and I no longer reported only to the firm's top management. With the firm's new structure, I was merely a part of the department—a move that made both the department head and myself rather uncomfortable. It didn't take long before I began to hear suggestions, including those from my new boss, that perhaps I might be better off working somewhere else.

Eventually, after four years, it became time to start looking for a job with another company. As I started to explore my possibilities (Chicago only!) and after an interview with a very prestigious engineering group, my very close friend asked, "Why not try opening your own business? After all, you could always work for somebody else." But I questioned myself: "What clients would hire me and how would I get the money to begin start the company?" Remembering American stories and tales, I wondered: *Is this still the land of opportunity?*

My first meeting with a principal of a major firm with whom I had personally established good relations was anything but encouraging. The man apparently knew "the business" much better than I, and apprised me of some important issues: Any contract I set up had to include both professional and general liability insurance. I had never thought of this! It cost a lot of money and could be obtained only by substantiating one's professional and business credentials. So, it was either try or quit, and quitting was not a desirable option. Taking to heart what the great jazz artist Clark Terry used to tell his students, "Keep on keeping on!" I was determined to make a go of it.

My next step: money and its providers, which in this case (as I was told) would be the banks. After having several doors slammed in my face, I finally met with a small bank whose VP was apparently impressed by my accent and my *chutzpa*, backed by a small amount of home equity and reinforced by some advice I'd given to him on how to keep his home's garage from cracking.

With all the financial logistics behind me, my first project came from a least expected source: one of the better-known Chicago structural engineers, Kolbjorn Saether, with whom my previous employer had run into a conflict. Learning that I had left the firm, he found my home number through the telephone book (some still remember the good old "White Pages"), called me and then hired me to consult on one of their projects involving a group of aging landmark buildings.

The second job, bringing the first check, was from a young entrepreneur Paul Kakuris solving erosion problems on the shores of Lake Michigan. He had been too small and deemed too financially unreliable for my former place of work to take a chance on.

My main goal of being able to make ends meet and paying my mortgage by making at least half of what I used to make was surprisingly met by the constant flow of small projects. Still, I had some sleepless nights, dogged by the constant gnaw of insecurity that every startup business is certain to feel: What if the next project doesn't come?

Despite the uncertainty of it all, I managed to maintain my presence at professional societies, which are always great networking places and potential source of clients. While checking my calls from a payphone (long before cellphones were a thing) during a change of planes in Charlotte, NC, I found an urgent message left by a former principal in the famous Chicago firm called Skidmore, Owens and Merrill. He had just formed his own company and was requested by SOM to submit a proposal for an unusual and technically challenging project.

Mobile Oil Corporation was planning to build a tall tower in downtown Chicago, using the existing foundation (caissons installed in the 1920s) of a still-functioning Montgomery Ward building they had acquired. The requested proposal included the investigation of existing foundation caissons (built in the 1920s) without an interruption of commerce within the operating store or its working areas in the basement—a tall order to say the least.

But the most challenging thing was the competition. Proposals had been requested from two organizations whom SOM trusted: one from my former employer and the other from the caller. The message the caller left was asking me if I'd be interested in being a part of his team. I vaguely remembered the caller's name, Michael Tylk, from my previous job. He was a true gentleman and brilliant engineer to whom I would forever be in debt, not only for his recognition of me personally but also for the pathways he opened to the success of my nascent company.

Here we were two competing groups: the established nationwide company renowned throughout the world of foundation engineering with dozens of years of daily fruitful cooperation with SOM... and Mike Tylk, who brought me in as a concrete consultant on his newly formed team. Flattered by the offer as a good sign, but feeling that I had no chance at this one, I submitted my proposal, but not before I hedged my bet by finding experts who could back me up by building and using the unique machinery needed to drill down 55 feet deep into concrete without disrupting MW retailers daily sorting of their merchandise.

The next call from Mike was even less believable than the first one a month earlier. This one was followed by a "confirmation letter" from SOM, awarding us the contract based upon our team's qualification and experience.

This contract really put me on the map, and I earned enough money to move my business from a garage to a real office with laboratory space. I was also able to hire a staff and buy new equipment. This was followed by an even larger project. I was now developing a broader client base, including New York and other places around the USA and foreign countries, including Canada, Mexico and overseas.

I have already mentioned the American loss of domination in putting up high-rise buildings, but working on many existing and historical structures around the country I was amazed by how advanced the Unites States used to be in the construction industry and how much we have fallen behind. The Americans were building bridges which were beyond the dream. One great example is the Golden Gate Bridge in San Francisco. Completed in 1937, this bridge is built to withstand earthquakes, tremendous winds, fog and perilously strong tides. The design and machinery of such civil engineering projects as Wards Island or Bowery Bay Wastewater Treatment plants in New York were 50 years ahead of anything built in the rest of the world. Not to mention the amazingly quick construction schedules. It took one year and 45 days to build the 102-story Empire State Building in 1930-31. The list of such projects is too long to mention in its entirety. This is why it amazes me that it now takes over three years to complete a one-mile road reconstruction project on the street where I live in a Chicago suburb.

And what about flying from the backward-of-my-youth China, getting to Shanghai Airport by a train at 260 miles an hour and arriving at JFK airport in New York with an eerie feeling of backwardness? Every major airport in Europe and Asia is conveniently connected with the city by a direct train, but after spending zillions of dollars on a new LaGuardia Airport terminal or "Big Dig" in Boston, one still has to jump between the buses to get into Manhattan or Boston.

With mostly private entities as our clients, I tried to stay away from government projects, as they all required a tremendous amount of paperwork, for which I had neither sufficient staff nor patience. Occasionally, however, we would have to get involved in state and city projects, working for private architects, engineers or contractors awarded those projects. What never ceased to surprise me was the openness and lack of concern from our clients about my foreign-born background, overseas education and omnipresent Russian accent. We were awarded projects in competition against people who had been classmates, lifelong friends and even relatives of our potential clients. I kept telling myself—*I finally live and work in a truly meritorious society!*

This was true, until that very singular day when I had a bit of a rude awakening. This unexpected wake-up call occurred when I was asked to accompany our client, who was proposing work for the city of Chicago and had listed us as a part of his team. Entering the meeting room at city hall, we were met by the city representatives plus, standing out, an ostentatiously dressed black gentleman. After being quite ambivalent during the technical presentation, this man turned to me and asked me very pointedly about the make-up of my company. After assuring him that we carefully selected our people and that they were all well qualified for this project, his attitude darkened and he lowered his voice to an accusatory tone, asking me if we had assigned any African-Americans to the project.

I had no idea who this man was. My answer was that we were colorblind and concerned only with our staff's abilities to do the job. This apparently set him off, and his subsequent reaction made me feel like I was once more back in the USSR facing a *Kommissar* who was demanding my Party loyalty. I had previously heard about the Affirmative Action programs in place all over the country but had never experienced them in my profession. So, this meeting and the entire attitude of awarding privileges based on anything other than merit certainly triggered a lot of thinking on my part, because it reminded me of some Soviet practices that were both insidious and extortive.

Later on, I actually benefited from this program by being hired to do the work for minority companies who were awarded these projects based upon Affirmative Action. Over the years, I also hired several black field technicians—one of them an Army veteran and another a born artist named Michael M., who later wrote me several letters of gratitude, followed by a later missal about his artistic accomplishments accompanied by an attached work dedicated to George Floyd. This was his letter:

> I spent a year painting this. It's 60 inches by 48. I call it "We The People." It's my statement about how things are in this country. There are 3 symbols in the painting. 1) Knelt down Colin Kaepernick (Black Lives Matter). 2) The American flag upside down. 3) The words "We The People" segmented.

To this, I responded accordingly:

> Mike,
>
> I'm not in a position to judge the artistic value of your year-long work. I have no qualification to do that. But since your work is a "statement" I feel myself compelled and rather qualified to comment on that statement and symbols you used.
>
> **Symbol 1.**
> When the United States National Anthem is played, I proudly get up and stand with the feeling of being much taller than my 5'6". The same goes for my wife and millions of others who have fought for the right and opportunity to come to this country (often-times penniless) and not kneel like the millionaire football player in your artwork.
>
> Our country is in trouble, which is your **Symbol 2**—the American flag upside down (this is what positioning a flag upside down means) and **Symbol 3**—the fractured We The People.

The *Chicago Sun-Times* reports that 18 people were killed on one Sunday, May 31, "making it the single most violent day in Chicago in six decades." Over the full weekend, "25 people were killed in the city, with another 85 wounded by gunfire." None of these deaths or shootings involved police, so there will be no massive protests over them, no tearful commentary on cable news and social media, no white politicians wrapped in Kente cloth taking a knee for photographers. Law enforcement has had next to nothing to do with these black homicides in Chicago. According to the *Sun-Times,* there were 492 homicides in Chicago last year, and only three of them involved police. So where are all of the BLM protesters when 25 blacks are killed by blacks in a single weekend? Indeed, the lives of these black people do matter.

Yes, our country is in trouble. Big trouble. What else can you conclude when you watch looters and rioters take control of our streets and the police are ordered to stand down. What else can you conclude when the dominant media, celebrities and politicians fall over themselves making excuses for law-breakers in the name of "social justice?"

America is a great country for everyone of every race who works hard and plays by the rules, and you, Mike, know and proof it very well.

I strongly suggest you to listen to the eloquent, forceful voices of black people like Larry Elder, Brandon Tatum and Jason Riley who are speaking out against the ugliness they are seeing and hearing: the destructive lies about our America. I also attached a link to Shelby Steele.

Here's what they are saying:

"One of the big #FakeNews narratives is that 'institutional,' 'structural' and 'systemic' racism remains a major problem in America, when, in fact, race has never been a more insignificant barrier to success in America." ~ Larry Elder

"Don't let the Media fool you! The majority of Americans support the police. Do not support the destroying of their city. The biggest problem with growing up black in America… IS not racism, police brutality, or black on black crime… It's the Mental Brainwashing." ~ Brandon Tatum

"Black activists and white progressives stress racism because it serves their own interests, not because it actually improves the station of blacks." ~ Jason Riley

Mike, I don't have to sell you my racial credentials, and I have never met or heard of a racist or hateful comment within a rather large circle of my friends and family members. And as far as the BLM movement is concerned: I see it as a far-left anti-Israel, anti-Semitic organization with a Socialist agenda. Having lived close to 40 years in the Socialist Soviet Union, I know a little about Socialism and am open to sharing my experiences with you and your friends.

As my email is getting too long, I would just add a few more words about the flag and your fractured We The People. As a young man living in Moscow, I used to take long public transportation rides on July 4th to the street where the American Embassy was located, just for the opportunity to walk under the American flag flying from the building while being closely watched by the KGB.

The inmates of the German death concentration camp Mauthausen secretly, with risk for their lives, sewed an American Flag in anticipation of their liberation. Not knowing the exact number of stars to affix, they sewed on 56 and waited for the American soldiers who, they prayed, might save them. That flag flew over the liberated camp.

The American Flag has been—for me and millions of freedom-deprived people around the world—a symbol of that freedom and hope. It could be compared to a lighthouse finally found by a lonely sailor lost for months in stormy seas.

And one more point. How is it that almost all troubled cities run by politicians from the same political party show no visible improvement in the lives of the people who keep electing them over and over? Having a two-term black President, two black Attorney Generals, with black and/or Democrat mayors of Chicago, Washington DC, Baltimore, Atlanta and other major cities, over-seeing the police and education departments, is it not time to look into the one-party system having a grip on people's lives? You well know, Mike, that Job Opportunities, Education and Strong Family ties are the main pillars of a successful life of black, white and yellow peoples, and not the political demagogues whom people in minority neighborhoods keep electing.

Mike, perhaps all those things coupled with bad schools in poor neighborhoods run by the corrupt Teachers' Unions (opposing teacher's tests and school choice) and fatherless homes could become your next art project (with the Statements).

My best to you,
Boris Dragunsky, PhD, PE, FACI

Nobody should die as George Floyd did, but in equal measure, nobody should ever live the way George Floyd did—committing eight crimes in eight years and serving four years in prison for aggravated robbery during a home invasion, one in which he held a gun to a pregnant woman's stomach while threatening to shoot her unborn child if she didn't bring him her money.

What I really loved about the United States was that it was the "melting pot" of different ethnicities, races, and religions. I saw mostly harmonious society with occasional prejudices expressed behind the back. One thing I could never tolerate were the racist remarks made towards blacks that I heard from time to time. How could I? Living through 40 years of prejudice as a Jew in Soviet Russia, I knew very well how it felt.

After all, almost all of my cherished musical idols were black jazz artists. As I used to say back in Russia: "My first love was Ella Fitzgerald, and one day when I meet her I will kiss her feet." I didn't get to kiss Ella's feet, only her hand and cheeks when I managed to sneak into her dressing room after the concert in Galveston during my Houston days. I told her about my dream too. (She refused to perform in Houston after the ugly racist incident years earlier).

Among my most faithful clients was Ken Eastman, who owned a small firm in St. Croix and hired me on numerous projects throughout the Caribbean. These jobs provided the greatest getaway in the winter months, when after leaving white piles of snow in Chicago I was watching white caps of Caribbean waves. I kept wondering if I should pay them instead of billing them for dwelling at these sea resorts. These were exactly my thoughts while passing a nude beach in St. Martin as I was on my way to a project.

Ken and his teacher wife were blacks originally from Trinidad and they were great hosts. Ken shared with me his hypothesis about Affirmative Action. In his opinion it was created by white racists who want to hold back black advancement by keeping the people of color less trained, and thus less competitive.

Once during his visit to Chicago, I invited him for dinner during the Jewish holiday of *Sukkot*. While sitting in the traditional *Sukkah* he asked about the Jewish traditions and why it took 40 years to cross the Sinai Desert. Learning it was to make sure that two generations of wandering would allow the Jews to get rid of the slave mentality developed during Egyptian captivity, and enter the Promised Land of Israel as free people without a "chip on their shoulders," he responded that this type of chip on the shoulder is exactly what was being promulgated by Affirmative Action.

Attesting to that and so many other things, Ken surprised me by confiding that he didn't want his two children living in the States—where his engineer son and doctor daughter would be looked upon as receiving their diplomas because of their skin color.

Ken was one of many entrepreneurial blacks I met in the course of my working years in the Caribbean. For example, a black driver sent to pick me up by a black plant owner happened to own his car rental company. But the most memorable group of people I ever came across was in Trinidad. Working on a trouble-ridden building, replacing a reportedly failed group of British engineers, I was invited by the client for a dinner at the home of his friends. Four or five couples gathered in the living room and amazed me with their erudition—extending from their knowledge of literature (including Russian), music and philosophy to their complete comprehension of the nuances of world politics.

Socio-economic contrast exists within every ethnic and racial group, but the prevalence of poverty, absence of family and rampant crime I so often encountered while working on projects in some parts of my own Chicago area really puzzled me a lot. Trying to understand it, I learned about segregation, Jim Crow, and the Civil Rights movement.

If you have always believed that everyone should play by the same rules and be judged by the same standards, that would have gotten you labeled a radical 60 years ago, a liberal 30 years ago, and a racist today."

~ Thomas Sowell

The print and radio/TV media have a lot of facts but little analysis and questions about this topic. WHY? Because they are very often loath to take on the controversy of independent thinking.

Going deeper, the first publication I came across was *The Moynihan Report. The Negro Family-The Cause for National Action,* published in 1965 and authored by former Assistant Secretary of Labor, Ambassador to United Nations and "Liberal Democrat" US Senator from New York, Daniel Patrick Moynihan. Among other things, the report concluded that the conditions under which black children were being raised—generally in single-parent households—were the leading cause of black poverty. A report in 1965 indicated that the percent of black babies born out of wedlock had, over the course of 50 years, dramatically increased from 25% (devastating at the time of the report) to over 70% now. These babies are handicapped at birth. What can a single, often poorly educated teen-aged mother give to their future teenager? That teenager will grow up on the streets among his/her peers who are most likely living in the same type of situation.

Former Chief Rabbi of Great Britain Lord Jonathan Saks (*zt"l*) quoted the famous saying of Edmund Burke…"To be attached to the subdivision, to love the little platoon we belong to in society, is the first principle…of public affection. It is the first link in the series by which we proceed towards a love to our country, and to mankind..." And Rabbi Saks continued by emphasizing... "*Strong families are essential to free societies...*"

When there is no family structure and a community that condones young (often teenage) girls having babies, all this tends to perpetuate a community that becomes both rootless and corrupted at its core. Without any sane points of reference or standards or quality education, all social groups—black, white, brown or Asian—revert to a kind of tribalism that becomes a seedbed for violence, gangs, crime and dysfunctional fatherless family environments.

According to FBI Uniform Crime Reports, black youths who make up 16% of the population, accounted for 52% of juvenile violent crime arrests, including 58% of arrests for homicide and 67% for robbery. What's more, 80% of these crimes are committed against other blacks...people of their own race.

American society has to stop making excuses and start seeking solid solutions like mature adults. Using big words and "catchy" political slogans doesn't do anyone any good. People need to take personal responsibility and stop blaming others.

In 1955, Milton Friedman introduced the idea of vouchers in an essay titled *The Role of Government in Education,* saying: "Governments could require a minimum level of education which they could finance by giving parents vouchers redeemable for a specified maximum sum per-child, per-year, provided they were spent on 'approved' educational services." In other words, parents are granted the authority to decide where the public funds for educating their children should go.

It took years to catch on, probably because in 1955 most people were satisfied with their public schools. When school choice measures were later passed in some areas, they almost always targeted poor children in urban districts. The rationale was that these kids needed help to escape rotten public schools that condemned them to life on the margins of the American Dream.

That changed with COVID-19. During the pandemic, parents saw their public schools put students last by shutting down and staying closed. When angry moms and dads showed up to complain, the National School Board Association asked the Biden White House to treat them as domestic terrorists. Attorney General Merrick Garland then sicced the FBI on them.

In his original plan, Friedman had been primarily concerned with education. But choice in education turned out to have far-reaching consequences

for politics, where Teachers Unions hold great power, propelling their organizer to be elected as a mayor of crime-laden Chicago.

No one is more aware of the threat the Friedman's proposal spells for "politics as usual" than Randi Weingarten, president of the American Federation
of Teachers. In a March 2023 speech at the National Press Club, she warned
that, this year, 29 states are considering school choice measures. In the words
of William McGurn: "As the vampire fears garlic, Teachers Unions fear giving
parents any say in public education and keep blaming the racial imbalances in
K-12 grades on racial discrimination."

Attending poorly performing schools in their neighborhoods, over 80%
of their pupils will lack proficiency in mathematics and reading skills. To use
the words of the black Lieutenant Governor of Virginia Winsome Earle-Sears:
"They are 'functionally illiterate,' meaning that they are unable to manage
daily living and employment tasks. How can our society progress if a such
large segment of our country cannot function in the world that is becoming
more and more competitive? Society doesn't help under-performing groups by
pandering to them or by holding them to lower standards. By lowering the
bar, we are losing the ability to jump."

Learning the minority statistics and hearing complaints from some ex-pa-
triots who have been now teaching in the US Universities, I wondered about
the general American standing in the world of school education to be shocked.
According to Pew Research Center quoting the latest results of the Program
for International Student Assessment, measuring the capabilities of 15-year-
olds, the US is 38th out of 71 countries in math and 24th in science. The 52%
literacy of adults at the 6th grade level presents another unflattering characteristic of the society we live in. While the majority of my American friends are
well read and highly erudite, I'm amazed at how so many people, considered
to be educated and affluent, lack the basic knowledge of literature, basic civ-
ics, world geography and history. And with all the information readily available without any obstruction! Many times, I was left dumbfounded when
the rather mature, college educated and financially well-established people I
encountered had no idea that Russia was fighting Nazi Germany in WWII,
and even naïvely queried me as to whether or not Stalin was really that bad?

While attending meetings with the foreign participants, especially my
European colleagues, many times I felt embarrassed when they spoke about
"American ignorance." Any country is only as strong as the people who live

in it. And the educational and intellectual decline of the USA is becoming increasingly apparent. It started with the erosion and eventual collapse, of the public schools in urban areas, which in turn fostered ignorance and apathy toward what amounted to responsible citizenship.

Ignorance of history will always result in the most inevitable and tragic form of accountability. Because it invariably ends in apathy and indifference toward one's own nation.

That is why I began this book in Chapters Two and Three with something of a history lesson (and even posted a couple of tables of statistics). I did so because the average American has precious little understanding of either World War I or World War II or how devastating a global conflict can be—and how close we all came to ending civilization as we know it. They have also proven to be fatally unaware of the politics of extremism and how very dangerous conceptions such as Fascism, "National Socialism," and Communism are at their very core, and how—at the cost of our humanity—they fail to function at all.

Immigrants like me have most often come to know and love America more than those born here because we have a point of reference and can compare now to then. The future of America represented by today's younger generation has little frame of reference. According to the survey conducted by *US News and World Report,* two-thirds of Americans would not pass the test required to become a US citizen (with passing score of only 60!). Only 13% of surveyed knew that Constitution was ratified in 1788 with the majority thinking it was 1776. The fact that colonists fought the British was known to 24% with 37% identifying Benjamin Franklin as the light-bulb inventor. Sixty percent of people could not name the countries America fought in WW II. The same survey found that people aged 65 and older were more likely to pass the test than those aged 45 and younger. One can only guess what that threshold would be for age 20.

As my friend Dr. Robert Licht wrote to me: "I blame diversity, that is the radical idea of equality. Think of it as a tax on excellence and intelligence. When you tax something you get less of it. Also of course we must recognize the Internet as anti-Darwinian; no need to compete for survival. This is the survival of the fitless."

My own dad, who never mastered English, easily answered questions translated to him during his Citizenship exam about the three branches of

Government, election cycle of US Presidents, the size of the United States Senate, and the number of Senators from each State.

One more thing with respect to citizenship: Apparently, the lack of patriotism among the average American-born citizen has a spillover-effect onto the development of it among many newcomers—especially those who come here for reasons other than searching for liberty and freedom. During recent permissive immigration policies they were pouring-in in droves, through virtually open borders, bringing with them closed minds and an overriding sense of entitlement.

How else one can explain the protesting crowds waving the Mexican, Salvadoran and Honduran flags on streets of Chicago? They are rife with selfish expectation and no sense of either commitment or patriotism toward their adopted country. It is not the same as flying Greek or Italian flags at cultural and food festivals of proud Americans of Greek and Italian descent. These are misguided protests of the perpetually disenfranchised, who are ignorant of their responsibility to the very nation that has taken them to heart.

Freedom, I had come to learn, is not only a right to be enjoyed, but also a responsibility to be cherished and defended.

And as President Ronald Reagan once said – **"Freedom is never more than one generation away from extinction."**

CHAPTER THIRTEEN

Reagan vs "The Evil Empire!"

Peace is not absence of conflict.
It is the ability to handle conflict by peaceful means.

~ Ronald Reagan

My dad's tireless efforts coupled with the rapid deterioration of the environment in the Soviet Union had helped to break the ice for me—so much so that my ex-wife had even applied for emigration, filling me with a renewed sense of hope that I would soon be able to see my now teen-aged girls. It was hard to believe that the application also included her mother and devoted Communist father!

My hopes for the coming reunion with my children were quickly dashed since they were refused almost as soon as they applied, giving me another, and one of the most important projects of my life. Determined to see them into the safe haven of the USA, I started appealing to the politicians I thought could be helpful, starting with my Senator and Chair of the Senate Foreign Relations Committee Charles Percy (R-Illinois). After my initial contacts and counseling with Senator "Chuck" Percy, I continued with local House of Representatives members, *et al.* I even wrote to the visibly physically and mentally "losing it," Soviet Premier Leonid Brezhnev.

This process of appeals went on for about two years without me being able to distinguish between Republicans and Democrats. At that time, this was still somewhat irrelevant to me because the ideological lines were fuzzier "back in the day"—at least partly in a good way. There were conservative Democrats then, and liberal Republicans. Such creatures still exist, although—even in the early 1980s—the "divide" was beginning to harden.

I still couldn't vote during the 1980 Presidential elections, which I watched, hoping that Jimmy Carter would lose, as he was known to me and other *refuseniks* from our times in Russia as a politically naïve, weak President, presiding over an astronomically high-interest rate economy, long gas lines, and a pathetic international policy dominated by Arab petrodollars (although facilitating the Begin-Sadat negotiations).

In the meantime, I also remained uncertain about his little-known oppo-nent—a second-tier Hollywood actor named Ronald Reagan. (Admittedly, I hadn't done my homework, because if I had, I would have realized that Reagan had been the best twice-elected Governor that California had seen in about 50 years. Under Reagan's stewardship, California enjoyed the best educational system in the nation, the most improved infrastructure in two decades, the lowest income taxes and the most business-friendly environment of any state in the union. Under Reagan, crime in California was down and household incomes were up. And he made no bones about taking on the Soviet Union during his speeches on the 1980 campaign trail. Given the impotence of the Carter administration, this proved to be strong tonic indeed. To anyone's way of thinking at the time, anything would have been an improvement.)

In truth, immediately after winning the 1980 election, Reagan put out the word early-on to the international community that he was someone not to be taken lightly. As evidence of that, and (behind the scenes) he let the Mullahs in Iran know through special envoy and soon-to-be Secretary of State Alexander Haig that once he took office, they were to release the US Embassy hostages…"or else."

So, from day one, and with the entire world looking on, the Ayatollahs in Iran announced the release of the hostages virtually by the time of Reagan's inauguration on January 21, 1981. This provided me with another, fresher look at the newly elected Ronald Reagan, and along with it, more than a modicum of hope.[31]

---

31   As a little touch of class so characteristic of Reagan, he even sent defeated rival and lame-duck US President Jimmy Carter over as Special Emissary to bring the 56 hostages back to the USA, thus allowing Carter to both share in the credit and show a sense of American unanimity to the world.

Then, 100 days later, tragedy struck at the heart of the American presidency yet again, and I was left once more in utter disbelief while driving back to the office. Another President had been shot—once again by yet another "nutcase" from Dallas, Texas—but fortunately not fatally this time. John Hinckley, the deranged son of a wealthy Highland Park, Texas, family had emptied his .22 caliber revolver into Reagan's entourage, striking the President twice and shooting then-Press-Secretary James Brady through the head. Proving tough, Reagan survived, and was out of the hospital in 10 days. He gained the respect of a nation by having done so—even doubling down on his rather strongly-worded rhetoric toward the USSR.[32]

With all the things and events going on around me, I still had to run my small company and make a living. Which reminds me of a story about an older Jewish man falling down and while being helped by passing people was asked if he was comfortable—he answered that he was "just making a living."

Part of the beauty of professional relationships built out of mutual respect is the personal friendships that can often grow from them. I developed great working relations with a number of clients, becoming close personal friends with several of them. Two of them were especially prominent structural engineers Jay Paul in Chicago and Dov Kamenetzky in New York with whom we worked on many interesting and challenging projects.

I soon found such personal relations and mutual trust to be making work and life feel more enjoyable, productive and rewarding. Another great feeling of satisfaction I had happened when the jobs I had created allowed the people working in my company to take nice vocations, buy cars and own homes. We were managing be competitive and financially successful by finding niches in our field and bringing in new technologies and equipment, which was not without significant financial risks, but the risk-reward paid off for us, almost every time.

We also became quite proud of our ability to provide a prompt response to our clients' needs and timely delivery of our reports, even when it required working long hours, weekends and holidays. This was a very important feature

---

32 Jim Brady survived as well, but never fully recovered from his wounds. As he'd been shot in the head, the bullet wound left him with slurred speech, aphasia, memory loss and partial paralysis that required full-time use of a wheelchair. In his name, however, Congress enacted The Brady Bill in 1994, the first act that required background checks for all gun purchases.

in a profession where clients often obsessed about schedules and constantly needed services to be delivered ASAP. The commonly used phrase—*I need it yesterday*—reminded me of a story about a fellow who came to a car dealership in Moscow during the Soviet times and wanted to buy a car. The salesman put his name down, informing the buyer that his car would be delivered… "Exactly 10 years from today."

Upon the news, the happy fellow asked: "Will that be in the morning or afternoon?

When asked that question, the salesman responded: "What difference does it make?"

The future owner responded: "You see, I have a plumber coming in that morning."

Well, this was not Russia—this was America! We were constantly striving to be ahead of a curve. I and others in our company were taking courses to learn new things at the time when computers, especially portable field laptops, were just coming into the industry and were a part of the new equipment, often developed in Denmark. Some of our engineers who had never opened laptops in their lives went on to become among the best in their respective fields, and would go on to develop into future IT masters.

Not everything was going smoothly all the time. The mishaps, mistakes, losing to competition, occasional late-pay or deadbeat clients and personnel problems often led me to those sleepless nights that any business owner might have to endure. Any conscientious owner's job is a 24/7 undertaking filled with a mixture of gold and garbage—maintaining the just right balance is the name of the game.

I was now a year into my struggle to obtain my children's emigration. By reading now available-to-me papers and magazines and watching TV, I was becoming more attuned to the political divide growing in the country.

I loved Reagan's calling the Soviet Union "The Evil Empire," especially since this was exactly what it had always been. Watching Sunday morning TV programs, I saw much more persuasive and correct, in my opinion, views from conservative commentators, that fit with my rapidly solidifying views of world events. Most of these were better articulated by notable intellectuals such as George Will, Jean Kirkpatrick and William F. Buckley than by most other panelists. These were generally civilized discussions with rather objective anchors that always seemed to end in a positive accord.

It was also during this time that I had been invited to "share" my Soviet life experiences at several organizations and clubs. With my affinity for the military, the invitation to speak at a dinner for retired Navy and Marine senior officers at the Chicago Yacht Club was one of the most exciting events I could remember.

The dinner theme was the Soviet Union, and presentations began with a lecture by a guest speaker who was a retired Admiral. He described his trip through Russia and being fascinated with the vast permafrost region. His explanation of the permafrost as the area where, "As long as you drill, you are still in ice," was met by a comment of one of the officers sitting next to me: "I used to have a girlfriend like that." (My presentation was met with somewhat fewer laughs.)

Springing out of my regular consulting work, I also found that this aspect of the business took on a more significant role than I might have imagined. It involved representing sides in various construction litigations and serving as an expert witness. This led to many hours of interaction with legal professionals and me wondering how come lawyers still managed to charge for the time they spent correcting their own mistakes made during filings.

Testifying in court in front of juries was always a stomach-churning exercise for me. Still, especially in smaller Wisconsin and Michigan towns, I felt the juries I faced were sincerely fascinated and embraced a certain level of trust for somebody like me—foreign-educated and presenting findings to them with an accent. The lawyers by my side very often felt the same way.

As a counterpoint in my life, I learned that in the early 1980s Uncle David was being used even more flagrantly than ever by the Soviet Propaganda Machine—especially when it came to anti-Israel and anti-emigration hysteria frequently promoted on Soviet TV and radio shows. In fact, it had finally become enough of a global issue that it even got the attention of America's second longest-running independent news broadcast show, CBS's *60 Minutes*. Noted for hard-nosed journalism, it featured the sacred triad of unimpeachable integrity in reportage: Harry Reasoner, Morley Safer, Ed Bradley, plus the face of the *60 Minute* franchise, Mike Wallace.

Ever aware of that, I received a call one day from the office of selfsame, "pull-no-punches" Mike Wallace, asking me if I would be willing to be interviewed on an upcoming *60 Minutes* segment alongside Uncle David. I would be basically challenging him during his upcoming May 1985 visit to New

York City. He was coming there at the invitation of the American Communist Party (CPUSA, which was still in existence at the time).

From this possible media confrontation, a Hobson's Choice arose for me. The chances of getting my daughters out of the USSR and into the USA could take a decided upturn. However, publicly engaging in a confrontation with my own uncle in the front of the entire world would have doubtless been the last thing I was looking for.

As it was, Fate intervened when I was informed that the proposed CBS interview had been canceled "for the time being"—the underlying cause being that Colonel General Dragunsky had been denied a US visa in retaliation for the Soviets having canceled a visa for some American official.

All these events were unfolding while the Soviet Union was now busily preoccupied with arranging a series of funerals scheduled for its aging, mentally diminished leaders called General Secretaries of the Communist Party. At this juncture they were all dying at 11- to 16-month intervals. Beginning with the death of Leonid Brezhnev, 78, in 1982 (possibly facilitated by reading my letter to him ☺). The USSR followed this with a game of "Premier Musical Chairs," first with Yuri Andropov, 71, in 1984 and Konstantin Chernenko, 74, also in 1984, when it was commonly rumored that, after the third "Official State Funeral," the Politburo had decided to issue funeral coupon books as a kind of "package deal."

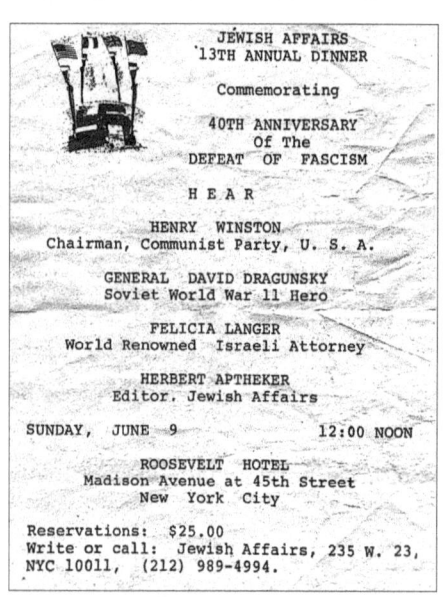

JEWISH AFFAIRS
13TH ANNUAL DINNER

Commemorating

40TH ANNIVERSARY
Of The
DEFEAT OF FASCISM

H E A R

HENRY WINSTON
Chairman, Communist Party, U. S. A.

GENERAL DAVID DRAGUNSKY
Soviet World War 11 Hero

FELICIA LANGER
World Renowned Israeli Attorney

HERBERT APTHEKER
Editor, Jewish Affairs

SUNDAY, JUNE 9   12:00 NOON

ROOSEVELT HOTEL
Madison Avenue at 45th Street
New York City

Reservations: $25.00
Write or call: Jewish Affairs, 235 W. 23,
NYC 10011, (212) 989-4994.

Finally, seemingly weary of the stodgy seniority that was taking its toll in the Central Committee, they settled on a relatively "teen-aged" newbie in the form of 54-year-old Mikhail Gorbachev. This happened in March of 1985, and in June of that year I was already happily on my way—flying to Vienna to greet my liberated twin daughters, their mother and grandmother. (Their grandfather, my former father-in-law, had died a short time before.)

Living for eight years in two countries as different as Russia and America brought me to the realization that my ex-wife and I were thinking and behaving as two people coming from different planets. Unfortunately for all of us, our inability to reunite proved particularly heartbreaking for my 16-year-old girls, because they came to the realization that there would be no reconciliation in the offing.

On the other hand, one of my dreams did come true, the first morning I was able to see my daughters off to the school bus. The girls, Sonya and Olga, were easily managing their new environment in all the ways that only the young can do.

A few months later they even got jobs in a local McDonalds (sometimes with me in the background helping them to understand some specifics orders coming from the rapid-fire demands of a young American suburbia).

Sonya and Olga in their finest MacDonald's garb.

A day after their high school graduation, I had to leave for Moscow as a part of US-USSR exchange taking place more frequently in the construction industry. This was the beginning of a new form of *Glasnost* introduced by Gorbachev, but with the old Soviet apparatus still in place. My visa (which I doubted would ever come) was issued minutes before the workday's end, preceding my morning departure from Washington, DC, and leaving me with only a few hours to get ready. Apparently, I was the first recent emigrant to receive permission to visit the Soviet Union as a "foreign citizen."

It was an emotional landing in Moscow, where I still had my father and brother (and Uncle David) living. I showed my American passport to what now presented itself as a very attentive and welcoming immigration control, followed by proceeding to a newly-built complex with a hotel strictly limited to Westerners (mostly Americans) where all guests were required to present a hotel pass. That's why I was surprised to see the lobby bar full of hospitable, attractive, young Russian women when I returned in the evening. I guessed the KGB payroll still remained intact, allowing them to rather blatantly continue using these "lovely ladies" as a tool to infiltrate the Who's Who of foreign visitors.

Once I'd arrived, my dad was very happy to see me but was still burdened by deep concerns about the risks of my being back since he, like many others, was taking Mikhail Gorbachev's freshly introduced "reforms" with a grain of salt. After 70 years of the totalitarian nightmare that had preceded this seeming paradigm shift to openness, who wouldn't be inclined to anticipate that it might return overnight?

These fears were still ingrained in the Soviet psyche when I attended our exhibition stands, where all of a sudden, I saw my former friend and colleague standing at a distance with tears in her eyes. She was afraid to approach me even after all this time. In a short time, I also saw the Deputy Director of my former Institute passing me and—without turning his head—he simply whispered: "You look good, Boris!"

Back in my room, I was amazed to see the TV programs revealing the ills of present Soviet society and criticizing the party and local elected officials—all accompanied by favorite descriptions of Western technological achievements and news from all over the world without the customary Soviet propaganda twists. This, for me, was something hard to believe.

Even with these breakthroughs, the USSR had also fallen into disarray. Compared to the US dollar, the Russian ruble had tumbled in value to such a degree that my wine-enriched lunch with my cousin in a top Moscow Georgian restaurant cost me around three dollars. People were selling everything for next to nothing and trying to make a buck wherever possible. With no taxi-cabs in sight, on my way to see my dad I caught a private car driven by a fully uniformed Red Army captain looking for some extra cash to supplement his plummeting salary.

I didn't dare call my uncle during my entire visit.

Landing in Zurich on my way back to Chicago, I experienced a sense of both relief and joy at being again in the West. The cocktail I had while changing planes had never tasted better.

My next trip to Moscow was in June of 1991 to visit my dad and brother, who were still caught up in the emotional maze of trying to leave the country. And this time, six years into Gorbachev's governance, I also felt sufficiently safe (even in gang and crime-laden Moscow) and finally took it upon myself to reconnect with Uncle David.

By this time Colonel General David Dragunsky was retired and living the life of a gentleman-civilian, somewhat at peace with himself. In that new, more-relaxed incarnation, he made me feel as if I'd gotten back my own loving uncle. The feelings were mutual, and our visits were filled with his emotional memories of my perished grandparents and all the past trips we'd taken together. It was then that it struck me: his transformation had at last fallen into sync with the changing times around him.

He was inquisitive about my new "American life" and the life of my children in our adopted country, asking me to encourage my dad (the brother he hadn't spoken with for over 10 years until recently) to leave and join me in the United States. Now in his 80s, my uncle had mellowed considerably and that restored the warm feelings I'd had for him when he

A photo of the first and last reunion with my now civilian Uncle David, after 20 years of "Cold War". (Picture of my perished grandmother in the background). And it all happened to be in Moscow on July 4th.

was in his 30s and 40s! These were the happiest days I'd ever experienced in my Moscow life.

As Gorbachev's process of *Glasnost* (Openness) continued, a good number of Soviet citizens were allowed to travel abroad to visit their relatives or move for good. Many such visitors came to the United States expecting to see their hosts, who were themselves relatively new immigrants, as millionaires. But not all of them were, and they had a hard time supporting the unfathomable appetites of their guests for gadgets and clothes to be taken back to empty-shelved Soviet cities. With all the delight of seeing their long-missing relatives, the welcoming hosts began calling them "Gorbachev's vacuum cleaners" or "Gorbachev's Avengers".

In July of 1991, I was welcoming the arrival of beautiful and vivacious Aunt Elena and her family. This time I had more room to host them before they resettled in their own dwellings in Chicago. My cousin Mila and her husband later went on to open and run a successful international travel agency. Her brother Vadim, with whom I share an identical palate of tastes, became quite an IT expert.

Now with both of my master-baker aunts around and actively competing, I was periodically treated to their melt-in-the-mouth specialties: Maria's eclairs and Elena's napoleons.

Before Elena's family moved out, I woke them up one morning to watch the scene taking place on television. Tanks stationed next to the famous Hotel Ukraine (and my uncle's apartment I had just visited) had their turrets aimed and then fired into the Moscow White House—the seat of the Soviet government. This turned out to be an attempted *coup d'état* by the Communist hardliners to seize government control from Mikhail Gorbachev. Although the coup failed in the end, it severely diminished Gorbachev's power and prestige and helped to elevate Boris Yeltsin to the apex of Soviet politics.

During my last visit to Moscow, I witnessed the process of internal disintegration within the Soviet Union, which in turn resulted in the end of the country's existence on December 26, 1991. It brought an end to the administration of General Secretary (later President) Mikhail Gorbachev's effort to reform the Soviet political and economic system in an attempt to stop a period of political stalemate and economic backslide.

Aftermath of the failed coup d'etat by Soviet Hardliners in 1991.

By late 1991, amid a catastrophic political crisis, with several republics already departing from the Union—along with the waning of centralized power—the leaders of three of its founding members declared "the Soviet Union no longer existed." Shortly thereafter, eight more republics joined this "Defection to Autonomy." In the wake of that, it was game over for the Gorbachev regime.

Gorbachev, who resigned in December 1991, didn't come to power to end Socialism or to dismantle his Soviet "union." As a younger and better educated person he was able, unlike his predecessors, to realize the insurmountable problems the country had been facing and was looking for ways to save it. But by the end, he was facing a "tech-revolution" in the West, where the first casualties were the information lock-downs that had so strongly characterized the Soviet Union of the past. Now, the revolution, headed by the Cold War warrior Ronald Reagan talking about the "Star Wars," left Gorbachev with a Solomon's dilemma he wasn't willing to make.

With the Soviet priorities of being a dominant military power decidedly on the wane, Gorbachev knew his nation was bankrupt and couldn't keep pace with America's fast-developing new technologies. He was leading a government that was heading into the "Abyss."

A study in pathos in the midst of this, Gorbachev was like a man running along a platform while watching his train already leaving the station. There were two ways of catching it—by running faster than the train (the West) or by slowing down the train. Gorbachev's strategy was to try to slow down the train by negotiating in good faith with the USA and Europe.

His attempts to do so were first recognized by the "Iron Lady" of British Empire, Prime Minister Margaret Thatcher, who shared it with her best friend and, as it turned out, a highly receptive Ronald Reagan.

"Mr. Gorbachev, tear down the (Berlin) Wall!" was the demand Reagan made in a speech entirely resisted not only by the US State Department but also by political "experts" all over the world. In truth, they proved to be the first hammer blows that brought down not only the Wall but also the Iron Curtain it represented…and with it the entire Soviet system.

In 1991, Boris Yeltsin replaced Mikhail Gorbachev as the first-ever *popularly elected* leader in Russian history. Along with the many other reforms he introduced, he even attempted to outlaw the Communist Party, a party he had openly quit in July of 1990.

Once, while at a July 4ᵗʰ party picnic at my friend's house in Chicago, I asked one of the attending guests, a professor of economics moving to teach at the University of California, Berkeley, what the difference was between Moscow and Berkeley universities? The answer I suggested was, "There are no Communists in Moscow University."

Back on the home front…

After their graduation from high school, my daughters moved to California where their mom received a position to teach Russian in the Department of Defense School of Linguistics. After attending a local college for a year, they were both accepted into prestigious George Washington University in Washington, DC. I didn't think this was the right school for them, since they excelled in math and other disciplines not strongly associated with GWU. But what did I (or any other father of teenagers) really know?

CHAPTER FOURTEEN

"A Hero's Repentance"
The Captive Mind Redeemed

"I will insist the Hebrews (Jews) have contributed more to civilize men than any other nation. If I was an atheist and believed in blind eternal fate, I should still believe that fate had ordained the Jews to be the most essential instrument for civilizing the nations ... They are the most glorious nation that ever inhabited this Earth. The Romans and their empire were but a bubble in comparison to the Jews. They have given religion to three-quarters of the globe and have influenced the affairs of mankind more and more happily than any other nation, ancient or modern."

— John Adams, Second President of the United States

A s I previously mentioned, even in 1991 my dad, Zalman, was still barely talking to his brother after nearly 15 years of no communication. He even called Colonel General David Dragunsky, twice Hero of the Soviet Union, "a disgrace and shame on Jewish people."

My father had good reasons for saying just that. In 1983, David had willingly agreed to serve as Chairman of a KGB initiated and controlled Soviet propaganda organ called the Anti-Zionist Committee of the Soviet Public, the core of which contained many well-known Soviet Jews who were members but, to their credit, members "in name only."

While in this post, David had signed many declarations of this Committee—some that he had written and some that were written for him. As it was, he was a frequent soloist in the most vicious chorus of anti-Israeli

215

sentiments, defending the official position of the committee opposing the emigration of Jews from the USSR, and justifying it by stating that Israel's policies of emigration of only select Jews from the USSR would cause problems for those Jews that remained. Despite Gorbachev's *Glasnost* and *Perestroika* and the genuine thaw in relations between the USSR and Israel in the late 1980s, David Dragunsky remained as head the Anti-Zionist Committee until his death in 1992.

As I noted earlier, my uncle was fully retired by that time, a civilian who was clothed and well taken care of by his wife, who was now exceptionally friendly to me. In retirement, he still retained all his perks, including a plush apartment in a prestigious building and a black Volga car with a chauffeur, but had lesser access to "closed doors" stores. The latter played somewhat favorably during my brief stay in Moscow. Now it was my turn to treat my uncle to the things that were just a click away from my American Express card. I was happy to present him with a Phillips electric shaver and a host of other "goodies" of his choice.

When my cousin Alla was traveling from Chicago to visit her parents still living in Russia, my uncle, through my dad, asked if I could send a Chicago Bulls winter sport jacket with her for his 5-year old grandson—which I dutifully did, packaging it along with other American luxuries and "goodies." A week later, on Sunday afternoon, I placed an order for an overseas telephone call and, after waiting for an hour, was connected with my uncle in Moscow. I wanted to make sure that the things I sent were exactly what he asked for. It was late evening in Moscow, and our conversation lasted close to an hour.

After thanking me for all the great gifts, he went on to pointedly tell me how proud he was of me, and that my father and my children should be proud as well. He also added that he wished that my father, his brother, would be able to leave the country and join me in America, even as he belittled himself for belonging to a generation of "political prostitutes," and openly confiding that, "History will judge people like me harshly." In his own words, everything had changed and he had changed; too bad he was too old now to change his circumstance.

Overwhelmed and hardly believing what I just heard, I invited him to visit me in Chicago, insisting, "Everything will be taken care of."

Despite my encouragement to come, he emphasized his many concerns about his age. I insisted at the end of our conversation that I would do everything to facilitate his visit, finally wishing him goodbye until we were to meet again soon in Chicago.

These happened to be the last words spoken by the Three-Star General of Tank Forces, Twice-Hero of the Soviet Union," and mainly my uncle, David Abramovich Dragunsky, *A"H*. It was almost midnight in Moscow by the time we finished our call.

The next morning, Uncle David woke up as usual and peacefully passed from this life to the next while waiting for his breakfast to be served.

"Generation of political prostitutes"

Upon hearing the devastating news of my uncle's death, I replayed his words non-stop in my mind. What a revelation and a verdict to the 75-year-long nightmare! The following night, around 2 a.m., I was awakened by a telephone call from Moscow. Doubtless shaken after learning of it, my brother Alex delivered the sad news that our uncle David had passed away, and that a State funeral had already been scheduled for him on the following day.

Struck to the heart by the tone and tenor of our last conversation and his last words to me, I was honor-bound to be at the funeral and determined to do so, even though it would take place in just 24 hours. I also realized that I would be trying to get into the same bureaucratically-burdened, red-tape tangled Soviet Union where it often required months just to get a visa to enter.

I sat, seemingly frozen in time. I had a business to run—with a hefty schedule of previously booked appointments, including several reports due to be delivered the next day. But I would set all that aside, and did, starting in the middle of the night.

My first telephone call at 2:30 a.m. was made to the Soviet Embassy. The on-duty, hardly-awake gentleman quickly responded, "The US Embassy doesn't issue visas," and that I should, "ask the Consulate." After hearing the reason for my request and the name of the deceased, he promised to relay it to the Consulate when they opened in the morning. Hearing no outright denial even as a consideration, I got dressed immediately. Packing a warmer coat since it was already cold in Moscow, and not forgetting my prayer book, I went to my office. There, I wrote-out instructions to my secretary, and went to Chicago's O'Hare Airport to catch the first available flight to Washington, DC.

By the time I got to the US Consulate, with the help of my daughter Sonya who was living in DC, it was close to 10 a.m. The reception gate of the Consulate had a small window, a long line of visitors and a lonely public telephone hanging on a dilapidated wall behind a single bench. I pushed my way to the window and requested an emergency visa to attend the funeral of my family member. I was told they required an "official letter." After asking the young lady attending the window if the official obituary in their newspaper could suffice, she called her boss. Obviously, the Consulate had never received the promised notice from the Embassy.

Now all I needed was a fax from somebody in an official position in Moscow, two passport photographs and $250. In the Soviet Union of 1992, a fax machine was as common as a yacht in landlocked Czechoslovakia. Still I had no choice but to try to get it. Miraculously, the hanging payphone allowed me to get through to my uncle's phone and I asked his surprised wife, Eugenia, about something for which she hadn't a clue. She promised to inquire about it from a friend, who was a minister of something-or-other. Hanging-up the phone, I was less than optimistic about the fax affair, but nonetheless started searching for a place to get my photos. This turned to be a workout all its own, requiring me to go running winter dressed through a 90-degree, hilly and humid Washington, DC. Pushing away a much more valuable client purchasing a Canon camera, I convinced the camera salesman in the store to promptly develop and reproduce my photo instead.

Running uphill back to the Consulate, photos and cash in hand, I found the gates already closed. (Standard Consulate hours at the time were 10 a.m. to noon.) Like a victim unfairly locked out, I felt no small sense of rage—and started to shake the iron gates of this "iron wall." With a bit of Divine intervention I've yet to fully comprehend, I left the Consulate gates 30 minutes later with the visa folded neatly into my pocket. I was fully exhausted but had a sense of relief I'd seldom known before.

The only flight that could deliver me to Moscow in time was an Aeroflot Boeing from New York's JFK Airport, departing around 6 p.m. From my starting point, I had about 4 hours to get to JFK and buy a ticket. As I arrived at the Delta counter to buy the ticket for the flight which might have brought me to JFK in time, I was slammed with the news that the flight had just been canceled. Chasing through the (at that-time-much-smaller) Reagan International

Airport, I was able to catch another flight that brought me to JFK, but at a different terminal.

Trying to get to the correct terminal, I took a wrong inter-terminal bus, but the driver was kind enough to radio another upcoming bus that picked me up and then dropped me off in exactly the right place. By that time, the Aeroflot flight had been delayed—just long enough to help me to buy a ticket and settle-in for a nine-and-a-half-hour flight to Moscow that was scheduled to arrive around 10 a.m. Moscow time.

Connecting with my still-in-Moscow cousin (the only one left in Russia), I knew the official State ceremony was going to take place at the Soviet Army Palace at 10 a.m. This was a ceremony I was obviously going to miss and didn't really care for. The important issue for me then was the knowledge that I could still attend 12 p.m. cemetery funeral with the help of my cousin and his car.

We landed in Moscow on schedule and I impatiently got ready to be first to get out of the Boeing 747, which had stopped about 50 feet short of the tarmac. After few minutes, which seemed much longer, an announcement came that there was broken glass at the tarmac approach and we were waiting for a cleanup crew to arrive shortly.

Three hundred curious people sitting on this giant plane, having just finished an overseas night flight, were eagerly awaiting the "emergency" glass removal operation, only to behold a peasant-looking older lady with a broom crawling on her knees, scoop-collecting glass pieces while being "supervised" by three grim-looking, fur-hat clad men standing around with their hands in their coat pockets. While nobody could believe their eyes, I was getting more and more agitated, tortured by the knowledge that I might be late.

After close to an hour delay, I finally debarked from the plane only to find the automatic glass doors leading to the terminal were not too automatic—they were in fact closed tight. After manually prying the doors apart and going through the border control, I was finally sitting in the passenger seat of my cousin's car, repeating "pedal to the metal" the whole time he drove.

I arrived at the Novodevichy Cemetery and got permission to enter this official government burial site. There, I found the funeral procession for my uncle, which happened to be 100 feet away from Nikita Khrushchev's grave and monument. Not even my father knew I had arrived it was a shock when they found out. I got there just in time to hear official tributes and farewell words from several Generals, relatives and friends. As all the speeches came to an end and the lowering of the casket was about to begin, I came up front, wearing a *kipa* (traditional Jewish head-cover) and asked them to wait as I opened the prayer book and recited the *Kaddish* prayer. Keep in mind yet a this was 1992, and words of *Kaddish* hadn't been heard in public in Moscow for more than 70 years.

My uncle loved to be surrounded by "bohemian" type people, and after the funeral procession concluded, I faced a long line of careworn, red-eyed faces belonging to my uncle's friends and comrades. Among them were well-known artists, poets, actors and public figures—all of whom were thanking me, many with tears in their eyes, for bringing back their childhood memories of their traditional Jewish grandparents.

After the funeral, I found myself—the only blood-relative of General David Dragunsky—invited to the wake held at the location of my uncle's last posting: the Vystrel Officers School. To top off the honors given to this former "bad guy and traitor," I was seated at the head table between my uncle's wife and the Defense Minister of the Russian Federation, General Pavel Grachev, who, with the help of several vodka shots, became very talkative and friendly. As our conversation progressed, I asked him about the rumors circulating in the American press that seemed to be impossible: China had acquired two Soviet ballistic missiles by somehow "stealing them."

The General leaned toward me and squarely stated: "You Americans are stupid and naïve." He went on to tell me that after leaving the East Germany and other Eastern European satellite countries following the collapse of the Soviet Union, the troops had returned to their Russian bases missing more than a half of their tanks, artillery pieces (even planes!), plus almost all ammunition and other supplies. No uniforms and footwear came back either—it had been sold virtually down to the last item. According to the Defense Minister, everything was stolen and sold on the black market. As he spoke, I came to learn that the army no longer had the petrol to even fuel their tanks. Later that week, I saw several Generals' uniforms and festoons of medals set out in the open at a Moscow market—there to be sold for a mere "fistful of dollars."

While still at the cemetery, I reached out to one of the funeral attendees, my uncle's close friend—a famous sculptor named Lev Kerbel, questioning him about my uncle's future monument.[33] When he told me that they were all financially broke with neither money nor materials available, I offered to commission him and pay him in US dollars to do it. This proposition was warmly welcomed, and an impressive monument decorates my uncle's resting place.

But it is obviously not how a Jew, regardless his rank in society, must be buried and how a graveyard monument should look (with cremation strictly forbidden, body wrapped in a white shroud and placed in a modest casket made of easily disintegrating material…and a stone placed atop the grave a year later).

In something of a strange juxtaposition, a few yards away stands a memorial to the Soviet aviator, "Killed in Action Protecting the Motherland Skies". Keeping the name of the Action undisclosed, it was a tribute to the pilot shot down by the Soviet rocket sent to intercept the Gary Powers U-2 plane, a chain of events that, through Colonel Tereshenko had sent to my place of work, assisting me in my emigration to the USA.

Walking to visit my uncle's grave, I also had to pass the monument of former Soviet Premier Nikita Khrushchev—something that engendered feelings of both gravity and relief for a Soviet

My next and final meeting with my Uncle in the Novodevichy Cemetery, Moscow. This monument has the inscription: "Twice-Hero of the Soviet Union, Colonel General David Dragunsky".

---

33 Lev Kerbel was a highly lauded Soviet sculptor commissioned by the Soviet government to create sculptures of Karl Marx, Vladimir Lenin, Yuri Gagarin and many other politicians and public figures. His works were often sent as gifts to Socialist and Third World countries across the world—from East Germany (Marx) to Cuba (Lenin).

222 ഇ *Back in the USSA*

Union that no longer existed…and for men, now forgotten, who were heralded in their day.

The almost 75-year reign of Soviet rule made sure that the passing three generations would lose any signs of the heritage their ancestors developed over 5,000 years of Jewish history, instead to be molded into an average conformist, "Homo Sovieticus," whose vestigial points of pride—such as our ethnicity, customs and religion—had been judiciously eradicated, to be replaced by the new "Marxist-Leninist man."

Succeeding in the physical detraction from Jewish traditions and prosecuting any observance, particularly in large cities, they failed to understand that there always remains something Jewish in every single Jew.

The relentless anti-Jewish assaults, especially during the Stalin Purges of 1930s and anti-cosmopolitan propaganda war of 1950s, have caused in the minds of Soviet Jews one turbulent effect: that his or her Jewishness was made to be felt as one of the central factors controlling his or her personal destiny. I witnessed these "Jewish remains" through the tearful eyes and tortured expressions of the famed Soviet artists, public figures and all others still living the lives of loyal Soviet citizens.

Virtually from the beginning of the USSR, Soviet Jews were punished when they expressed their Jewishness—their open commitment to being Jewish was an act of both masochism and martyrdom.

Example: The 1952 "Night of the Murdered Poets" with 23 leading soviet Jewish writers, poets and artists artfully assassinated on Stalin's orders in the basement of Lubyanka (remember my invitation to Lubyanka?) signaled the "final solution" to the Jewish culture. Even in the lull of the Khrushchev years, fraught with a kind of "benign neglect," not one Jewish applicant was admitted to Moscow State University in 1977-1978—with Jewish enrollment in the institutions of higher learning dropping from 111,900 in 1968-69 to 44,000 in 1980 *(Simcha R. Goldberg. Jewish Acculturation)*.

However, in a survey conducted by Professor Robert Fain—even back in 1979—among the 70% of university graduated Jews who considered themselves Russians and being content to stay in Russia, it was found that 96% would buy a book on Jewish history if available; 87% would visit a Jewish restaurant, again, if available; 80% expressed a desire to learn the Jewish language; 50% would want their children to attend Jewish schools or courses; 34% said all five of their best friends were Jewish; 78% expressed preferences for their children to marry Jewish. It also revealed a strong revival among the youths with positive attitudes towards Jewish holidays, religion and synagogues prevailing among the responders. (Source: Elisa Alterhand, Tel Aviv University, April 4, 1979).

All these Jewish sentiments have been expressed, not by *refuseniks* or others who declared their intention to emigrate, but by the people with no intention to emigrate. Naturally, one should expect much higher levels of "Jewish interest" among the people who broke all the emigration barriers, lost their jobs, risked their own wellbeing and obtained all degrees of freedom, including their Jewishness, crossed "the pond" and finally settled in the country of their choice—the "Golden Medina" of the United States of America.

But don't rush, and hold onto your expectations.

First of all, the communities receiving and helping to resettle the Soviet Jews were shocked by the lack of knowledge and desire among most émigrés to learn such basic things as Jewish history and Jewish traditions—*kashrut*, fasting on Yom Kippur, *Brit Milah* (circumcision), not eating bread (and grain derivatives) on Passover, Bar Mitzvahs and Bat Mitzvahs, etc. It seems that the lack of desire to learn the values denied them by the repressions of a Soviet society has been the most surprising.

However, one can justify such a lack of desire when considering the challenges faced by the Soviet refugees. Just like all refugees, they have virtually been dropped from the sky into an alien environment. The majority of the newcomers came with little or no command of English and its nuances. As a result, some seemed to go into a period of mourning for the rich culture they loved and lost. Moreover, their resettlement was compounded by having to deal with material needs to the exclusion of all else. The refugee's openness to all-things Jewish, if it ever existed, had been pushed way down on the list of priorities. The fragile thread of Jewish attachment was found to be under tremendous stress during this process, giving way to the simple struggle for survival. This particularly affected professionals like MDs, engineers, lawyers, accountants *et al.* in their need to overcome language and other barriers in order to leverage their qualifications in this totally new environment.

The other problems with the Soviet Jews, until this very day, is that they remain on the fringes of a rich Jewish life and traditions—even after settling and acquiring the highly accessible comfort of an American lifestyle. There are different ways to take advantage of these newly attained freedoms—either to forgo your Jewishness because, unlike in Russia, nobody will remind you that you're Jewish, or to embrace, learn and practice your 3,500-year-old history. Unfortunately, a preponderance of former Soviet Jews tend to select the former.

Upon their arrival, there were very few people around to help them to overcome the 70-plus year Soviet attempts to erase all traces of Judaism from human consciousness. Neither the majority of American Jewish religious leaders nor the professionals and volunteers with whom they were in contact through the absorption process have been sufficiently conscientious in their need help with this.

These contacts comprising the majority of the left-leaning seculars and/or reform denominations were held in contempt by the people who had just escaped from the Socialist "paradise," finding more understanding and sharing their ideas with people more conservative and thus associated with the opposite American political party and leaders they have come to admire.

The other part of the American religious leaders, the traditional Orthodox rabbis and their congregants, who were politically closer to these newcomers, appeared to be too rigid, "speaking Greek" to those people who possessed little or no knowledge of Judaism. They also demonstrated close to zero interest in providing a badly needed, gradual process of education while making Judaism and Jewish history attractive to mostly well-educated and secular people. This made new emigrants feel uncomfortable in this strictly observant environment.

In his 1980 interview, Rabbi Zalman Posner of Nashville compared the Soviet émigré to a Jew who was raised in captivity from infancy. The obligation towards this Jew, as regards the Talmud, are to educate him from *Aleph-Bet*. However, the obverse side of this obligation must also be felt by those performing it—the sheer elation to be felt in the returning home of a Jew. And that is this: These teachings must also be a joyous celebration and not done merely by rote—something devoid of passion, pride or commitment.

The *Chabad* movement was just growing and coming to full force recently as the only Jewish religious organization looking forward to take-on Jewish acculturation, some of them with specifically designed Russian programs. *Chabad*, being a Hassidic movement, originated in Russia. Their spirited Shabbat and holiday activities make everybody, including secular émigrés, feel at home. Chabad rabbis and congregants don't demand the newcomers to be more Jewish than they are…simply being Jewish is deemed sufficient. There is no judgment, but rather the offering of a wide range of classes.

Invitations to a Rabbi's home to witness and share the traditional celebrations of Shabbat and other Jewish holidays also provides a role model to anyone who wants to learn and observe. And many do, indeed. But again, at the time when hundreds of thousand Soviet Jews arrived upon America's shores in the early 1970s and '80s, *Chabad* was only beginning its fruitful mission, leaving out many newcomers driving and eating on Yom Kippur, consuming bagels on Passover, and serving shrimp appetizers while grilling cheeseburgers in their suburban backyards.

And above it all, there is a very good (some say 75%) chance that they will all be celebrating the marriages of their children to brides and grooms who are very nice, beautiful and well-educated—but not Jewish. Just like many of their American Jewish neighbors.

By now it was 1993, one year almost to the day after Uncle David's funeral brought together the final pieces of what remained of my family, as my father, my brother Alex and his wife had landed in Chicago, Illinois, USA—"The Land of Lincoln." My dad, who'd grown up in poverty, was constantly worried about his children's financial well-being and was an unhappy camper whenever I took him and others to a restaurant and paid everyone's tab. (As much as he worried back in 1993, I'm glad he doesn't have to see the 2023 restaurant prices!)

Being involved in high-rise restoration projects throughout Chicago, I was able to find nice senior apartments along Lake Michigan's shores near Lincoln Park for my dad, my brother and Aunt Elena. This way, I could visit them all with just one hard-to-find parking spot.

My dad became a proud American citizen in 1998, passing the (interpreted) questions during his final citizenship interview with "flying colors" and celebrating it with a vodka infused luncheon in Chicago's own Russian Tea Time. He departed this earth in 2002, ten years after his younger brother David and still holding a grudge against him for his role in the Soviet propaganda machine.

My brother Alex, still looking up to his older brother Boris, remains a jazz enthusiast, an avid soccer fan and a passionately opinionated political observer. He is now retired after a brief career in IT, and happily residing in a Lake Shore Drive apartment with his wife.

"Life is Beautiful" as the 1997 Italian movie once declared. And it was about to become even more so...

CHAPTER FIFTEEN

"It is not good for man to be alone..."

"A good marriage requires falling in love several times. Always with the same person."

~ Mignon McLaughlin

The Torah begins by reminding us seven times that all that G-d created was good. Then we are told that one thing in G-d's world that wasn't good: "It is not good for man to be alone." (Genesis 2:18).

My status of being single and leading the adult single's life was not sitting well with some of my closest friends, especially the ones who have been religiously traditional and married from the time they were in their 20s. I think they wanted to "get even" with me for staying a bachelor for so long... and were, for a long time, very actively looking for ways to do it, but without much success.

Admittedly, I wasn't much help to them. I was really busy with my work. I traveled a lot and had to refuse a number of their generous dinner and party invitations because I was out of town or with other friends. I was also becoming more interested in the Jewish life and traditions. One such tradition—Shabbat dinners on Friday night, watching women lighting the Shabbat candles, followed by sumptuous home-cooked dinners, libations and lively conversations into late hours—had, for me, become the most attractive tradition of all.

Finally, after declining the invitations to one such dinner given by Joy and Jack Siegel, I received a call the following Sunday from Joy gently admonishingly me that I had just missed a great evening and probably the opportunity to meet a very lovely guest: a lady whose company she thought I would enjoy. But, as Joy quickly mentioned, not all had been lost, since she could share with me this particular lady's telephone number.

Somehow compelled to follow suit, I called her later that week. It was a somewhat hesitant call that resulted in talking to an answering machine. A couple days later, my answering machine was doing its work. With the help of the latest achievements in communications technology in the of summer 1995, in couple of weeks I was speaking to the "lively" mellow voice of a lady, who, after hearing my references to Joy, agreed to a dinner date. Making sure that I would be recognizable, she asked me about the color of my car, to which I replied: "What color would you expect from a Russian? Red, naturally!"

When I pulled up at her house in my red convertible, two pairs of eyes were watching me opening the door and driving away—one from her son and the other from the future daughter-in-law.

The lovely lady's name was Emilia, and she was a widow, having lost her husband to cancer. She married him at the age of 21 in Israel where she lived after leaving Poland. She had two children: a married daughter and a "dating" son. She kept a perfect kosher home, scarcely knew the venerable Chicago city neighborhoods such as Old Town where we went for dinner, and liked the music of the movie we went to see after dinner: *One Sunday Morning in Harlem*. The latter was about the efforts to gather and photograph as famous jazz musicians on Sunday in the morning hours as possible (close to 100), with some of them just coming out of all-night gigs in the Big Apple.

This was as much as I was able to learn about Emilia before she summarily dropped me. (At the time, I felt that she wasn't "dating material," and I was "too single" for her taste.)

My busy schedule and preoccupation with running a company, coupled with an abundant cultural life in the lively Chicago Summer of '95 helped me get over the rejection, but wasn't sufficient to overcome my being both peeved and intrigued by this very attractive, sexy, honest and winsome lady. Apparently, she hadn't forgotten me either—as a month or so later, we were together again, enjoying the Hubbard Street Dance Company at the end of Ravinia Festival season.

By this time, I had come to learn a great deal more about Emilia that recounted to me a life that was a testament to several things—not the least of which were tragedy, resilience, innovation and courage. Emilia was born two months after her parents, aged 26 and 20, had left the bunker in which they, along with 14 other Jews of different ages, had successfully hidden-out from the Nazis for over two years. This numbered them among only 250 survivors out of the more than 20,000 Jews living in the Polish city of Przemysl.

As a town, Przemysl was unique in that it was situated on the San River in the former Lvov district of Eastern Galicia on the border with the former Soviet Ukraine. The river became a line of demarcation, as the Germans and Soviets were dividing all specified territory as part of the spoils of the Molotov-Ribbentrop Pact. Almost as if it had been specially cursed, World War II reached Przemysl on September 7, 1939 when the first bombs from German planes struck the city with a vengeance. The Germans entered Przemysl for the first time on September 15, 1939. Repression and humiliation aimed at the Jewish population began almost immediately. The Germans started to arrest members of the Jewish intelligentsia: physicians, lawyers, industrialists and merchants, refugees from the West and Jewish political activists.

People were removed from their homes or seized outright on the streets. They were then driven together to be shot in the woods surrounding the city and buried in communal graves. The first mass executions of Jews took place between the 16th and 19th of September of that year, at several places on the city's outskirts. On September 22, 1939, an official communiqué was issued that specifically defined the San River as the demarcation line between German and Soviet troops. On September 26, the Red Army entered the city. In accordance with the Molotov-Ribbentrop Pact, the Germans left that part of Przemysl on the east bank of the River San on September 28, 1939.

Before their withdrawal, the Nazis burned down the Old Synagogue, the Hassidic prayer house, the New Synagogue and a part of the Jewish Quarter. On September 26, 1939, Jewish inhabitants of the German side of the River San were ordered to move to the Russian occupied section of Przemysl. It was further determined that any Jew found there after that time would be killed immediately.

The border was set along the River San—with the left bank under German control and the right bank under Soviet control. Many families were separated by this border. Under Soviet rule, in April and May 1940, approximately 7,000 Jews were deported from Soviet occupied Przemysl to the Soviet interior. From there, the living conditions for the Jewish population deteriorated rapidly. Jewish community institutions, factories and shops ceased to operate, and their assets were "nationalized." All privately owned houses were transferred to the city administration by an edict of Eminent Domain.

The German attack on the Soviet Union on June 22, 1941 resulted in the complete Nazi takeover of Przemysl (yet again) on June 28, 1941, and along with it, full occupation of the city. Within a few days, the *Gestapo* arrived and initiated its usual long list of anti-Jewish measures. The Nazis immediately began rounding up Jews for any number of charges, offenses and infractions and shipping them off to "labor camps." Jewish high school pupils were summarily ordered to clean the streets, load rubbish onto carts and pull great piles of it through the town for everyone to see. Posters appeared everywhere describing the Jews as germs and lice. Shortly thereafter, the local Security Police and *Gendarmerie,* under the command of the regular police, assimilated Polish and Ukrainian "helpers" as forced labor.

Then, in the winter of 1941, German police, along with ethnic Germans (Volksdeutsche) and Polish "Blue" Policemen officers started to accost and harass all Jews wherever they found them, cutting away furs and fur collars from the coats of all Jewish men and women they came across in the streets. They also removed winter boots, mainly from women, leaving them barefoot in the street. They also entered Jewish houses and removed furniture, pianos, carpets, silverware and china. Adding further injury to insult, the German response to any kind of transgression by Jews grew even more severe. For example, for wearing the armband on the right arm instead of the left or visiting the market during prohibited hours, Jews were beaten brutally and imprisoned for lengthy periods or were sent to the central prison at Rokitnianska Street where they were usually killed.

From spring 1942, there began consecutive mass shootings of Jews at the Jewish cemetery. Finally, all Jews were forced to move into the ghetto, from Przemysl itself and the surrounding villages in the Przemysl area. In the summer of 1942, in Przemysl, as in all the larger towns in the Krakow District, the systematic extermination of the Jews began.

The establishment of a sealed-off ghetto was announced on July 14, 1942, after which all Jews had only until the following day to enter the ghetto. By the time of the closure of the district on July 15, 1942, 22,000 to 24,000 Jews lived in the ghetto. The Aktion Extermination was carried out from July 27 through August 3, 1942. *Schutzpolizei* and *Gestapo* units, together with their henchmen, surrounded the ghetto. On the first day, 6,500 Jews were deported to Belzec extermination camp. The elderly, the handicapped, the sick and some children—approximately 2,500 in total—were taken in trucks to a forest on the outskirts of the city where they were shot on the spot and buried in mass graves.

On the second day, another 3,000 Jews were deported to Belzec, to be followed on the final day by another 3,000. At the end of the *Aktion*, the Jews were forced to pay for transportation costs as well as for the new barbed-wire fences around the ghetto borders.

But sometimes humanity could show up and win, even wearing a long uniform.

In 1942, Wehrmacht officer Dr. Albert Battel faced SS trucks heading to deport hundreds of Jews. He blocked the bridge with armed soldiers and said simply: "Not today." What happened next changed everything.

Albert Battel stood on the San River bridge that morning, watching the SS convoy approach. Truck after truck, engines growling, heading straight for the ghetto.

He was forty-nine. A lawyer before the war. A Wehrmacht officer who followed orders and kept his head down. But something inside him snapped that day. When the lead truck reached the bridge, Battel raised his hand. His soldiers lowered the barrier. "This bridge is closed," he told the SS commander. The man's face went red. "On whose authority?" "Mine." Battel had no authority to do this. None at all. He was blocking his own government from carrying out official orders. But he stood there anyway. And his soldiers stood with him. The SS officer screamed, threatened, demanded passage. Battel didn't budge.

"Any man who tries to cross will be arrested," he said quietly. The SS convoy, engines still running, blocked by German soldiers pointing rifles at other German soldiers. The SS commander had no choice and ordered his trucks to turn around. But Battel wasn't finished. He climbed into his own military truck and drove straight into the ghetto. Battel started knocking on doors. "Get in the truck," he told them. "Now." He loaded dozens of people into Wehrmacht vehicles. Grandparents who could barely walk, mothers carrying babies, children clutching toys they'd never see again. He drove them to the Wehrmacht barracks. Fed them. Posted guards to protect them. For hours, he moved Jewish families out of that ghetto under the cover of "military necessity." Every minute, he could have been shot for treason. Every decision could have been his last. But by nightfall, dozens of people who should have been on death trains were sleeping in German army beds instead. The news hit Berlin like a thunderbolt.

Heinrich Himmler himself wrote Battel's name in his files. Called his actions "inexcusable fraternization with Jews."

They blacklisted him from the Nazi Party. Started court-martial proceedings. Destroyed his career. Battel never apologized. After the war, survivors started looking for him. The officer who saved several hundred of us, they said. The German who said NO. On January 22, 1981, Israel honored Albert Battel as one of the *Righteous Among the Nations.* The highest honor they give to non-Jews who risked everything to save Jewish lives. He never lived to see it. Battel died in 1952, unknown in Western Germany trying to rebuild his life but denied the right to practice law as a former Nazi officer. He never wrote a book about that day. Never gave interviews. Never sought praise. But what he did on that bridge proves something important. In a world that felt completely broken, Albert Battel showed that humanity could still win even wearing the wrong uniform and standing alone. And sometimes, that's all it takes to change everything — one bridge, one officer. And one word: *No.*

From September 1943 until April 1944, further deportations to Auschwitz followed. During this entire period, the Germans continued to hunt Jews who were in hiding. Between September 11, 1943 and the end of April 1944, 1,000 bodies were discovered in bunkers, murdered by the SS under Josef Schwammberger and the *Gestapo.*[34] The camp was destroyed at the end of February 1944, which meant in theory that Przemysl was now officially *Judenrein* (Jew-free). But in fact, there were still some hiding in bunkers in the town and its environs, maybe as many as 120. Between March and June 1944, three or four bunkers sheltering 40-50 Jews were destroyed. The last

---

34 Extradited and returned to Germany in 1991, accused Nazi war criminal Josef Schwammberger, at his trial, testified that he had witnessed the mass shootings of over 1,000 Jews by the *Gestapo* when he was concentration camp commandant in Nazi-occupied Poland, but denied that he had been personally involved. "I had nothing to do with those killings, Therefore, I cannot tell how many had been shot," Schwammberger had the audacity to tell the court. The Austrian-born Nazi was charged with at least 45 counts of murder and with complicity in the murders of 3,377 people, most of them Jewish inmates of the Przemysl, Mielec and Rozwadow slave-labor camps in Poland.

hiding place was discovered in May 1944 near Przemysl where 27 Jews were shot. The Polish family of the Kurpiels, who had helped the Jews, were also executed.

In early July 1944, the front was rapidly approaching Przemysl and on July 23, 1944, the town was bombed by Russian aircraft. On July 27, 1944, the Russians captured the town, on the exact anniversary of the first *Aktion* some two years earlier. Immediately after the liberation of Przemysl, the few Jewish survivors left their hiding places. At first there were some 100 people, but during the next few days, this number rose to about 250, with Emilia's "expecting" parents among them.

During that time they were hidden by an ethnic Ukrainian who apparently was somehow connected to one of the German-collaborating local forces and was considered exempt from suspicion. He had, during that time, managed to successfully hide 16 people, comprised of several family units, in his well-camouflaged basement. He secretly supplied them with food and whatever meager necessities their money could buy.

Within the two-year period of this ordeal, some people came before the strict ghetto enforcement, some after, and some even having escaped their dark underground confinement went back to the open-air ghetto not being aware their final destination would be the gas chambers of Auschwitz, Dachau and other death camps. Among them had been the twin sister of my future mother-in-law, Regina. The questions I asked both Emilia and Regina will probably be on the minds of anyone who reads this: How in the world can any human being survive, hiding for two years, without access to daylight, privacy, basic sanitary facilities and under the constant fear of being discovered? How could anyone maintain their sanity and composure, living under this Sword of Damocles—the prospect of sharing the cruel fate of their own perished parents and siblings, of being sent to the gas chambers and ovens, or being shot and buried in open graves?

And yet they had. For two long years, these people had survived to go on after they had been liberated. Emilia's parents succeeded—not once but twice—in starting new lives: once in after-war Poland, under Communist rule within this viciously anti-Semitic society; and a second time later on by arriving penniless in their 50s to the United States, with no command of English and working night shifts, washing hospital dishes while establishing their own business, and going on later to live an opulent life.

Their guardian and savior, remembered by his name, Ryscko, emigrated to New Zealand and is named "Righteous Among the Nations" by the Yad Vashem Memorial, the second such person after Dr. Albert Battel for saving Jewish lives in Przemysl.

While Emilia was waiting to be born in the Przemysl underground bunker, her future husband, Morris Blaustein *z"l,* was a teenaged slave working in an underground Nazi ammunition factory at the notorious Dora work camp. He was taken there after living in the Lodz ghetto where he lost his father, and then in 1943 was shipped in a cattle car to Auschwitz with his mother and two sisters. He saw them for the last time as they were separated—finally and fatally—at the entrance of the camp. (His last recollection of his mother and sisters was seeing them taken away, later to be gassed and burned, while the able-bodied 15-year old Morris was sent to work in different labor camps before the liberation from Bergen-Belsen by British troops.)

It was exactly the place where teenaged Morris had been separated forever from his mother and sisters, that his and Emilia's teenage son, Ron, had recited the Jewish prayer, the *Kaddish,* when their extended family from the US, Sweden and Israel came to visit Auschwitz. In Morris's own words: "This was his way of getting even with Hitler."

After marrying in Israel and coming to the US, Emilia and Morris made sure that both their children received an academically-solid "Jewish" education, graduating from Chicago's Ida Crown Jewish Academy.

In August of 1998, I was finally honored to become the husband of a great woman who also brought me a friend and an eternal optimist mother-in-law...and, as a bonus, made me a stepfather of two bright recent college graduates whom I promised I would always cherish their father's memory.

This time, sparing nothing, I had a real traditional Jewish wedding with my father and Emilia's mother walking us to the *Chuppah* where we exchanged rings and vows. I crushed the glass—all to the cheers of 200-plus guests, shouting of *Mazel Tov!*

Our next ten years together produced two beautiful and brilliant granddaughters and three handsome and talented grandsons. We also had to babysit two sweet dogs always trying to sneak into our bed. They were a great addition to the family. Later on, my twins added a granddaughter and grandson to the list of our grandchildren.

Emilia instantly became a great companion in my professional life, joining me on many business trips and professional, social gatherings—and quickly forming friendships with my colleagues and their spouses.

Since both of us came from Communist-ruled anti-Semitic societies, we were also becoming more and more involved in American, and especially Jewish, political and religious organizations. Now we both enjoy a wide circle of old and new relatives and friends of different backgrounds—Jews and Gentiles, born in the US, Poland, France, Israel, Soviet Union, Latin America and other countries.

Spending time with all these people has left us with a lot of food for thought, as we both embraced a deeply-held desire to uphold a strong and prosperous United States—one with its unwavering support for a safe and flourishing Israel.

Traveling the world, we have always made sure that we visited Israel as often as we could (until we settled in our own apartment), spending time with our relatives and friends who represent a broad spectrum of the Israeli society—from Israeli born "*sabras*" to recently arrived "*olim,*"—from professionals to homemakers, from strictly observant to secular, from well to do businessmen to pensioners. All this gave us a great deal of perspective and a chance to compare divergent peoples with a commonality of cause—especially Jews, American, Israelis, and people who came to those countries from Russia, Poland or somewhere else.

As a result, our joint experiences gave life to a political passion and a shared conservative philosophy about the trends that we see, as well as ways that we all might make our world a better place…

CHAPTER SIXTEEN

The USSA:
Amerika Upside-Down Cake

"When you see that in order to produce you need to obtain permission from men who produce nothing—when you see that money is flowing to those who deal, not in goods but in favors—when you see that men get richer by graft and by pull than by work, and your laws don't protect you against them but protect them against you, when you see corruption being rewarded and honesty becoming a self-sacrifice then you know society is doomed."

~ Ayn Rand/*Atlas Shrugged* 1957

Ayn Rand was a political paradox and yet, in her way, also a philosophical paragon to so many of us in that she was an early departure from Stalin's USSR who clearly read all the warning signs as she and her family fled to the USA in 1926 to embrace the American Dream. Jewish born Alisa Zinovyevna Rosenbaum in St. Petersburg, Russia, Rand was an avowed anti-Bolshevik who became one of the founders of the Hollywood Anti-Communist Association. An advocate of Capitalism and American democracy, she became increasingly horrified in the 1930s Socialistic frameworks that POTUS Franklin Delano Roosevelt was insidiously embedding into US political and economic systems.

Her first work of fiction, a novella called *Anthem,* was said to have inspired George Orwell's *1984.* Her early novel, *We the Living,* was penned about a pair of lovers who escape from a totalitarian Soviet Union, and the price they pay to do so. Her novels *The Fountainhead* and *Atlas Shrugged* formed the basis for her philosophy of Objectivism. Both were a paean to the Individual vs. the Collective—the democratic virtue of a Meritocracy as it stood against the tidal wave of totalitarian concepts. And each one, in its expression, was written as a warning against the culture of codependency sewn into the fabric of Communist governments depicted in the USSR and Red China, especially in the 1930s, '40s and '50s.

All of her works provide cautionary tale against the epidemic of socialist measures applied as "daily bread" baked into our modern society in ways that would soon become American political traditions. Along with them, the belief as she expressed it: "You cannot correct a problem without acknowledging that there is one."

This particularly applied to the USA as she saw it unfolding, and even more so in the America as it is in danger of becoming today. Many forms of Government have been tried, and will be tried in this world of sin and woe. No one pretends that Democracy is perfect or all-wise.

Indeed, as Winston Churchill was oft quoted as saying: "Democracy is the worst form of Government except for all those others that have been tried." He also noted that: "The main vice of Capitalism is the uneven distribution of prosperity. The main vice of Socialism is the even distribution of misery."

(British Prime Minister Margaret Thatcher once cannily observed: "The problem with Socialism is that eventually run out of other people's money.")

Many generations of the immigrants coming to the United States were right to call America "The Golden Land," or as Yiddish speaking Eastern European Jews termed it: "The Golden Medina."

Admittedly, the majority of them soon learned that there was no gold in the streets, as some of them may have imagined, which meant that they had to struggle, and struggle hard. But there was another, more precious kind of gold in America: There was freedom…and in that omnipresent *Freedom,* there existed *Opportunity.* Blessed with these conditions, the children, grandchildren and great-grandchildren of these immigrants flourished—and not just financially— to an extent unmatched in the history of any people.

Back in 1977 when I landed on the shores of this country I was only too well aware that there was no gold on the paved and often easily-flooded streets of Houston, Texas. But I had hope. And Hope is the food of life. I also had Gratitude; a great deal of it. I was grateful for the chance to make a living and become an integral part of the society that was ready to give me the one quantity that cannot be measured in coin: the Golden Horizon of Limitless Possibilities as they existed every day in this wonderful country.

For me, this banquet of potential for accomplishment was everywhere to be seen. Opportunities inevitably come with changes. And changes were developing along with my own personal transformation as well as the changes I was witnessing in the people, their attitudes and social behavior, and in the government branches and officials they were choosing (or thought they were choosing) to elect.

And yet, even then, the warning signs were everywhere.

With all the excitement of my new life, I couldn't ignore the national hangover from the post-Vietnam souring of the American state of mind. That, followed by the Watergate scandal, the first ever resignation of a US President, and the incompetence of the Carter Administration that followed, seemed to have left everyone with, what I felt, was a diminished feeling of pride of being American.

In 1979, President Jimmy Carter even described it as, "A Great National Malaise" that had swept over the country. (One, BTW, that he more than helped to foster.)

It took several years for me to see Americans once again become proud of being Americans. It started to take root once more when I was already living in Chicago and Ronald Reagan (POTUS #40) came to reside in The White House.

Reagan brought a return to national pride. And with it the belief that Patriotism was a demonstration of character—and not a character flaw. This was a man who stood up for his country and reminded us all that we needed to do the same. This was a man who actually "Made America Great Again." With Reagan at the helm, Americans were once more made to feel proud. We were not the world's villains; we were the final bulwark against them. Interest rates fell. Financial Markets soared. Employment was full. And our military bulged with new weaponry and applicants in all branches of the services— well-trained and well-paid as all servicemen (and women) should be.

(The ultimate statement and final blow to the USSR was Reagan's initiation of "Star Wars," a defense technology that was a quantum leap over any other in history. This was simply too much for the Soviets to be able to compete for military superiority. And their new leader Gorbachev saw the handwriting on the wall.)

Today, 25 years into the new Millennium, the question remains: "Is the America of Ronald Reagan still the USA of today?"

Are American citizens still proud of the country they were born in and live in? The best barometer for this remains the willingness of this nation's young adults to serve in her armed forces (as it was during the years of Reagan and Bush 41). After losing over 58,000 lives in Vietnam, America lost close to 7,000 men and women in Iraq and Afghanistan with close to 75,000 wounded and another estimated 90,000 suffering from TBI (Traumatic Brain Injury) or PTSD (Post Traumatic Stress Disorder). The brief aberration of a unified Operation Desert Storm notwithstanding, not one of these wars ended with pride and victory parades like this country saw in 1945.

As someone raised in the family of a Soviet general and being around his top-ranking comrades, I can attest that the communist adversaries quickly understood and exploited what General Colin Powell once said: "As soon as they tell me [war] is limited, it means that they don't care whether you achieve a result or not."

These timid, equivocal American political and military strategies in the years after the Korean War have led to other conflicts for which our countrymen paid with blood and lives without achieving any of the noble goals that only America could fulfill.

The US spent 16.9% and 8% of its economy on defense during Korean and Vietnam wars. But after the explosion of government domestic spending the Pentagon now gets a mere 3% of GPD. Also, today the US military is facing its greatest recruitment crisis in 50 years. Military leaders report that they are struggling to meet their enlistment targets because more than a half of young people in America do not care for the armed forces or for what they represent. And most potential recruits simply do not meet even the basic military standards required, due to reasons of poor education and physical shortcomings, obesity being one of majors.

In 2018, Navy Secretary Richard Spencer complained to Congress that 1,100 high school districts had banned all Military Recruiting Officers from their campuses. The same goes for some universities where uniformed soldiers have been assailed and spit on...like the recent assault on a servicewoman passing through the California Berkeley campus.

Fortunately, today—as opposed to the protest racked Vietnam War years— civilian mistreatment of our military is the exception. But what is not exceptional has been the elimination of the draft and the diminishment of the career corps of soldiers, sailors and marines. Initiated under the Nixon administration in January, 1973, to fulfill a campaign promise, it was originally thought that this new "volunteer army" would encourage a leaner-meaner military by empowering better-trained, better-equipped and better paid professionals in all branches of the Service.

What it has done instead is spawn a generation of Metrosexual Males who look upon service to their country as an inconvenience they simply cannot afford. Drafts still exist in a good many countries, even Switzerland, among a long list of other nations. When they do, it has proven to strengthen a nation's resolve. When required to serve their countries, boys become men, men become better men—and both men and women become better citizens with a sense of pride in having fulfilled their obligation to their nation.)

America simply can't afford not to be a military superpower, as she is the last best hope for saving Western civilization and freedom in the way that our parents and grandparents knew was essential to our National Character. In today's world, military superiority is the best way to preserve peace and prosperity. And in order to maintain the military prowess the country needs to have the economic and moral upper hand.

> *"You can always count on Americans to do the right thing—after they've tried everything else."*
> ~ Winston Churchill

Winston Churchill offered the above left-handed expression of admiration for the American mindset as a cynical but somewhat pointed admonition against complacency...one that also proved to be prophetic when first made (in 1951). It is here that I confide that my 48 years of observations include more than 30 years of deep concern for my adopted country. Going back— among the reasons for the military enlistment problems—there now exists both a lack of patriotism and a decline in education, which are in turn rooted in the same soil.

Education is crucial to economic growth, and yet that is where America has fallen the fastest. In 2020, US schools ranked 30th in the world, a 13 place fall compared to the 2000 rank of 17th). The US is 11th in math and science among the top 79 countries ranked by Organisation for Economic Co-operation and Development (OECD). This is especially disappointing when realizing that 40% of high school graduates didn't go on to attend college.

This also makes me wonder what kind of education their college-bound peers received. Even schools as respected as Harvard, arguably the top of the mountain of collegiate academics, has relaxed standards and in 2018 decided to be politically correct and eliminate a grading system in favor of issuing pass/fail grades in all its graduate courses. I worry that the United States is doomed as a country when I see statistics documenting 71% of all US citizens under the age of 50 failed a basic exam about American history.

The exchange of ideas, freedom of discussion and being open minded are critical for education in a free society, but American colleges and universities seem to be becoming institutions of indoctrination rather than knowledge. While the percentage of college graduates who have registered as either Democrat or Republican are roughly equal (31% to 26%) in the United States, that is not the case for college and university staff. In 2019, the Center for the Study of Popular Culture found that upper level administrators at 32 elite colleges were overwhelmingly registered as Democrats with 1,397 compared to Republicans at 134. What's more, not a single department at any of the 32 schools even remotely approached parity. The closest any school came was Northwestern University, where 80 percent of faculty were Democrats and 20 percent were Republicans.

At Ivy League Brown University, the ratio was 30-to-1 Democrat. The researchers also could not identify a single Republican on the faculty at Williams, Oberlin, MIT or Haverford College. The imbalance is becoming even greater at the other 4,000-plus campuses across the country. The ratio of liberal seculars to conservative professors has profoundly changed, from 4 to 1 a few years ago to 17-to-1 today.

Here is the result of the indoctrination that includes both trends and biases: 55% of all US Millennials and Generation Z (those born after 2000) prefer Socialism over Democracy as a permanent form of government. Should this come to pass, thus perishes patriotism, successful recruitment for the Armed Forces needed to defend the country and Western Civilization in general.

Today, in the America we know and love, there has grown into being a Conspiracy of Guilt. It comes with a kind of culture shaming—for one's heterosexuality, white race, gender clarity, rewards for personal excellence, patriotism and even one's love of country. The US Constitution has been cherry-picked, our Founding Fathers villainized, and our institutions impaired—from our fundamental industries to those who protect and serve, our Police and all Law Enforcement in general.

What was once a proud Meritocracy is now under assault—24/7/365—by those for whom excellence is a challenge unless it is averaged-out. Our system of learning, K-12, has been hijacked by a kind of "handicapping" that has virtually sabotaged universal education as we know it. Teacher salaries have been frozen in place in proportion to other professions. Seniority has taken precedence over superior teaching credentials. Classrooms are overcrowded and Charter Schools have cut into Public Schools in such a way that the latter are now simply processing plants where poorly educated, sub-literate (predominantly minority) students are shoved out the door, diplomas-in-hand without a single clue as to what to do next. Traditions and discipline have given way to anarchy. And revisionist versions of history and language now prevail.

Nothing has underscored this educational aberration more emphatically than something called *The 1619 Project*. This project, created by Nikole Hannah-Jones, is a fabulist account of the USA that claims the true founding of America took place in 1619 when a ship with 30 slaves dropped anchor at the colony of Virginia, thus beginning slavery in America. (Ignoring the founding of the United States in 1776, it avers that America, its Constitution and economy, were all built entirely on the backs of slaves…when in truth by the inception of the US Constitution in 1787, 11 of the 22 States in the United States of America had already abolished slavery, as had all new "free territories" established in the West and Northwest.

Disregarding the facts and setting up this very slanted culture of victimhood called Critical Race Theory, this revisionist perspective of people and events has so completely infiltrated primary schools across the nation that it has been banned in some states in the South and Southwest as simply inaccurate, fictitious and over-the-top with both its militancy and hatred of the United States itself. Apparently, the initiators of this philosophy have lost all sense of something called "balance" when it comes to teaching American History—and have now succeeded to such an extent that what was once a nation of tolerance and brotherhood in the 1970s, '80s and '90s has now grown into one of racial division and permanent grievance during the decades of the New Millennium.

I say this sadly but with volumes of proof that this racial/cultural divide was particularly exacerbated during the 8-years of the Obama Administration from 2008 to 2016 and promulgated by Biden from 2021 to 2024. Rather than becoming the "unifier" he promised to be, Obama stoked the fires of racial division, first by bringing Iranian born Valerie Jarrett on board as Senior White House Advisor.[35] And second by appointing Eric Holder to be US Attorney General. Both proved to be provocateurs, especially Holder, whose attempts to politicize his office and use the IRS to persecute political rivals in the GOP, netted him twenty straight 9-to-0 rejections by the US Supreme Court—a record of rebuff and humiliation that still stands in the *Guinness Book of World Records,* and will probably never again be equaled in the annals of the Justice Department.

Holder was also noted for instituting "Fast and Furious," the insane strategy at the US/Mexican border of supplying Mexican Cartels with automatic weapons in the absurd belief that these weapons could somehow be electronically ID'd, thus providing a way to track these drug dealers down. (All it did was arm—cost free—some already fortified Mexican gangs with state-of-the-art AR-15s, and help make them even more dangerous than ever.) One of Holder's other legacies filtered down into the cities of America where his light-touch treatment for criminal behavior—unfortunately nicknamed "Crime and No Punishment."

And nobody deserves more credit for the "Crime and Punishment" implementation than the ultra-progressive's sugar daddy, billionaire George Soros.

---

35 Valerie Jarrett was instrumental in filling POTUS #44's foreign advisory staff with half-a-dozen Muslim "diplomats" who, on an ongoing basis, provided him with biased pro-Muslim Brotherhood and anti-Israeli policies that included the disastrous Arab Spring of 2010—a series of government coups from Algeria to Egypt that utterly trashed the political balance in the Middle East, led to an epidemic of radical Islamic extremism, and a chain reaction of backlashes that CIA Director John Brennan (a convert to Islam, BTW) admitted was the worst foreign policy decision of his career.

According to Google, Mr. Soros has spent at least $40 million over the last decade to help elect "social justice" or progressive district attorneys (DA) across the United States.

Soros figured out that local district attorney races were often "sleepy" contests with low spending, allowing relatively small amounts of money to have an outsized impact. In some cases, Soros-linked groups were the single largest source of funds for a candidate, comprising a majority of their campaign spending. Beyond direct campaign spending, Soros has funded support of policy organizations, think tanks, and advocacy groups that work to support the progressive, low or no punishment DA policy decisions which contribute to rising crime rates in cities once they are in office.

Soros-backed prosecutors have been elected in cities and counties across more than 30 states, including Los Angeles, Chicago, Philadelphia, San Francisco, St. Louis, and Boston. These district attorneys represent more than 70 million Americans, or over one-fifth of the U.S. population, and their jurisdictions account for a significant percentage of the nation's total crime volume.

Several of these DAs, such as Chesa Boudin in San Francisco and Marilyn Mosby in Baltimore, have faced recalls, resignations, or lost re-election amidst this criticism.

This Bail-waive policy for people who can't afford it, has by a 2021 ruling of the California Supreme Court also become law for the entire state, and has filtered down to cities like Los Angeles where LA has now become the Shoplifting Capital of the World— keeping in mind that most of these crimes are no longer even reported.

Even more outrageous are reparation payments proposed for blacks in major cities throughout California, and this state becoming the first to create a task force to study slavery's legacy and recommend reparations.

Governor Newsom signed a bill in 2024 for a formal, bipartisan apology for slavery in the state, and in 2025, a new state agency, the Bureau for Descendants of American Slavery, was created to oversee future programs.

For a clearer perspective, it is essential to remember that California was a free state and never officially had slaves. So, these are payments to be made to people who never suffered enslavement by people who never had anything to do with their persecution.

Both these permissive crime bills and legislated policies of subsidized race-shaming have become a trend in states from Oregon to New York. When this precedent comes down from the courts, how could anyone be surprised that crime is so high?

Nothing illustrates the advance of lawlessness and "racial blackmail" in America more than the Black Lives Matter (BLM) movement, Marxist in its thinly disguised contempt for American Democracy and its campaign to "Defund the Police." With a mandate for Socialism as a part of its founding charter, BLM has used public protest as a tool for extortion of our US government institutions and a license for bringing lawlessness to our streets.

Hinging on the tragedy of George Floyd in Minneapolis in May of 2020, BLM was—in the midst of the pandemic when everything was locked down—granted free reign to launch mass demonstrations in the streets. Once they did, turmoil was the result, in these COVID super-spreader events, trashing cities like Minneapolis, Chicago, Denver, LA and New York City to the tune of tens of millions of dollars…even as they virtually held downtown Portland, Oregon hostage for several weeks. Rampant looting and even mob invasions of private homes went on unopposed, while local police were ordered to stand down. All this took place while BLM continued to loot, injure and obliterate (many minority businesses, ahem…) And to make sure they were "well-funded," ultra-liberal super-donor and Move-on.org's "sugar daddy" George Soros dropped a large portion of $150 Million on them "to help give them added impetus." (So once again, it became, all about the money, and for BLM it has been a money grab ever since.)

So why all this concentration on anarchy, chaos and crime without recourse that is now pervading our major cities? The answer is simple: Anarchy is the handmaiden to totalitarian takeovers. And loss of personal freedoms (in the name of public safety) are as sure to follow as night follows day.

Make no mistake about it, we are already losing our personal freedoms in some very insidious ways. We have already forfeited so much of our Freedom of Speech. And nothing underscores this more than the attacks the PC Police, the "Woke" posse and the "Me Too" and "Time's Up" Gender *Gestapos* have invoked upon people in the public professions—including media, athletics, academics, entertainment and politics itself. These are the high-profile projections we see in the news every day—so frequently they are regarded with a passing nod and a yawn.

No better example of this than the last week of April 2023 when CNN talk show host Don Lemmon (no favorite of mine) got fired from his daily gig for simply observing that GOP presidential hopeful Nikki Haley was "probably past her prime." Not restricted to gender bias, former FOX media, conservative superstar Megyn Kelly was bounced from her show on NBC for simply observing (during the Minstrel Show flap over Virginia's Governor Glenn Youngkin's college antics) that Blackface as a form of satire might have been considered acceptable 30 years ago.

Perhaps nothing would summarize this uneven playing field for sexual discrimination better than the January 21, 2017, the day after POTUS #45 Donald Trump's inauguration, when millions of American women donned pink "pussy hats" or full vagina outfits and marched through the streets of America protesting his election, shouting: "Not my president!" as they walked up and down the boulevards of major cities from Philadelphia to Phoenix. Imagine if the shoe had been on the other foot and Hillary Clinton had won the 2016 election. What if millions of American men had hit the bricks in protest, wearing pink penises on their heads? None of us would have ever heard the end of it.

There is little doubt that the issue of gender equality, gender-norming, and gender blending has sparked a new crisis of consciousness that—like a phial of Nitro Glycerin—is volatile at best and (at its worst) ready to blow up in our faces at any time.

The people of America look to our military to form a bulwark to defend this nation against foreign enemies, even as we ignore the enemy within— even as feminists denounce "toxic masculinity" and work to provide "gender norming" for women in the US Army, as a means of lowering the bar for the physical demands of being a soldier or Marine. (Something that is NOT done in any other country in the world.)

Gender-blending and equivocal gender classification—such as gay, non-binary and transgender—has led to such sexual confusion in our K-12 schools that it has split our state educational institutions right down the middle where the mention of gay, trans, non-binary or LGBTQ issues are concerned. Half the states insist upon teaching gender-choice even in grades 6-9 where—all are agreed—the human brain is not even well-enough developed to make rational adult decisions. Other states (such as Florida) are insisting that gender choices be held off until the individuals reach the age of 21—and as such have faced rapid and vocal opposition in the US Courts.

The blade becomes double-edged here when it comes to all forms of athletics where Title-9 has granted women equality in university subsidies (scholarships) and proportionate funding even as they must now unravel the unwinnable conundrum of "men who have become women competing in a woman's world."

We all witnessed the event of 6'4" University of Pennsylvania swimmer Will Thomas managing, after becoming Lia Thomas, to set NCAA 500 free-style records at last year's Ivy League Women's Championship—thus jumping to the top of the women's rankings.

Tough luck girls, because when one of them, former University of Kentucky swimmer Riley Gaines, tells us that it is destructive for women's sport and that, "It shouldn't be allowed for males who think they are women." As her reward for such candor, she is insulted, physically attacked by activist mobs and branded as a bigot.

Where are the feminists protecting women's rights in sport and who pay the price for all this– hate, insults and violence? This is Gaines's heresy: to refuse to believe that trans women are women; to prefer the light of scientific and moral reason over the delusions of the mob. (*Spectator,* April 8, 2023, Brendan O'Neill).

And where are these same feminists, after all, when it comes to sticking up for women's rights for the more than half of the world's 800 million Muslim women who are officially second class-citizens just short of "house-slaves" in nations such as Iran, Yemen, Mauritania, Mali, Somalia, Sudan, some parts of Libya, Nigeria and (to be sure) Afghanistan? Marital slavery, traditional wife beatings for things such as burning dinner, and "honor killings" even in countries such as Iraq, Syria, Jordan and Palestinian territories are so commonplace they take place on a daily basis and yet are looked upon without comment by groups such as NOW and the Women's World Global Community Fund.

And yet criticism of Islam by anyone in the US ranks as the most unforgivable form of Political Incorrectness—and is considered by the "Woke Generation" to be the PC Naughty List Trifecta: racist, sexist and pan-nationally prejudiced in the extreme. In the USA today, in a classic assault on free speech, media personalities have been fired from their jobs for daring to cry out against the systemic abuse of Muslim women—especially where it involves some blatant abuses of Sharia Law practiced in our own country.

There is one bastion of Political Correctness that summarizes the assault on free speech more emphatically than any other—and that is in the world of Academia, not only in US Colleges and Universities…but also in American High Schools. A classic example would be the Cal Berkeley students who got firebombed with Molotov Cocktails in 2018 when they tried to interview Breitbart Editor and (gay) conservative journalist Milo Yiannopoulos—causing such a riot that the event had to be canceled. (It also got one professor suspended simply for defending Milo's right to appear.)

Then there was the absurdly ignorant firing of Wisconsin University professor David Howard who got bounced from his tenured position for using the word "niggardly" to describe a stingy historical figure, citing the reference as a "racist slur." The term, niggardly, actually Norse in origin, as *hnøggr*, very specifically means: "a tight or miserly person." But that wasn't enough for the Snowflakes of Madison. So, Howard was given his walking papers due to the illiteracy of the Wisconsin Chancellery and his own hypersensitive students.

It gets worse. What comes next is hauntingly reminiscent of both Nazi Germany and the Soviet Union. Today in America, we are going through an epidemic banning of library books—not just any books, but many classics of American and English literature: *To Kill a Mockingbird* (because it uses the N-word and is racially inflammatory), *Catcher in the Rye* (because it uses vulgar language and discusses masturbation), *Animal Farm* (because it expresses bias against Islamic Arab sentiments), *Ulysses* (because of its language and explicit sexual content), *1984* (because—I kid you not—it promotes Communism!!!) *Huckleberry Finn* (again the N-word as part of the name of one of the characters), *Slaughterhouse Five* (depicted sexual fantasies about women and politically incendiary depictions of WWII), *Call of the Wild, The Great Gatsby, Lolita, Gone with the Wind, Catch-22, Lord of the Flies,* Stephen King's *The Shining, For Whom the Bell Tolls*—the list goes on and reads like a literary Who's Who of American letters.

These are just the ones we know and love. There are hundreds of others that have been banned for reasons that vary from political insensitivity to sexually explicit content.

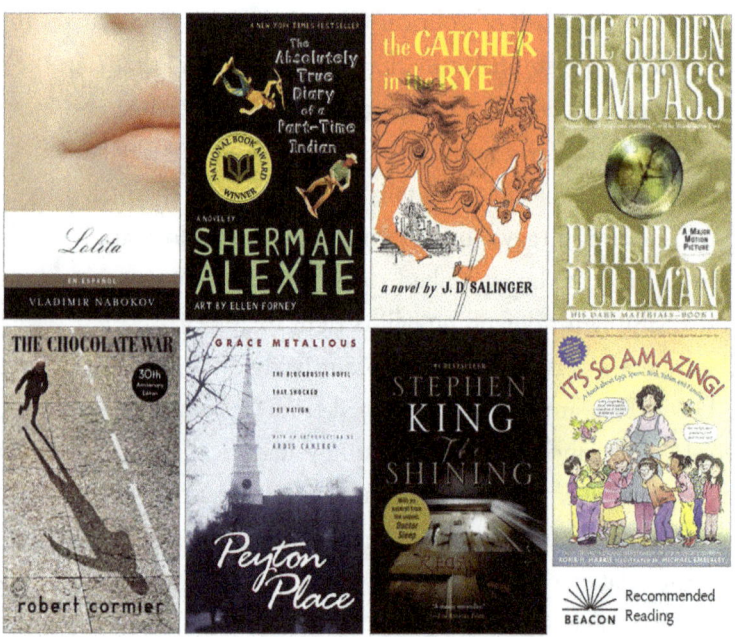

*A handful of international favorites among the more than 4,000 instances of
"banned books" in American public schools and libraries.*

The irony in all of this is that our moral outrage, especially in the world of
entertainment, is both duplicitous and selective. We villainize certain players
on the tableau of world history while we minimize or hide the sins of so many
others. A classic example is the *Shoah*[36] coming out of Hollywood. We've had
over 300 films and television series covering the atrocities of Nazi Germany,
Adolf Hitler's Third Reich and the universal pogrom it created during World
War II. Justifiably it focused on his persecution of the Jews. Yet, since then,
there has been little or nothing to cover the atrocities committed by the Soviet,
Chinese and other communist regimes in so many other ways.

Feature films about the dark days of the modern Soviet Union are a
classic example. Since 1950, there have been exactly 2 films to come out of
Hollywood that have covered the brutalities committed by Stalin or the madness and murders of millions during his 30-year regime.

---

36 *Shoah,* the Hebrew word for catastrophe, specifically meaning the killing of nearly six
million Jews by Nazi Germany and its collaborators during WWII. English-speaking countries
more commonly use the word Holocaust.

One is *The Death of Stalin,* a black comedy at best. The other, *The Way Back,* is Australian director Peter Weir's brilliant portrait of escapees from Stalin's Gulags and their long saga in trying to reach freedom in India. (A masterpiece that died due to a lack of distribution.) The only other films in the last 25 years covering those dark and dirty chapters in Russian history have been eight very good ones produced by Russian filmmakers.

As even greater evidence of the moral hypocrisy in the world of entertainment, other than perhaps the Oscar-winning film, *The Last Emperor (1986)* there has been not one—as in zero—films depicting the atrocities of Mao Zedong's regime in China. One during which an estimated 40 million were either murdered, starved or worked to death in labor camps. And the reason is simple: After Hollywood and Bollywood (India) China now boasts the world's third largest film market, film community and distribution for most of Southeast Asia. So, no one—least of all the major Hollywood studios—possesses either the will or the courage of conviction to piss them off.

Then there is the cancellation of entire films or film projects for fear they may offend another nation, its government or its heads of state. Classic example would be a film called *The Interview,* a black comedy where two bungling American patriots plot to take-out North Korean "president for life" Kim Jung Un and just mess it up. Already in the can in 2018, it got pulled from distribution and now sits on a shelf with other "radioactive" films such as Hollywood's *Ivan Denisovich*, a brilliant film based on Aleksandr Solzhenitsyn's eponymous book that got made but was so poorly distributed that no one ever saw it. So much for freedom of speech. Though no one is being sent to the Gulags, there are Gulags of a different kind—ruined careers, shattered reputations, and profound losses of income. There are lives that are being destroyed while society takes on a new role as Big Brother and the Nanny State in a marriage of convenience.

While we're on the subject of Nanny State, welcome to Affordable Health Care known as Obamacare. Or in the case of so many—"That was all we could afford." No question the quality of American health care has declined in the last 10 years, mainly because they have invoked the tenets of socialized medicine while also still being held hostage by American Pharmaceutical Companies ("Big Pharma"), creating a high-cost conundrum that will sabotage us in the end.

Twin Evils

Most of us—regardless of where we are born and live—love movies from different genres. Among the numerous movies produced by Hollywood and other worldwide studios there are masterpieces depicting stories of World War II, including the tragedies, suffering and extermination of 6 million Jews during the Holocaust perpetrated by Nazi Germany and its collaborators.

Movies like *Schindler's List, Sophie's Choice, The Diary of Anne Frank, Defiance,* and others are widely known, as are books about Nazi monsters like Hitler and his henchmen. The United States is home to many Holocaust memorials, including the Holocaust Museum in Washington, DC, which leaves a lasting impact on visitors. These stories are taught in American schools to varying degrees, and for Jewish families like mine, the history is deeply personal because we're only one or two generations removed from the blood related victims themselves.

But Nazi Germany had a grim twin: Soviet Stalinism. The two regimes fought each other, even though they shared ideological roots and methods of mass terror. An overlap of both Nazism and Stalinism was recognized as early as 1951 by Hannah Arendt in *The Origins of Totalitarianism*. We should remember their victims equally. As historian Gary Dreyer notes, understanding both is essential for a healthy society.

So, the question I've been asking for many years is: Should the 70-plus nightmarish years of the deadliest ideology in human history that spread through dozens of countries leaving 100 million dead and countless millions deprived of lives destroyed not warrant at least a few textbooks, movies, memorials, museums and field trips through the frozen Siberian GULAG camps and KGB torture chambers? And yet there are very few. Why were there no parallel trials of the KGB and GULAG sadists like the Nuremberg trials? *Doctor Zhivago's* cinematographic depiction of the depravations is closer to inconveniences of inclement weather in Miami Beach than to the reality faced by millions and millions of innocent Communist victims of Soviet Stalinism, or

Mao's Cultural Revolution and Great Famine. Where is the camera of the brilliant creator of Schindler's List, Steven Spielberg, when it comes to depicting the Communist atrocities? Perhaps left-leaning Hollywood doesn't feel comfortable to engage its talents and pockets for this purpose?

It took more than 30 years after the fall of the Soviet Union for Washington, DC to open a small museum dedicated to the victims of Communism, and only in 2022 did Florida become the first state to mandate high school education on the subject—allocating just 45 minutes to an ideology launched in 1917 that reshaped the world through terror.

This absence of education has consequences. A 2020 YouGov poll found that significant portions of Gen Z and Millennials view Communism or Marxism favorably, and many believe the Communist Manifesto offers more freedom than the Declaration of Independence. Even more alarming is the growing normalization of far-left authoritarian rhetoric in U.S. public discourse—attacks on Western institutions produces echoes of Cold War–era Soviet propaganda, and ideological narratives that increasingly resonate with younger generations. These parallels are especially visible in movements that label Zionism as racism or colonialism, mirroring long-standing Communist tropes. And as a result, the Capitol of Capitalism and the center of Jewish life elected a fervent anti-Zionist Socialist Mayor.

For those of us who lived under Communism, the reality is unforgettable and should be covered by more than 45 minutes in one state's classrooms. Visiting the former Gestapo and KGB torture chambers in Vilnius in 2018 was a chilling reminder to this author of how people were surveilled, tortured, and broken. These are experiences future generations need to see and understand so they are not repeated.

As Dreyer writes, an entire generation has entered public life with an understanding of history that is "a mile wide and an inch deep." Without confronting the full truth of Communism's crimes, that gap will only grow.

Discovering the American medical system and services was one of my most indelible experiences. I owe to my hospital stay for circumcision shortly upon landing in Houston. The hospital building, the equipment, the interior and services were, to me, nothing short of terrific, leading me to believe that I was somehow the guest in a luxury hotel and had mistakenly been taken for a Cabinet member—or some shiny celebrity. Several follow-up telephone calls by a hospital doctor after my discharge making sure of my well-being just confirmed my thinking.

Later, being in the company of my newfound friend and his medical colleagues allowed me to learn that these people were working unusually long hours, enjoyed tremendous respect inside their own community and made astronomical money (by my own standard at the time), but came to all that only after more than a dozen years of grueling education once they were deemed among the best in both their high school and college classes.

Having experienced their consummate professionalism convinced me that these people deserve all they make because they shouldn't be distracted by money worries while treating patients and solving life threating issues. This was, and remains, my thinking.

In my limited exposure to physicians in Houston and later in Chicago, I was always left with a sense of gratitude for their prompt, responsive office staffs and unfailing late evening follow-up calls by the physician himself. As my family and specialist doctors began to retire, often explaining that they had grown "fed-up" with the bureaucratic labyrinth of medicine as it had become, I began to feel the changes myself—while observing to my horror a new kind of hideous-hybrid of a medical machine that was hardly recognizable.

Dialing and touching numerous prompts to get to the physician and hearing a promise of a retuning call within 48 hours is no longer the uncommon experience for many of us. As research studies now indicate, the ongoing decline of Medical Care in the US, the increased inefficiency of quality of the care received, accompanied by increased levels of patient frustration—all these elements and more are warning signs for the decline in health care to come. As a result, we are already beginning to see more and more Americans opt-out of the public health care system and replace it with what is now referred to as Concierge Medical Practices. (IOW, doctors who, for a direct pay, actually do provide personal care.)

There is no question that the American hospitals remain superior to those in countries with Socialized medicine, as it was apparent to me in the UK, Canada and Israel. However, becoming more corporate structured coupled with the rising cost of medical education accompanied by declining doctors' income incentives, will likely tend to cut into this superiority, and has already created a system where the cracks in the quality of treatment are clearly beginning to show.

Those who can afford extra few thousand dollars a year will be opting for concierge doctors to guarantee a 24/7 professional response. The rest will be selecting prompts and probably seeing their medical care divided between haves and have-nots. This is particularly true of HMOs where the medical choices are sparse, where people never see their MDs but instead are counseled 90% of the time by Physician's Assistants or Nurse Practitioners.

Astronomical prescription costs, rejected surgeries, the unavailability of organ replacements—are all among the fates that await the US senior citizen, because universal health care in no way assures anyone of universal "equality" of Health Care. That is the Socialist paradox: where "free services" always come at a cost.

Equality is now the buzzword that runs our national mindset, when no one and nothing can be made equal by twisting legislation to make it so. Yet it is done on a daily basis: in the media, in the corporate world, in entertainment and especially in the legislative bodies of our governments—both on a state and national basis.

Equality is not a guarantee and never has been. It is the "equality of opportunity," that the United States Constitution promises us—to rise or fall, thrive or fail, according to our talents…and not for, "Each according to his abilities to provide for each according to his needs." (The Prime Tenet of *The Communist Manifesto.*)

Author Kurt Vonnegut once wrote a brilliant dark parody in short-story form titled, *Harrison Bergeron.* A dystopian classic, where time-future America's obsession with equality has removed Democracy from the equation, and where the President of the United States has been replaced by a Handicapper General. As de-facto leader of the nation, the Handicapper General's primary role in this dystopian society is to use government control, along with the power of the media and the military, to force "total" equality on everyone—by requiring the stronger, smarter, more individualistic civilians to wear physical and mental restraints in the form of devices that will impede their excellence, thereby assuring all citizens a harness of mediocrity in which no one excels…at anything!

In defiance of this, our (teenage) protagonist Harrison Bergeron literally breaks out of his prison, takes over a TV station and removes the electronic shackles on the staff, musicians and hosts—thus using the ensuing broadcast to announce that "Freedom is at hand!" To reward him for his efforts, The Handicapper General arrives at the television studio, comes onto the "live-show" and—on national television—blows him in half with a double-barreled shotgun. An on-air murder that everyone forgets two minutes later…because they have entirely lost the ability to either reason or remember.

Are we ready for a Handicapper General? G-d willing, not yet. But I lived in a country—the USSR—where things were just that way. And look around you. The signs are everywhere around us in the country that we love: "The USA. The land of the free. The home of the brave…where excellence is our banner and where Ronald Reagan's words today still echo in my ears: *"Freedom is always just one generation away from extinction."*

Extinct or around for another thousand years? It's up to us. It truly is up to us!

What once was great is now controversial as memories dim

History suffers from amnesia, and memories are short. And what is valid to one generation too often becomes meaningless to the next. So, at last we arrive at the crux of the matter. And it is here that I quote Thomas Jefferson with very specific intent. Because Thomas Jefferson—inventor, architect, scholar, multilingual diplomat, Renaissance man, patriot beyond measure, primary author of our Declaration of Independence, America's first Secretary of State and third US President—has now become a flashpoint for controversy in the brief but passionate chronicles of this nation.

The reasons for the condemnation are simple and single minded: because Jefferson—a man of his time, flawed but well-intended—was a slave-owner. Not only a slave owner, but one who kept a black mistress for the last 20-years of his life. Forget the fact, that it was he who first noted that the ills of slavery were something that, "this nation must soon be rid of if it is to live up to its democratic promise." Those infamous labels that have now been slapped on this phenomenal hero of the Republic have also been transferred in bulk to our other Founding Fathers—simply for the sins of having been men of a certain era.

"Most people on the Right have no problem understanding people on the Left because many, if not all were on the Left themselves when they were younger. And yet many, if not most, people on the Left find it inexplicable how any decent and intelligent person could be on the Right..."

~ Thomas Sowell, PhD[37]

Targeted and vocally villainized by Critical Race Theory historians, Black Lives Matter, "the woke progressive posse" in Congress, Bernie Sanders and Louis Farrakhan—Jefferson has become the new poster child for every flaw in our Constitution, our other founding fathers and the fact this bastion of Democracy was founded (in their words) on a lie! Built on the backs of slaves and designed solely for the aggrandizement of an elite (white) upper caste, they have now determined that, "America is a nation constructed of falsehoods."

These are the new poison pills poured on a daily basis into the ears of our Millennials and Generation Z, done so with revisionist histories and a conspiracy on the Left to seize power "by any means necessary." Sadly, it is succeeding because the Republicans appear at a loss to defend it. When they do—when they take a stand or make a legislation to reinforce "traditional values"—they are denounced in the liberal press as relics of repression, and dinosaurs of a bygone era.

So much of this is reflective of a Two-Party System that is coming apart at the seams. The GOP, well-intended with its heart very much in the right place, is so wrong-headed because it seems intent on cannibalizing itself. Reasonable people at the center-right are being attacked by the alt-right who pride themselves on their inability to compromise on anything at all. Meanwhile the Democrats are licking their lips and planning on establishing a one-party system where "loyal opposition" will become an artifact of the past. Once that threshold is crossed—

---

37 Honors graduate of Harvard, Columbia, and the University of Chicago (where he received his PhD in Economics), Thomas Sowell is a prize-winning economist and a recipient of the President's National Humanities Award.

as the progressives are conspiring to bring it to bear—it will be "game over" for the dynamics of democracy. And do not doubt their intentions for a minute.

For every reasonable moderate in the Democratic party, there are two Progressives, like those that nearly took over in 2016 when Bernie Sanders' storm troops put up a nasty stink. The pot has been brought off the boil since then, but "the stew" remains the same. Past perceptions are selective, but for those who were there we have an indelible image of a moat having to be constructed around the Wells Fargo Center to keep out Bernie's Band of militants who were not allowed to be seated." That kind of radicalism still bubbles just beneath the surface. And though it is the January 6th rebellion—the Proud Boys and the Oathkeepers *et al.*—that gets all the press, there is a rising new guard of progressives that are simply biding their time. They're far less interested in creating a government *for* the People than they are in creating one that comes *at* the People."

Dog-whistle terms such as "Tax the Rich," "Reparations for Racial Injustice," and "Socialism is the only system of government that works," are catch-phrases straight out of the Communist Manifesto. Yet they have taken root in the Democratic party today and are as much of party policy as oxygen to a lung. The challenge is that it has broad appeal, it makes socialism sound appealing if you missed the last century, which as it happens many on the left did.

He can almost make socialism sound appealing if you missed the last century which, as it happens, he did.

Emilia at Bush 43's pre-inauguration party, chatting with Marla Maples, Donald Trump's wife number 2, and her escort, one-time Chrysler CEO Lee Iacocca on January 20, 2001.

*Emilia and I get a prime pass to George W. Bush's swearing-in,
January 20, 2001.*

CHAPTER SEVENTEEN

America and Israel: A Love Affair. "It's Complicated."

"The state of Israel is a speck on the map of the world;
it occupies a continent in the American mind."
- Walter Russell Mead

"Israel was not created in order to disappear:
Israel will endure and flourish. It is the child of hope and home of the brave.
It can neither be broken by adversary nor demoralized by success.
It carries the shield of democracy and it honors the sword of freedom."
- John Fitzgerald Kennedy"

Our life histories and experiences may be considered somewhat different from others in that they provided both Emilia and me with perspectives that were bound to diverge—not only from our American-born friends but also from our own relatives and some in our inner circle. More than anything, this certainly applies to our support and passion for our historic homeland in Israel. Something that any committed Jew must feel in his heart and his soul.

In the United States of America, Israel has enjoyed full bipartisan support for a relatively short period of history. Since its establishment, and through the 1970s, it came heavily from the Democratic side of the aisle. Initially, it was the Democrats who were the party that championed Israel—especially when it was born in 1948. In contrast, support for Israel within the Republican Party was rather limited, if not even moribund at times. The Republican domestic and foreign policy agendas did not encourage supporting Israel, which at that time was a country with a decidedly socialist bent.

Indeed, during its first 30 years, Israel was run by various left-leaning socialist-oriented parties. Originally in 1948, the far-left Zionist factions that coalesced in Israel's MAPAM (United Workers) Party looked favorably upon the Soviet Union, adorning its dining halls in *kibbutzim*—with Stalin's portraits, and with the NKVD successfully recruiting leading MAPAM members prior to Israel's formation as a member state. Even in the early days, however, the MAPAM were at loggerheads with mainstream Zionists who openly embraced the West. As David Ben-Gurion told the first US Ambassador to Israel, James McDonald: "Rome would become Communist before Jerusalem."

The almost weekly oscillations of American policy, thus ostensibly depriving Israel a proper means of defense, was fueling feelings of disgust regarding the West. The shallow sympathy for Soviets was helped by the West's own reluctant reception of Israel, but fed a malicious narrative during the late-1940s among American opponents of Zionism in the State Department, the CIA, and the Pentagon that a Jewish state would become a Soviet satellite, infiltrated by Soviet agents in the guise of Jewish refugees.

While the United States had recognized Israel's independence, it had also mandated an arms embargo on the entire Middle East, until JFK provided Israel with a HAWK missile defense system in 1963. However, the life or death Six-Day War was fought by Israel mostly with French military equipment.[38]

In a point of irony, in the 1960s Israel was not looked upon as America's number-one ally in the Middle East — that was Iran, the only other non-Arab nation in that region at the time. Although a Muslim nation, under the Pahlavi regime, "Persia" also cultivated close but quiet ties with Israel, resulting in an informal strategic alliance. While seeking closer bonds with the West

---

38 In the strange mélange of Middle East politics it was actually Morocco, the birthplace of Mohammed, that held absolutely no love for either Nasser or the UAR, supplying Israel with most of its French-made armaments. It was also reported by one of LBJ's Joint Chiefs of Staff 10 years later, that President Johnson had secretly shipped additional reinforcement arms through a third party (Iran) immediately after the war, and in 1968, the US Congress approved a contract to supply Israel with an entire air-wing of sophisticated F-4 Phantom jets.

and striving for modernization, Shah Mohammad Reza Pahlavi (r. 1941-79) viewed Israel as a natural ally. Israel's independence, strength and progress fascinated the Shah. Its ongoing conflict with the Nasser-dominated Arab world and opposition to Communist influence in the region further provided the Shah with the kind of buffer he felt he needed politically in the region. The Shah also believed that, through relations with Israel, Persia would benefit in the United States, gaining the support of American Jewry, the Congress, the media, the business community, as well as the administration. This relationship began in effect in 1959 and intensified throughout the 1960s when Prime Minister David Ben-Gurion coined the "Periphery Concept," (one that basically stated, "The enemy of my enemy is my friend"). This translated into a close, though informal, co-alignment with Persia.

This all fell apart during the years of the Carter administration when, in 1979, his State Department led by Persian antagonist Cyrus Vance undermined the Shah to such a degree that he had to abdicate, leading to Iran becoming a rogue nation under the Ayatollahs, and a principal Soviet ally in the region.

As I have been observing Israel-related issues since my arrival in the US in 1977, and I have noticed different motives in support for Israel among the people I have met. The Democrats, who were the majority of my neighbors and other Jewish people I knew, supported Israel out of sympathy for a poor, small, underdog country populated by Holocaust survivors. The affinity for Israel among my Republican acquaintances stemmed from the respect for shared Western values—seeing Israel as an ally in democracy and freedom, and with tremendous respect for Israeli Defense Forces (IDF) that had always showed phenomenal valor in the face of overwhelming odds.

It is difficult to credit any single Israeli political leader (although Netanyahu stands out) with the change in support among Republicans. This support began with President Ronald Reagan, his Secretary of State George Shultz, election of Menachem Begin—the first post-MAPAI Labor Israeli leader, as well as a growing number of neo-conservatives, the majority of whom were Jewish. As an example, Republican Governor and current US Ambassador to Israel Mike Huckabee started organizing trips to Israel in 1981, 15 years prior to the first election of Netanyahu as Prime Minister.

Sadly, a growing number of Democratic candidates and officials have slowly but openly distancing themselves from Israel. This trend is turning support for Israel into a partisan issue—with the Republican Party firmly in Israel's corner, while more and more Democrats seem to show sympathy toward Israel's ene-mies...with a special affinity for the Palestinians (and Hamas).

The Democratic Party today is not the political party of the Kennedys, Scoop Jackson or Daniel Patrick Moynihan. Emilia and I repeatedly asked ourselves how 75% of Jews (all Democrats) proudly supported and voted twice for Barack Obama—the same Barack Obama who was for over 20 years a member of the United Trinity Church of Christ in Chicago. A church that was run by a minister (and former US Marine [go figure]) Jeremiah Wright, who never hid his contempt for the Jews during his weekly sermons. Sermons that were virtually always riddled with Anti-Semitic invective, while the Obama family sat dutifully on the front row.

Even during his campaign run, Obama openly declared his adoration of the man, claiming that Jeremiah Wright was like an uncle to him. This is the same Pastor Wright who honored the notorious Jew-hater and Black-Muslim Louis Farrakhan with his, Man of the Century award. Apparently, Pastor Wright also chose to overlook the fact that Black-Muslims have, since the days of Elijah Mohammed and Malcom X, advocated the second-class citizenship of women, the abolishment of Christianity, the establishment of Sharia Law, and the complete segregation of the races.

This was never really lost on Barack Obama who, upon entering the White House in 2009, immediately shored up ties with some of the most radical Muslim heads-of-state in the Middle East.

As the late Sheldon Adelson, a major Republican donor, explained in a 2012 article in *The Wall Street Journal* that he had left the Democratic Party because it had changed, becoming home to "a visceral anti-Israel movement, especially among rank-and-file Democrats."

The viciously anti-Semitic Ilhan Omar (a refugee of Al Shabaab-dominated Somalia, mind you), who took the US House of Representative seat of the equally anti-Semitic Keith Ellison, Deputy Chair of the Democratic Party, openly declared, "Death to Israel," while on the campaign trail. Today, Omar is a tenured member of the House Foreign Relations Committee. Just a few years ago, 16 Democrats (and one Republican) voted against House Resolution HR246 opposing the Boycott, Divestment, Sanctions (BDS) movement, a Palestinian-led movement for freedom, justice and equality.

Many Democrats accused Netanyahu of going behind Obama's back and accepting a Republican Speaker of the House invitation to address Congress on the Iran Nuclear Deal (also known as the Joint Comprehensive Plan of Action). The Prime Minister of Israel came in front of the United States Congress, accepting the invitation of the Speaker of the House, who has as much right to invite people to the Congressional podium as the President does to the White House.

Obama, in addition to numerous Democratic members of Congress, including the entire black caucus, turned their backs on the Prime Minister of Israel. Yes, the Republican Speaker felt the importance of addressing such a life and death issue for Israel as the upcoming Iran Nuclear Deal and the handing over of billions to the Israel-hating regime. And what about stabbing Israel in the back during the last days of Obama administration by failing to veto a UN Resolution condemning Israel? This was the same Barack Hussein Obama who, during his eight years in office put a lot of daylight between the United States and their longtime ally Israel (the United States' only true ally left in the entire Middle East) even as—to the horror of the West—he bowed to Saudi King Abdullah during their first meeting in 2009.

Why is it that Jewish Democrats don't ask about the morality of such elected Democratic congresswomen as Alexandria Ocasio-Cortez and her colleagues, Rashida Tlaib and Ilhan Omar, all of whom are outspoken Israel haters? Where are the questions about the defamatory verbiage pouring out of their mouths?

During the 2016 Democratic Convention, I remember hearing a loud chorus of boos that echoed through the hall when the majority had passed a pro-Israeli resolution. In fact, not a single one of the announced Democratic candidates running for office showed up to address the American Israel Public Affairs Committee (AIPAC) meeting I attended in 2016. To add insult to injury, former Alaska Democratic Senator Mike Gravel, a notorious Israel opponent in Congress, tweeted, "Long Live Palestine!"[39]

---

39   At this point it both alarms and enrages me to recall that arguably the most brilliant US Presidential Candidate of his era (and a personal hero of mine), Senator Robert F. Kennedy, was assassinated by a Palestinian radical named Sirhan Sirhan. The same Sirhan who openly boasted that he shot Senator Kennedy to punish him for his Pro-Israeli policies. Even then—during one of the most politically inflammatory periods in American history—his political affiliations and Palestinian radicalism were quite intentionally minimalized by the US press corps. This was the beginning of a silent complicity and journalistic anti-Israeli bent that prevails in the media even to this day.

Yes, there is an apparent paradigm shift in the American Left: Its position in support of Israel has eroded, and an anti-Jewish movement has taken its place, led by a self-hating, multi-billionaire Jew George Soros and his support of such anti-Israeli groups as J Street, Jewish Voice For Peace, T'ruah, Code Pink, BDS, MoveOn.org and others.

Israel is a free, relentlessly self-analyzing democratic society. One doesn't have far to go to listen-in as Israeli political activists openly criticize her policies and leaders. Questioning of Israel should never be confused with the lies and misinformation that constantly infiltrate the major media networks and US press corps these days.

Throughout history, the catalog of fabrications about Jews is long and outrageous and is matched only by the suffering that has followed their pronouncements. It is not uncommon to read about any number of all-powerful Jewish groups as being part of the Israeli or Zionist lobby and somehow mysteriously playing the man behind the curtain, manipulating American foreign policy to meet its own selfish ends. The best example was the fantasy book, *The Israel Lobby*, published by John J. Mearsheimer and Stephen A. Walt in September of 2007.

Another ridiculous claim often propagated by anti-Israeli sources is that Jews control the media, acting as puppet-masters by turning it into a strong pro-Israel propaganda tool. This completely ignores the fact that the two most pro-Israel media organs today are the cable channel FOX News and the newspaper, *The Wall Street Journal*. It takes a lot of imagination to cast their owner, Rupert Murdoch, as a Jew.

Presumed Jewish prowess is often projected into the erroneous, even funny, perception of the size of the Jewish population in the world. Here I have to share my own experience with a Chinese taxi driver in Sydney, Australia. Recognizing his riders as Jewish, he started to complement us for our power and possession. He sited basically everything, perhaps except for the sun, which is so plentiful in his new home country. After refusing to answer my repeated question: How many Jews do you think are in the world? He finally admitted that he realized there were "not that many," and he finally gave me his guess of *300 million*, but probably not more than that.

When I told him the actual number was around 15 million, he was taken aback and then thought I was showing him my "Jewish humor." His completely unreasonable guess of 300 million was recently beaten by a man driving my Israeli neighbor in Moldova who estimated the total Jewish population to *one billion!*

But most shocking was the book by former President Jimmy Carter titled *Palestine-Peace: Not Apartheid,* where he draws parallels between Israel's action to protect her people from the attacks directed to eliminate the State of Israel and the racist oppression of black people by the white regime of South Africa. These false analogies promulgated by the former POTUS lend legitimacy to more broadly-based movements that take the same dangerous direction. (Even as a now "beloved" ex-president, Jimmy Carter remains a pro-Arab asset, frequently speaking at BDS functions and even a Muslim Brotherhood 100th Anniversary Banquet in 2012.)

As former Secretary of State George P. Shultz wrote: "The United States supports Israel not because of favoritism based on political pressure or influence but because the American people, and their leaders, say that supporting Israel is politically sound and morally just." *(US News & World Report,* September 17, 2007).[40]

Or as a historian Walter Russell Mead noted in his recently published book, *The Ark of a Covenant*: "Israel occupies a unique place in American foreign policy because it occupies a unique, and uniquely charged, place in the American mind."

As Mead highlights in his book, long before modern Israel came into existence, the fate of the Holy Land and the Jewish people was a subject of enormous interest, fascination, and speculation for Americans, and how this is still reflected in the American-Israel relationship today.

America's long immersion in biblical Christianity and in a theory of progress that is both secular and religious is a matter of record. And the fact that Americans have built on those foundations has given the Jewish people and the Jewish state a distinctive place in both American historical consciousness and political thought. The state of Israel is a speck on the map of the World, and yet it occupies a continent in the American consciousness—one that has brought about a bond that cannot be easily broken.

---

40 Admittedly, I was originally quite nervous when Reagan appointed this former head of Arab-connected Bechtel Corporation as Secretary of State. But Shultz actually turned out to be OK. ☺

The proportion of Jews in the US population is decreasing in very mea-
surable ways. Just before the establishment of Israel in 1948 there were 5.2
million Jews living among 129 million Americans. Today, we have the US
population of 330 million (2.6 times increase) while the number of Jews
remain practically the same (at 5.7 million).

So, 70%-75% of Democratic voting Jews comprise roughly 2.8 million
adult voters. With only 2/5th of all US Jews who have ever visited or care
about Israel, nobody knows how many real voters there are. With 50% to
70% of intermarriage and low birthrates among secular, reform and conservative Jews in the US, the only growing sector is traditionally religious Jews
and immigrants (secular and religious) from the former Soviet bloc countries
who predominately vote Republican. Yet, with the current Jewish population
holding relatively static at 5.7 million, it is predicted that within 20 years we
will be superseded by Muslims as the second largest religious group. If these
predictions hold (and by all indications they will) it means that Jews will be
playing less of a role in consistent support for Israel.

What are 2.8 million active Jewish voters in comparison to the 60 million
Evangelical (most voting Republican) unconditional supporters of Israel? John
Hagee's Christians United for Israel alone has 5 million members (voters).

Israel itself as a country has been undergoing a remarkable transformation
from a state-controlled semi-socialist economy to the free enterprise start-up
nation. "Most Israelis today, including a large percentage of the socialists who
formerly backed state-owned companies, now regard these firms as a drain on
the nation's resources."[41]

The original settlers in Israel, then called Palestine, belonged to various
workers' movements which at the time were believed to summon and promote
the socialist dogma that capital was ruthlessly exploiting labor.

This, they believed, could be eliminated only when the means of production were owned and controlled by the socialist state. Thus, they founded the
Federation of Labor—*Histadrut,* which set out to control means of production and create places to work, often in areas critical to the possible occurrence
of war—thus playing a pivotal role in the defense of the nascent Jewish state.

---

41 Source: Macabee Dean, "Israel: The Road from Socialism," September 1, 1989,
Foundation for Economic Education (fee.org).

This philosophy was rejected by the forerunner of Likud, Israel's largest party today, which came to power in 1977 electing Prime Minister Menachem Begin…and in 2003 began to implement drastic economic reforms.

In 2002 only 54% of Israel's adult population participated in the work-force—the lowest participation rate in the developed world. Today it is 74%. Twenty-two years ago, Arab birth rates in Israel exceeded Jewish births by 2 to 1. In 2021, the Jewish birthrate exceeds the Arab with respective fertility rates of 3.27 with an Israeli-born father (and 2.85 to 3.00 in Judea and Samaria). "The unique growth in Israel's Jewish fertility rate is attributed to optimism, patriotism, the Jewish high regard for raising children and a healthy 'frontier mentality.'" (Yoram Ettinger).

Israel surged from a $37 billion economy in 1988 to $610 billion in 2025, and from an 8K GDP per capita to a $60K per capita, outstripping Great Britain and France. And by the year 2025, it ranked among the "Top 12 Most Efficient Economies World."

People who visited Israel during its early years witnessed Israel's lack of adequate roads and transportation system. Today, the same people are stunned to see nation's infrastructure and its continued growth. The roads, tunnels, multi-layer bridge interchanges, light railway in Jerusalem, the Trans-Israel Highway, the railway system connecting Ben-Gurion Airport with all major cities, subway construction in Tel Aviv—all have made it an infrastructure standard by which others are now measured. The entire country looks like one large construction site…with omnipresent crane towers lighting the skylines at night.

On a personal note, my comment to Emilia the last time we landed in Israel, was that they should change the sign in the Ben-Gurion Airport from *Bruchim Habaim* (Welcome) to the *Hard Hat Area*. However, with all this construction and prosperity, Israel still has a housing problem where too many Israelis are still living (by American standards) in substandard conditions while paying exorbitant prices for them all. Building permits and construction activities halted by the COVID-19 epidemic came at a hefty cost, while the continued influx of new immigrants from Ukraine and Russia as well as other countries definitely aggravated the housing problem.

The notorious Israeli bureaucracy developed during the socialist years of a very young Israel still lingering and able to cause headaches. Although this is currently being fought and successfully reduced—there are still enough government entanglements remaining to trouble everyone along the way. Even now, we are still met and blocked by minions of that bureaucracy who live by the old saying: "We are paid to come to work. If you want us to work, we need to be paid overtime."

Prior to enacting the economic reforms in 2003, there were 56 multinational corporations with R&D centers in Israel. By 2025, this number rose to 500 with many of these companies having Israel as their prime R&D facility.

American Intel, Microsoft, Cisco, IBM, Apple, Johnson & Johnson, Google and Facebook— all have established research and development centers in Israel, leveraging Israel's brainpower, in order to increase US production and expand US exports and employment.

The rise of Israel's economy is a critical component in securing its power and influence in that perilous neighborhood, facing, all the while, the threat of a nuclear Iran. And a powerful economy gives Israel the means to develop and acquire the most sophisticated weapons, thus compensating for her small area and population (precisely comparable to that of the state of New Jersey).

As Walter Russell Mead writes in his book, *"Israel did not grow strong because it had an American alliance. It acquired an American alliance because it had grown strong."*

In 1948, Israel was misconstrued by the State Department as a burden upon America, too feeble to withstand an all-out Arab military offensive, jeopardizing US ties with the Arab World and potentially becoming a pro-Soviet asset. This false claim of the "Israel Burden" is often alluded to even to this day. As a classic example: In 2016, a Brookings Institution survey found that 76% of Americans (55% Democrats, 24% Republicans and 41% Independents) still consider Israel a burden although for the obvious lack of the facts or simply prejudice.

Far removed from what is often misperceived as one-sided American assistance, the most compelling evidence of "mutual interest and benefits" for both Israel and America (along with other American allies) has been thoroughly researched and presented by my friend, author and Israeli Ambassador (ret.) Yoram Ettinger. Based on 50 years of Ettinger's detailed findings, the facts below underscore the reality that the USA does not extend any annual foreign aid to Israel, but rather makes an annual investment in Israel, which yields close to a 400% annual rate-of-return:

Since the Six-Day War of 1967 (in the height of Cold War with the Soviets) Israel has emerged as a formidable force-multiplier for the US when in June of that year Israel devastated the United Arab Republic (UAR) pro-Soviet Egyptian, Syrian and Jordanian military, while Egypt was on its way to become the pan-Arab leader, aiming to topple the pro-US regimes of the Arab oil-producing countries—all of this done at a time when the US had just become heavily dependent upon the Persian Gulf oil. The resounding Israeli victory spared the US a huge economic and national security setback, and denied the USSR a dramatic geo-strategic gold mine.

In December 1969 a secret intelligence maneuver called Operation Rooster 53, highlighted Israel's unique intelligence and battle tactic capabilities, which they in turn shared with the US. An Israeli commando unit snatched from Egypt an advanced Soviet P-12 radar system, which was a new technology that had managed to station itself throughout the world. This Soviet radar, thoroughly studied and dissected by Israel, was later transferred to the US, as were additional Soviet military systems, enhancing the capabilities of US intelligence, special operations forces and US defense industries.

According to the late Democrat Senator Daniel Inouye, Chairman of both the Senate Appropriations and the Senate Intelligence Committees, the value of the captured Soviet radar to the US defense industries and armed forces amounted to around *$3 billion.* Upon his evaluation, Inouye summarized by noting that the scope of intelligence shared by Israel with the US, far exceeded the intelligence shared with the United States by all NATO countries combined.

As a follow-up in 1966 and again in 1989, Israel acquired MIG-21 and MIG-23 Soviet combat planes by means of defecting Iraqi and Syrian pilots. The advanced technologies from these planes—as well as the planes themselves—were shared with the US, impacting the global balance of power, and enhancing the performance of the US Air Force and aerospace industries.

As a result of the benefits derived by the US, a team of 50 experts arrived in Israel following the 1973 Yom Kippur War, collecting information that benefited the US militarily and industrially, bolstering the US defense of Europe in the face of Soviet threats.

(I remember only too well my uncle's surprise when he and other Soviet generals were shown American M48 and M60 tanks captured by the Egyptians in the first days of the Yom Kippur war and given to their Soviet bosses, who found them inferior to the Soviet T-55 and T62 tanks. One can look and compare the American tanks manufactured before and after the Yom Kippur war to see the revolutionary difference in their height, weight and maneuverability alone.)

The list of American benefits from Israel's military and intelligence successes is long and impressive one, only a few of which we are listing here. And again, as both Walter Russell Mead and Yoram Ettinger observe: Israel's posture of deterrence is not growing stronger due to the recent peace accords with Arab countries. Arab countries concluded peace accords with Israel due to the fact that Israel's posture of deterrence is growing stronger.

Ambassador Ettinger writes: "The US does not extend foreign aid to Israel. Rather, the US makes an annual investment in Israel, which yields to the American taxpayer an annual R-O-I (Return-On-Investment) of *several hundred percent.*"

Here are just a few examples:

- While Israel is a most grateful recipient of a few hundred US military systems, it serves as the battle-tested, cost-effective laboratory of the US defense and aerospace industries, which employ—directly and indirectly—3.5 million Americans.

- Moreover, Israel's Defense Forces have served as a battle-tested laboratory for the US armed forces, enhancing the performance and efficiency of the US Military at various levels.

- A field-tested Israeli laboratory enhances the economy, national security and homeland security of the US. For instance, Israel's Air Force flies the Lockheed-Martin-manufactured F-16 and F-35 combat aircraft, providing the US manufacturer and US Air Force with lessons– on a daily basis–that involve operations, maintenance and repairs. These lessons are integrated into a multitude of upgrades for the next generation of the aircraft, bolstering the performance of the US manufacturer and Air Force.

- In fact, the F-16 has been improved due in large part to several hundred Israeli-driven upgrades (cockpit, fire control, wings, fuel tanks, and so many others). In so doing, the Israeli Air Force has saved Lockheed-Martin an estimated 10 to 20 years of Research & Development that would otherwise have cost billions of dollars—thus improving the global competitiveness of Lockheed-Martin as a builder of modern jet aircraft, and increasing its multi-billion-dollar exports while expanding Lockheed-Martin's employment base.

- Realistically, similar mega-billion-dollar windfalls are enjoyed by Boeing, the manufacturer of the F-15 combat aircraft (through flight-tested upgrades) by the Israeli Air Force.

- With its unique national security challenges, Israel is a Triple-A-Store for Lockheed-Martin, Boeing, Raytheon, G.D., Northrop Grumman, L3Harris Technologies, G.E., Oshkosh, Honeywell and many other US defense and aerospace industries, serving as a multiplier of export to countries that have come to presuppose that Israel's use of these military systems will continue to be a most reliable stamp of approval.

- According to a former Head of US Air Force Intelligence, General George Keegan, the US would have to establish *five CIAs* in order to procure the intelligence provided by Israel. The annual budget of one CIA is *around $15 billion.*

- Israel is extending the strategic hand of the US by securing vulnerable pro-US Arab oil-producing regimes and deterring terrorism, with no US troops on its soil (unlike NATO countries Japan, South Korea and [until recently] Germany).

- According to the late General Alexander Haig, NATO's former Supreme Commander and US Secretary of State, and Admiral Elmo Zumwalt: "Israel is the largest US aircraft carrier, which does not require American soldiers on board, cannot be sunk, and is deployed in a most critical region (between Europe-Asia-Africa and between the Mediterranean-Red Sea-Indian Ocean-Persian Gulf), sparing the US the need to manufacture, deploy and maintain a few more real aircraft carriers and additional ground divisions, which would cost the US taxpayer some *$15 billion* annually."

In conclusion, the US-Israel strategic relationship constitutes a classic case of a mutually-beneficial two-way-street, which enhances the economy and defense of both countries, benefiting Israeli and American taxpayers alike.

As Ambassador Ettinger concludes: "Israel is neither foreign to the US, nor does it receive aid. Israel is not a beneficiary of US foreign aid, but a beneficiary of an annual US investment, which yields to the US taxpayer a hefty annual Return-On-Investment."

There is, however, one aid-recipient that abuses money sent by American taxpayers, and does so with profligate impunity: That is the United Nations Relief and Works Agency (UNRWA). Founded in 1949, the UNRWA (dedicated to keeping descendants of Palestinian Refugees in a condition of permanent statelessness) received $830 million of US taxpayer money from the Biden Administration over the last two years, which represents one-third of the international support it receives each year. This agency employs 30,000 individuals, while its schools offer a curriculum and philosophical structure designed to inculcate its students with a hatred for Jews…and Jewry itself.

As a classic example, in June 2022, under pressure the UNRWA announced that it had placed six of its Teachers on Administrative Leave for emphasizing the murder of Jews and destruction of Israel as a part of their daily curriculum.

According Hillel Neuer, Executive Director of UN Watch, an independent non-governmental organization based in Geneva: "Teachers who call to murder Jews must be barred from the classroom for life…while these temporary suspensions are just a slap on the wrist, further investigations and penalties should be enforced."

In response, the UNRWA tried to pretend that this was an isolated incident, but the repercussions were much farther reaching than that: because the temporary suspension only served as a dog-whistle to the Palestinian staff and to terrorist organizations like Islamic Jihad, which pressed UNRWA to reject the UN Watch Report—that they don't really object to the virulent antisemitism of their teachers, which UNRWA and its donors know only too well pervades the agency.

According to Neuer, UN Watch had, at the time, exposed more than 120 UNRWA teachers and other staff who praised Hitler, glorified terrorism and spread Anti-Semitism, while the UNRWA was not able to provide the name of a single teacher who had been fired. In fact, quite the contrary occurred: the suspensions provoked a sharp response from Palestinian groups that falsely portrayed the teachers' open calls to slaughter Jews as, "instilling Palestinian national pride." To further add fuel to the fire, a coalition that included the PA, Hamas and the Islamic Jihad, known as "The Joint Committee for Palestinian Refugees," called on the UNRWA "to immediately rescind its procedure of suspending six of its employees, and not to respond to US-Israeli pressures and dictates."

Over the years, the UNRWA has routinely deflected criticism of Anti-Semitism in its educational materials with the excuse that it is only repeating material from its host countries, specifically the approved textbooks of Jordan, Lebanon and the Palestinian Authority. And a 2021 study showed that the UNRWA's own material used during the COVID-19 Pandemic was rife with bigotry, hate-speech and the glorification of terrorists. A spate of tributes, including one to the infamous Dalal Mughrabi, who carried out the Coastal Road Massacre that killed 28 Israelis and wounded dozens of others. Other UNRWA generated materials promote the ongoing armed struggle against Israel, even as it encourages martyrdom of various kinds. Textbooks routinely demonize Israel and Jews. And one even described the firebombing of an Israeli bus as, "a barbecue party."

Despite this condemning report by The United Nations Watch group, donor nations—including Germany, Sweden, Japan, the EU and the UK (and, until recently, the USA) continue to pour-in funds to keep the UNRWA well on its course of racial and ethnic animus toward Israel. They do so even as they remain purblind to the true dynamics of ongoing terror and peril the average Israeli faces on a daily basis in the Middle East.

They continue doggedly on this path with at least some knowledge that rogue nations such as Iran are surreptitiously constructing a nuclear missile system that blatantly emblazons the label "Death to Israel" on every armament they construct. They also cannot help but be aware of the terrorist culture that thrives in the midst of daily Palestinian life as it currently presents itself, especially among Palestinian Muslims.

In his book, *Son of Hamas,* Mosab Hassan Yousef, son of former Hamas No. 2, gives a laundry list of reasons for his defection to Christianity and the inbred madness of the cult of terrorism his father headed-up. In it, Yousef begins his exposé by recounts of having borne witness to a Palestinian Muslim woman who straps her nine-year-old son into a backpack bomb, covering him in a jacket and sending him off to blow-up a nearby Israeli shopping mall (himself included). Her logic: that her little boy would die the "Death of Flowers," ascending bodily into *Jannah,* Mohammed's concept of the highest heaven—with 72 virgins to attend his every need.

This is the kind of insensate madness that is woven into the fabric of the Hamas-driven, radical Jihadist mindset—one that Israel is expected to take into its bosom every single day. The EU, the US and most of the UN know this and yet they turn a blind eye, in what can only be described as an epidemic of appeasement to Arab petrodollars. It is a kind of economically-rationalized Stockholm Syndrome that continues to paralyze the West, even a rapidly growing sector of American Jews.

American and Israeli Jews,
with Russian-speaking Jews in-between

According to the Pew Research Center (April 17, 2023) the United States and Israel today are home of an estimated 80% of the world's Jewish population. Jews of both countries have deep connections and an estimated one-third of each nation has traveled to the other.

However, the majority of American Jews differ from their Israeli brothers and sisters on a very wide range of issues, especially when it comes to the so-called peace process. The former are optimistic in their support of a two-state solution, still believing in the (now defunct) Oslo Accords, even as the latter are skeptical and no longer believe that a peaceful co-existence between a secure Israel and an independent Arab Palestine is even possible. Also, while the majority of Israelis believe that Jewish developments in Judea and Samaria (West Bank of Jordan River) are essential for its security, American Jews look at those areas as the "occupied territories" that are hurting Israel's security and reputation on the world stage.

Also, the most common view among Israeli Jews is that the US is not supporting Israel enough (except for 2017-2020) with American Jews quite always satisfied with the support level, and with many factions often believing it is more than is actually needed.

The widest gap, however, is the ideological divide that has now broadened and deepened further between the two communities.

While 49% of American Jews describe their ideology as liberal, or moderate (29%) and only 19% as politically conservative, 55% of Israelis are in the center, 37% on the right with just 8% on the left. Although, these qualifications of liberal/moderate and conservative in the US and left/center/right in Israel very often represent different sets of values in each country.

The propensity of American Jews to be on political left was addressed by intellectual and editor of *The Commentary* magazine, Norman Podhoretz, in his 2009 book, *Why Are Jews Liberal?*, where he describes the mindset of many American Jews, who overwhelmingly identify as Democrats despite the party's waning support for Israel and protection of anti-Semites within its own ranks.

It is not for nothing that someone described to me the services of largest denomination of American Jews in a Reform temple as: the Democrat Party at prayer. (By the way, more traditional Jewish denominations call their house of prayers as Synagogues and avoid using term, Temple, due to the haunting memory of that most tragic set of events in the History of the Jewish people: the destruction of the Temples in Jerusalem, the First [in 586 BCE] by the Babylonians and the Second [in 70CE] by the Romans, which led to the almost 2,000-year Jewish Diaspora and exile of Jews from their ancestral homeland—until they were finally able to declare a reunified State of Israel in 1948.)

Quite some time ago, American Jewish institutions became a part of Democratic Party establishment by openly opposing Republicans and doing the Democrats' bidding. The best recent example is the May 2022 event planned to take place in the Museum of Jewish Heritage in New York City. The Museum canceled the Tikvah Fund conference because it had invited the Florida Governor Ron DeSantis to share his experience in Jewish education along with his tireless efforts in combating anti-Semitism in Florida.

Claiming to be non-political after having Progressive House Representative Alexandra Ocasio Cortez speak there just a short time prior to the event, the Jewish Heritage Museum pulled the plug on the foreigner governor's invitation for no other reason than pressure from "woke progressives" on the new Left.

Below is the letter I was compelled to send to the Museum:

> *Mr. Kliger, my family and I, who escaped the ideological prison of the Soviet Union many years ago, are appalled by your decision to cancel the Conference organized by Tikvah. You know well that the excuse given by the Museum as being non-political is bogus; just look up the roster of speakers who have enjoyed the Museum's podium in the last few years.*
>
> *To me and many others who dreamed of this country as a beacon of freedom and openness, you are playing a dangerous game by canceling public figures whom you disagree with. It mirrors exactly what we escaped from— the communist ideology where the accusation of being out of line with the Party meant things that I'm sure you are well aware of.*
>
> *It seems that the Museum of Jewish Heritage ignores the true meaning of its name. Isn't our Jewish Heritage the direct opposite of the cancel culture so prevalent these days and which you're apparently emulating? Just a month ago, you were probably enjoying the story of the four sons at the Passover Seder. Not all of these sons are the favorites of the Haggadah authors, but they are welcome at the table.*
>
> *This, to me, is our Jewish Heritage.*

For about a century, Jews have been a reliable piece of the Democratic base, usually delivering two-thirds or more of their votes to the party's presidential nominee. For Republicans, the 1980 election was the high-water mark, when Ronald Reagan won approximately 40% of Jewish votes.

Hamas's October 7, 2023, onslaught, in which some 1,200 people were murdered in Israel and 251 hostages were taken, and the groundswell of anti-Israel criticism from progressive groups that followed, made it seem like a political change could be possible. Donald Trump predicted that he could match Reagan's 40% and famously said that Jews would be to blame if he lost.

And still, Kamala Harris won the Jewish vote 71% to 26%.

It is quite the contrary when we see the New Americans coming into the Jewish community today—our friends and relatives who have lived in the Soviet Union or other Communist bloc countries, who have struggled to come to the United States looking for the diametric opposite of their previous societies.

Meanwhile, in both countries, traditional observant Jews tend to lean more to the right, while American-born secular and "reform" Jews are center or liberal-leaning. Many American Jews, especially "liberals" identify with Jewish denominations that have a minor, if any, presence in Israel, such as Reform (35% of American Jews) and Reconstructionist movements. *Masorti,* which is the official name of the Conservative movement in Israel, is close to, but not a direct equivalent of the American Conservative denomination, currently attracting 18% of all Israeli Jews.

There is one more group of Jews in both the United States and Israel with a strong tendency toward being politically conservative while tenuously connected to religion and its observance: Russian-speaking Jews from the Former Soviet Union *(FSU)*. With 1.3 million of today's Israelis and 750,000 resettled in the USA, they do not exactly fall-in with either the Israeli or the American Jewish pattern.

Regrettably, the story of their modern-day heroes—refuseniks who risked life, limb, family and careers as they fought to leave the Soviet Union for a new world of freedom and opportunity—is a saga largely unknown to younger American Jews, with the possible exception of the extraordinary Natan Sharansky. These worthy Epics of human rights legends who have profoundly influenced Israeli Society, politics and American Jewry more often than not go unrecognized, underestimated and unsung.

While half of all Israeli Jews identify as secular (*hiloni*), four out of five FSU-born Jews in Israel identify as non-religious. For an American Jew, who thinks secular Israelis identify with left ideologies, shining a light on secular Russian Jews is a surprising experience, as these immigrants and their children take a hard-turn politically to the Right once they see the Left-leaning liberals whose ideological extremism reminds them of the place they escaped from—

even as it proves too weak in defending the Western ideals of Freedom and Democracy they came for.

Politically, the first generation of FSU immigrants found their political voice in the secular and right-of-center *Yisrael Beytenu* party of Avigdor Liberman. Even as the second generation has come of age while joining other parties, they maintain their right-leaning outlook and traditional conservative values. But despite being Israel's most prominent Jewish minority, their political power has been diminished by the second generation, gravitating to many other parties. When they voted as a block, *Yisrael Beytenu* received 15 Knesset seats at its peak and was the political kingmaker in Israel's coalition politics; but in the last election on November 1, 2022, it received just 6 seats.

As Harriet Sherwood wrote in *The Guardian*, "They have influenced the culture, hi-tech industry, language, education and, perhaps most significantly, Israeli politics…Some came to pursue the Zionist dream. Some came to escape antisemitism. And a large number came for better economic prospects. They brought culture —art, literature, theatre, music— and new entrepreneurialism. And their children continue to reshape the Jewish state."

Researcher Lily Galili, writing for the Brookings Institution, said: "The over one million people who immigrated to Israel from the FSU in a wave from the beginning of the 1990s have changed Israel to its core — socially, politically, economically, and culturally. Within the first years, they formed what has become a large secular nationalist political camp that secures right-wing rule to this day."

Meanwhile the voice and political power of the right-leaning conservative Jews from FSU in the United States can only be felt during local elections, and within districts that contain heavily Russian-speaking and/or highly "observant" populations. When it comes to the State and Federal levels their impact is minimal (except in Florida) since the Jewish population is concentrated within the urban areas of the heavily "blue" coastal states, such as New York, New Jersey, Connecticut and most certainly California.[42]

---

42 Prof. Jonathan Sarna of Brandeis University, the preeminent historian of American Jewry, commented in a recent article in *The Jerusalem Report*, "The divide between US and Israeli Jewry".

CHAPTER 18

737 Days and One Nightmare

In Israel, in order to be a Realist, you must believe in Miracles."

~ David Ben Gurion

A drone view shows a depiction of U.S. President Donald Trump and the words "Thank You", on the day Israeli hostages, held in Gaza since the deadly October 7, 2023 attack by Hamas, were released as part of a U.S.-brokered hostages-prisoners swap and a ceasefire deal in Gaza between Hamas and Israel, near the U.S. Consulate in Tel Aviv, Israel October 13, 2025.

Monday, October 13, 2025, was the day when nine million of Jews in Israel woke up and lived as one single emotional family. We, like our neighbors, had our TV and all other gadgets tuned to the news in the anticipation of the final release of all living and dead hostages from Gaza dungeons and a visit by U.S. President Donald Trump to formalize a ceasefire agreement. Were the hostages really coming home? The Jewish world and his friends scarcely dared believe it. Was this long nightmare finally over?

We were watching on split screens how the Air Force One was approaching Israel from the Mediterranean Sea, flying along the Tel Aviv coast where a massive sign thanking President Trump was erected, and landing at Ben Gurion Airport and how the United States President was being greeted by Israel Prime Minister Netanyahu, and President Isaac Herzog before departure to Jerusalem, to the Israeli Knesset.

At the same time, we were watching beginning of hostage handover and release of 20 living Israelis and transporting them by Red Cross vehicles from Gaza into Israel. Simultaneously, Israel began releasing 2,050 Palestinian terrorists as part of the negotiated deal-the appallingly high price Israel was having to pay for the hostages living and murdered. In Knesset Trump spoke forcefully in his Trumpian style about ending the war, bringing home all the hostages living and dead, creating a new reality in Gaza and working on bringing greater stability to the Middle East.

People of Israel finally could breathe again after great suffering over these past two years. Too many of our best and brightest have lost their lives; too many will be reciting the Yizkor memorial prayer for the rest of their lives for relatives that have made the ultimate sacrifice.

All this was happening on the eve of the Jewish holiday of Simchat Torah, heightening the emotional and religious significance of the day's "miraculous" events — exactly two nightmarish years after the tragic Simchat Torah day of 2023 when Hamas committed the worst atrocities against Jewish people since World War II.

The Nation was celebrating with thousands of Israelis gathered across the country to honor the return of the captives. These were bittersweet moments with a lot to remember.

On October 7, 2023, over 3,000 Hamas, Palestinian Islamic Jihad (PIJ) and his Gazan sympathizers breached Israel's borders by land, sea and air, launching a brutal assault on civilian communities across the southern region. It was meticulously planned attack and executed with the intent of indiscriminate massacre of Jews. More than 1,200 adults, elderly, infants and music festival attendees brutally killed and 251 taken hostage to Gaza. As former mayor of Bal Harbour Gabe Grossman compared these numbers in terms of the United States population, that equaled to more than 40,000 Americans murdered and 9,000 kidnapped in a single day.

The atrocities included widespread torture, mutilation, raping women in front of their husbands and children, burning babies alive and other barbaric acts. These acts were committed with clear ideological intent enshrined in Hamas founding chapter calling for the annihilation of the Jewish people and Israel. These terrorist acts didn't stop at Israeli or Jewish citizens. Foreign nationals from over 40 countries were among murdered and kidnapped, including 31 Thai agricultural workers. Among numerous victims were the members of local communities who were Israeli activists helping people of Gaza, including our friend's a former schoolmate, retired teacher who dedicated own time and finances to driving several times a week the sick children from Gaza to hospitals and doctors in Israel.

As Morson and Shapiro recently wrote in The Wall Street Journal — unlike the Nazis who tried to conceal their crimes, and the Soviets pretending there was no GULAG and denying the terror and famine because Hitler and Stalin knew that what they were doing was wrong or, they were sure that others would think so, today's mass murders can expect our elites to cheer their atrocities.

October 7, 2023 displayed something different. Far from hiding its brutality, Hamas advertised it, filming and broadcasting sadistic cruelty. Just recall the enthusiasm of one of terrorists calling his parents from the phone of an Israeli woman he had just murdered, imploring his parents to open up WhatsApp and "Look how many I killed with my hands. Your son killed Jews!" he told his father as his parents overjoyed." My son, G-d bless you," his father said and "I wish I was with you" his mother added.

And it took not more than 24 hours on October 8, 2023 for the world at its college campuses and other public squares to light the anti-Israel flames, celebrate Hamas atrocities as a "success" and call for "global" intifada" with the Palestine from the River to the Sea (often without being able to name or location of those bodies of water.)

The questions on many minds remain how Israel, the country renowned for its intelligence, could have been so wrong about Gaza, how it left itself so unprepared, how it was caught so completely by surprise? These questions still hang in the air and need an answer through a thorough investigation. According to The Jerusalem Post editorial this wasn't just an operational failure; it was a conceptual debacle. It destroyed the belief that Israel could contain those sworn to its destruction by relying exclusively on hi-tech technology and replacing manpower, that deterrence and diplomacy could substitute for vigilance.

For nearly two decades Israeli military convinced itself that it could manage its enemies-keep Hamas boxed in by fences and sensors, deter Hizballah by fear of devastation, and even contain Iran through covert operations. As economy was booming, life was good, quiet became the ultimate goal and the people responsible for her defense preferred not to look too closely at what was happening just a mile or two away. That quiet turned to be an illusion shattered by October 7. Israel misjudged Hamas by assuming it would not do anything crazy for fear of provoking a devastating Israeli response. But Hamas calculation was not Israel's. It was ready to sacrifice Gaza population so that Iran and its "ring of fire" satraps would join and rain hellfire on the Jewish State to consume it.

After October 7 and the failures that allowed 1,200 Jews to be slaughtered, Israel rebuilt, regrouped and responded with might. It dispelled the often heard complains of the Israeli public about the today's young people as being spoiled and disengaged. But this young Israelis proved it wrong and saved the country.

On October 7, 2023 thousands of young Israelis caught abroad, many of whom were on post-army "big trips" or working/studying, did not wait for a formal call-up, immediately packed their bags and faced arduous journeys, having to take multiple flights via intermediate cities, crossing the Mediterranean on freight ships, with some walking to cross the border after arriving to Jordan to join their military units or volunteer for civilian aid efforts. Many left jobs in the tech sector or other industries, with reports of over 150% of those called up reporting for duty, demonstrating an overwhelming eagerness to serve. Men and women well beyond their draft age were lining up to sign for service. My cousin in his 50th was one of them. But while being ready to leave his comfortable job and home in Modiin he received a devastating rejection as his past heart problems surfaced in his record. I saw how upset he was. This was all driven by an unwavering commitment to defend his country, to protect the family and friends.

Alongside the official military mobilization, an "army" of civilians rose up to support the war effort, filling logistical gaps and boosting morale. Close to

50% of Israeli citizens formed a vast network to acquire and deliver needed items, from basic necessities like underwear and protective vests to specific military gear, which were sometimes lacking in official supply chains. Groups like "Brothers in Arms," initially a protest movement, transformed into a civilian "war room," using apps to coordinate aid requests and shipments to where they were most needed. Thousands of citizens engaged in cooking, baking, and delivering hot meals to soldiers in the field, helping to supplement rations with a "taste of home", creating improvised mobile showers in Gaza battlefields and providing a significant morale boost. Our neighbors and friends like many other groups organized barbecues for entire bases, sometimes providing the first substantial meal soldiers received in a new location. One of our close friends delivered a suitcase of hard Romanian salami from Chicago to a Negev airbase. I cherish the time when I had a chance to be a part of these events – from weekly deliveries of thousands of freshly cooked and baked, kosher certified (all military kitchens are strictly kosher) Shabbat meals to the soldiers at the front lines to equipping the mobile showers with generators or arranging weekend retreats for the weary fighters.

Following the October 7 attack, over 200,000 Israelis were displaced from communities along the Gaza (and Lebanon) borders. The cities and inland areas became temporary homes for thousands of people displaced from Gaza envelope for months. Response and generosity of the Israeli population was incredible. In our own community a number of volunteers worked tirelessly to provide living accommodations, financial help and household items small and large for displaced families. Some people, including us, opened their apartments free of charge for extended time to these people in need. After the family we hosted left and we came back to our apartment we could witness the generosity extended to our "tenants". After they returned back to their apparently large home they left behind so many gifted items – from several sets of dishes to electric appliances to bedding that we had to spend quite a bit of time to distribute, store or dispose of.

Israel dismantled Hamas's military infrastructure built over last 15 years with 500 miles of sophisticated tunnels, eliminated Hizballah's leadership, including Hassan Nasrallah, decimated Houthis in Yemen and their leadership, and destroyed Iran's nuclear ambitions. "The axis of resistance"- Iran's network of terror proxies, which they called "rings of fire" spanning from Gaza through Lebanon to Syria, Iraq and Yemen- has collapsed, at least for the immediate future. Israel demonstrated military, technological and intelligence prowess that shocked the world. Who will ever forget 5,000 beepers exploding simultaneously in the hands of Hizballah terrorists trained to rain 120,000 to 200,000 rockets and missiles on Israel.

These were all Iranian proxies and satraps with the main culprit "sitting out" direct military confrontations with Israel. In the interim Israel conducted targeted assassinations and electronic strikes against Iran's nuclear infrastructure, removing key IRGC commanders (Salami, Hajizadeh) and scientists (Feghhi).

But on April 13, 2024 (after the end of Shabbat) came the first direct Iranian attack on Israel which was a blatant attempt to disrupt my birthday celebration as we began driving for a night out in Tel Aviv's Shablul jazz club. As I left our neighborhood and stopped to get the Waze directions (GPS was blocked those days with the iPhone in our apartment showing my location mostly at Beirut airport) I received a warning message of incoming drone attack from Iran. By the time we were already in bed, the Iranians decided to greet me also with missiles. None of the 170 drones, 30 cruise and 120 ballistic missiles caused the sirens to go off in our neighborhood but made the night waiting for them and staring on the phone screen. The second Iranian assault in October killed one person, a Palestinian Arab in Jericho.

And then comes June 13 of 2025. Iran is the country 75 times larger than Israel with the ten times larger population and is over 1000 miles away with hostile counties in-between. With Iran openly declaring its readiness to destroy Israel unleashing its huge military arsenal, Israel launched a synchronized opening strike on that day combining fighter jets and on-the-ground intelligence assets hitting senior military commanders and nuclear scientists all within minutes. More than half of Iran's arsenal was gone in less than two weeks. All this might have seemed unthinkable: the distance too far, Iran's defenses too advanced, the threat of retaliation by its proxies too grave, its nuclear facilities too deeply buried, Israel's arsenal too small for success. Yet, Israel did it, pulling off an operational masterpiece. On June 22, the United States formally entered the war with "Operation Midnight Hammer," launching bunker-buster strikes on three Iranian nuclear facilities (Natanz, Fordow, and Isfahan). The result-the devastating blow dealt to Iran's nuclear and military infrastructure, severe damage of enrichment facilities, weapons depots, and command centers, setting back Iran's nuclear program by years. The hundreds of billions of dollars that the Islamic Republic spent on its nuclear program disappeared in minutes, leaving the regime and its supporters in shock. The losses extended beyond hardware. The deaths of more than 30 senior commanders, tens of scientists, and hundreds of IRGC personnel eroded the credibility of the regime, its leader, and his praetorian guard, the IRGC. The war additionally exposed the limitations of Iran's partnerships with Russia and China. Despite Tehran's rhetoric of a "Look East" strategy, Moscow and Beijing offered only symbolic support during the crisis.

Israel operation against Iran was named "*Rising Lion*" after a biblical prophecy that the people of Israel would rise like lions from adversity. Israel's June 13-24, 2025, campaign exposed critical vulnerabilities in Iran's military and internal structure, while demonstrating Israel's (and American) superior military capabilities. One of these F-16 pilots, a man we know, in his early 40's, father of 4, and Executive of a large international hi-tech company, had described to us his experience during his missions over Iran as he could clearly see the Russian supplied S-300 air-defense system without being effectively seen or bothered by them. It is not uncommon for him to land after a mission, go to a secluded space at the base and conduct his "normal" business as usual. I guess - *only in Israel.*

Iran retaliated by launching over 500 ballistic missiles and more than 1,000 suicide drones towards Israel, using the codename "Operation True Promise III". With the 90% interception rate by Israel's air defense systems, some missiles managed to struck buildings, hospitals and military targets employing in the last days of confrontation cluster munitions in populated areas, a violation of international law. The omnipresent Israeli humor produced an announcement after one of these salvos – *Iran says they hit the Mossad building in a missile strike. Luckily, nobody was there… They are all in Iran.*

Tragically, the war inflicted Israeli casualties which included 32 civilians and one off-duty soldier killed, and over 3,000 wounded.

The war did not, however, lead to the collapse of the Iranian regime or force it to abandon its nuclear and missile programs. **Wounded animals are dangerous, especially ones which cannot be tamed. As Tehran has proven of being one of them, President Trump and Prime Minister Netanyahu took the stage to neutralize that animal.**

Saturday, February 28, 2026, was a typical Shabbat morning in Yr Yamim and the most of Israel — complete soundlessness, nothing moves. As I was ready to leave for the 8:30 a.m. synagogue services, the deafening silence was replaced by an ear-piercing siren. To say that my wife and I have our hearts sinking is to say the least, as we didn't know what was happening. Was the siren warning us of already incoming missiles or something else? As I quickly turned on my phone, we learned this was the beginning of a joint American-Israeli attack on Iran. The Iranian response came about fours later with another siren during the pre-planned Shabbat lunch at our friend's home a few blocks away. It was amazing to see the life around us as we walked outside — everything and everybody acted as if nothing happened.

The world knew that after the 12-day war of 2025, Iran was extensively rebuilding it nuclear infrastructure, ballistic missile and drone arsenal as well as regional proxy network, such as Hezbollah, Houthis and others.

On December 28, 2025, Iranian streets in 200 cities were filled with protests followed by a brutal crackdown where over 30,000 protesters were killed and thousands of others were arrested and later executed. In the meantime, intelligence was reporting Iran's preparations for attacks on American Middle East assets and Israel.

A massive February 28, 2026 U.S.-Israel joint preemptive strike (Operation Epic Fury/Lion's Roar) targeted Iranian military facilities, nuclear infrastructure, and key leadership sites, killing Ayatollah Ali Khomeini along with 30 senior military commanders and 11 nuclear scientists. The timing of the initial strike was a result of real-time intelligence providing a unique opportunity during a rear leadership meeting in the underground headquarters.

This was the climax of a 47-year-old conflict involving the U.S. and Israel which began on November 4, 1979, when Iranian Muslim Revolutionaries stormed the US Embassy and Foreign Ministry in Tehran, seizing 69 Americans and holding 52 of them hostage for 444 days.

The Operation Epic Fury has documented an unprecedented military synergy and cooperation (personal, social and operational mutual respect) between the US and Israel. Israel's Air Force (IAF) has contributed to the US Air Force in the areas of Command-Control-Communications, out-of-the-box battle tactics, avionics and maintenance. They underscored the benefits derived from the frequent joint US-Israel exercises, which feature daring and innovative maneuvers conducted by the exceptionally, intensely experienced Israeli pilots, whose do-or-die attitude is a derivative of Israel's "narrow geographic waistline" and unique seven-front-threats.

Yoram Ettinger wrote about the highly intense use of combat aircraft during Epic Fury — in addition to Israel's ongoing wars against Hezbollah,

Hamas and Houthi terrorists in Lebanon, Gaza and Yemen and the pro-Ayatollah terrorists in Iraq — has highlighted the "Israeli Turnaround Time Factor," which has been a decisive force multiplier that yielded sustained high-volume strikes that outpaced Iranian initiatives. This refers to the IAF's exceptionally rapid aircraft servicing, rearming, and preparation between sorties — using fewer but seamlessly-choreographed ground crew personnel, including female technicians — which extend to 1,000-1,200 miles each way.

The relentless attempt to minimize the Ayatollah's missile launching capabilities, requires sorties that involve exceptionally intense 34+-hour missions. US combat pilots attest to the fact that the IAF operates at a pace that "shatters global standards, sometimes flying up to three daily strikes." Operating under a flying-or-eating (no sleep) policy during much of Epic Fury, the IAF managed to convert speed on the ground into more strikes in the air.

US combat pilots emphasized the fact that the IAF offensive dispatched 200 aircraft simultaneously in one night, hitting 500 targets 1,000-1,200 miles away, sometimes with no midair refueling (facilitated by the F-35's innovative external fuel tanks, developed by the IAF and Lockheed-Martin), and returning without a single collision/loss. The IAF has also revolutionized the air force's battle tactics through the Israeli-upgraded F-35, which is equipped with sensor fusion, electronic warfare, and data-sharing capabilities, which allows other combat aircraft to hit targets without exposing themselves as much.

The United States demonstrated overwhelming military superiority, employing two giant aircraft strike groups, 13,000 aircraft, including 1800 fighter jets with stealth F-22 and F-35 and B2 and B52 bombers among them — and this is only 10% of US Naval power. And who can forget the ability to shown by high-precision, awe-inspiring missions to rescue the American F-15 crew from the Iranian jaws.

While Iran tried to hijack the world's oil shipping route through Hormuz Strait, the European countries and NATO members, the same countries which depend on that oil, refused to join the US in securing this area, showing their cowardly faces.

As Hizballah renewed its military operations against Israel at Iran's request, Israel had to mobilize 300,000 sons and daughters to defend its northern communities as well as other parts of Israel from Hizballah rocket and ant-tank fire. And again, young people were ready to defend their country with unprecedented enthusiasm. Our friends' five grandsons and granddaughters, three of them students and young parents with no obligation to serve, fought the army offices to be accepted and joined different branches of the armed forces.

The United States Armed Forces had thirteen (13) troops killed and nearly 400 wounded by mid-April of 2026 during Operation Epic Fury, most of them while stationed on American bases in Gulf countries that had been subjected to Iranian missiles and drones. Bombing cities and oil facilities in UAE, Kuwait, Saudi Arabia, Qatar and even Turkey was probably a huge strategic miscalculation of the Iranian regime.

On Passover Eve (Erev Pesach) of 2026, our Rabbi Mendel Wuensch wrote in his weekly message: *"Many Israelis (for the past three years) and Americans (for the past seven weeks) are frustrated with the lack of a "knockout blow" against the Iranian axis. Even the spectacular achievements of the beeper-and-pager attacks against Hizballah, of the opening decapitation of the Twelve Day War, and of the beginning of this war don't have that kind of finality. This victory doesn't feel complete. We fought, we prevailed, and yet something inside us knows the accounting isn't fully settled. There is relief, yes. There is gratitude, yes. But there is also grief, and confusion, and a quiet voice asking: why didn't it end cleaner?"*

As Zvika Klein recently wrote: not every war can be the Six Day War of 1967. At the same time, military victory can change regional maps, turn foes into friends, and end decade-long conflicts.

Ronald Reagan did not tear down the Berlin Wall when he demanded it from Gorbachev on June 12, 1987. He made it impossible to maintain. The pressure made the Soviet system unsustainable, and 29 months later on November 10, 1989, the people of East and West Berlin were dancing together on top of the Wall.

Trump and Netanyahu did not tear down the Islamic Republic and its Revolutionary Guard ... yet. But, they made it impossible to maintain.

Whether the Iranian walls will actually fall depends on what happens inside Iran, and on whether the diplomacy is executed with the same nerve as the war.

The operation was a success. The recovery is someone else's fight.

Resilience

As Iranian ballistic missile barrages had become the new nightly normal across Israel since June 13, 2025, Israelis were forced to seek shelters wherever

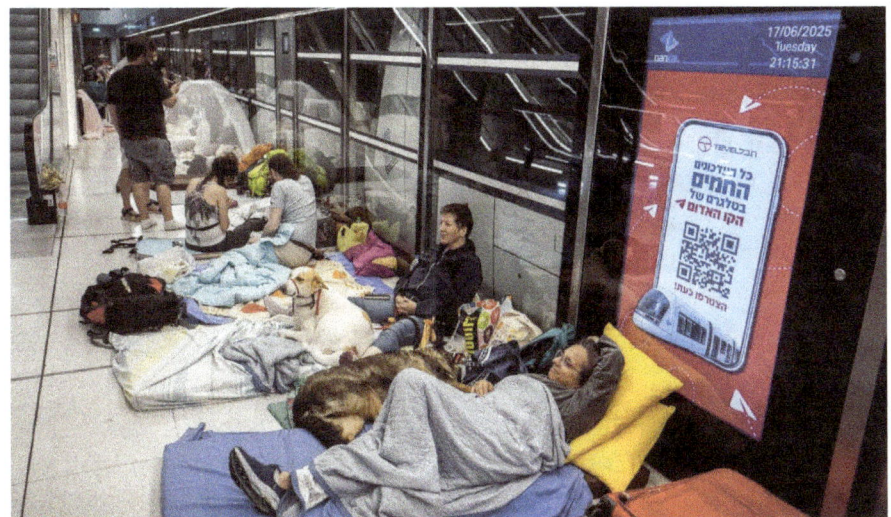

People take shelter in an underground light rail station in Tel Aviv during ongoing missile attacks from Iran, June 17, 2025.

they were available. Every building constructed since 1992 is required to have a safe room (mamad) like our apartment in Yr Yamim - but plenty of people live in apartments and houses without them. When the air-raid sirens go off, they have to run to public shelters. From subway stations to underground parking garages, residents were transforming public spaces into improvised shelters - and unlikely communities. Like everybody around us, we were used to be glued to the smartphone, scanning for alerts. Notifications tell you when to stay near a shelter, when you have 10 minutes or 90 seconds, or sometimes less to reach safety.

Polina Fradkin wrote a letter that I think should provide the reader with a feeling of the bomb shelter experience during the rain of Iranian missiles. A 30-year-old Tel Aviv resident was born in near-Siberian Russia and raised in the suburban Michigan, describes how the siren went off in the middle of Shabbat dinner which she hosted for her friends. With grabbed wine glasses and filed into her bedroom, which is a safety room (Mamad), they all sat and joked about being the whole Israel in a nutshell: two young religious women chanting psalms; a married gay couple cracking jokes about whether the missiles would interfere with their Pride plans; a marine biologist home for the weekend from reserve service in Gaza; teenage girl; an American tourist, and her immigrant fiancé, who moved to Israel to escape Maduro socialist dictatorship. The 12 of them were in the safe room for about an hour and a half with a friend providing periodic news updates to those, including herself, whose phones were shut off for Shabbat. They held their breath while being told how many and where missiles had fallen and how many people were injured. At one point, someone had a panic attack, other meditated. One of the religious girls was praying naming out loud the Jewish tzaddikim, "holy people," such as Rabbi Nachman of Breslov and the Lubavitch Rebbe. Her secular friends contributed their own - Sheldon Adelson and Amy Winehouse. They made L'Chaims (toasts to life), told stories, prayed, and laughed and at some point, all sang "Hatikvah" ("The Hope") - Israel's national anthem.

She tells her readers that when Israel is deep into an all-out, existential war—about what life is like here, to show what the Jewish people have built, and why this place—this nation—is worth defending. The Talmud saying: *"All of Israel is responsible for one another"* is an explanation why, the moment a single lands here, everyone and their mother tries to match her/him with their single, eligible relative, why trust is built-in to Israeli society, how when she stopped after a hike at 1 a.m. at the Negev gas station, a woman parked next to her and asked if we could keep an eye on her five sleeping kids while she went to the bathroom. That responsibility is also why, in Israel, your work will take care of you beyond paying your salary, why the CEO of her small private company sent an email offering a stipend to anyone who needs to rent an Airbnb with a safe room, why the COO ended the call by reminding the company: "We are the Jewish nation and we will survive anything". When she went to see one of the missile-impact sites in Tel Aviv - a printing shop known as "the print shop next to the sex shop" she found both shops with windows smashed and boarded up, and about 50 yards down the street from the impact site, she ran into friends, sitting at a cafe that was slammed with customers, making origami swans and laughing at the oddity of their lives right now. As Polina writes - Life in Israel is life at its best. It's miraculous, full of purpose, full of people willing not only to defend but celebrate with every guest invited to Shabbat dinner, every Frisbee thrown on the beach, every marriage contract signed and every child born.

The final word should go to Zohara, a young friend of Polina with whom she talked while waiting for the light rail. The 8-year old girl was going to school (naturally) without adult supervision and asked a thousand questions about the war before saying *"America is the strongest country in the world, physically,"* adding, *"Israel is the strongest country in the world spiritually."*

Little Zohara explained why life in Israel is worth defending—and why Polina's grandparents have stopped asking if she is ever planning on moving home. *"They know she is already there...".*

People, like my widow cousin, who live in older buildings with shelters located in the basement had own indelible experiences. She told me ...you keep your shoes next to your bed, never lock your building door, so that strangers caught in the street can take cover. You run to the underground shelter where an intimacy takes shape, it becomes something more than protection — a community of the strangest sort. When the explosions of missiles and interceptors are heard overhead, you begin to truly see the people whom you'd shared an elevator with, in silence.

A neighbor is no longer just the guy who nods; he's a father of two, with strong political views different from mine. You find out who has snacks, who panics or is stoic, and who insists on tuning up the radio to hear every report. Left, Right, religious, secular, Ashkenazi, Mizrahi, immigrant, native-born – the sirens flatten the social structure. Everyone is equal under threat. In the end, the experience confirms the cliché about Israel: It is a land of almost unbelievable contradictions and resilience, which doesn't surface loud or heroic. It's understated, practiced, shows up in flip-flops and pajamas, with a thermos in one hand and a dog leash in the other.

When the all-clear notification arrives and everyone shuffles out, someone always says the same words, taking it in turns to say what's on everybody's mind: *"See you in a few hours! Take care."* And my cousin admitted to me recently — she is missing those nightly pajama comradery "parties" full of stories, gossips and shared homemade goodies.

And then were Houthis sending their ballistic missiles and drones since October 2023 and resuming the attacks after the 12-day war with the most of them intercepted by Israeli air defense systems. Well aware of their inability to penetrate the Israeli skies and inflict physical damage, Houthi rebels concentrated on the disrupting the life routine through the alerts and siren warnings. The sirens were coming sporadically-once or several times a week, mostly in the middle of the night or during morning and evening rush hours when people sleep, parents take children to or from the childcare centers and people travel to and from schools and work. As example, my phone still has stored alerts received at 2:53, 4:09, 5:02, 6:18, 8:01, 9:17, 10:49 and 11:50 am, as well as 1:01, 5:55 and 7:30 pm.

Israelis, even children, got used to what became almost a routine. During one of our visits to a family in Jerusalem our dinner was interrupted by an alert of incoming Houthi rocket followed a minute later by a siren. It was amazing to see all four kids from age of 4 to 12 getting up and orderly descending to a lower floor apartment's shelter where we all spent about 10 minutes playing the prepositioned games.

After February 28, 2026, and, not being able to hit military targets or simultaneously fire large salvos, Iran concentrated their ballistic missile fire, often using cluster bombs, on major dense population centers such as Tel Aviv, Jerusalem, Bnei Brak, Bet Shemesh where any remnant of an intercepted missile had a chance to hit a building. Firing one or two missiles with a total of about 500 ballistic munitions was causing multiple warnings and sirens sending people to the shelters throughout days and nights. Many older neighborhoods had no apartment mamads or elevators, so there was a tremendous stress on families with children, seniors with limited mobility and everybody else when the alert or siren sounded.

During the 40 days of the war a total of approximately 40 Israeli civilians and military personnel were killed and about 8,000 injured, some critically, by ballistic missiles and drones. Reports indicate between 6,295 and 9,000 Israelis were forced to leave their homes. Over 31,000 residential buildings in Israel sustained damage during the conflict. The Israel Tax Authority received 30,000–36,465 claims for damage to structures, vehicles, and personal property. As of late March 2026, thousands remained in government-funded hotels in cities like Eilat, as many homes were rendered uninhabitable by direct missile strikes.

The war has also demonstrated to the Israeli population again and again that adhering to the instructions of the Home Front Command during the warnings and sirens is a life saver. Unfortunately, a few people fell victim to their own complacency and even recklessness — often the result of "siren fatigue" as nine out of 10 warnings and sirens were followed shortly by a message of "the event is over".

People wonder may what it says about a society that must brace for war with such frequency. How do you build normalcy on top of emergency? With

Iranian salvos and Houthis attacks our life in Israel was and is more than the news. It is the encyclopedia of extraordinary true stories all around us. Living here means accepting unpredictability, balancing daily routines with sudden disruption. The people adapt quickly - knowing how to shelter, relying on family and friends and strangers, and keeping hope for peace alive.

Two Years Later

The astonishing changes since the first publication of this book in the fall of 2023 is the why I'm attempting this edition to reflect those changes, some of which I have never expected to see, especially in the United States.

While Israeli Jews were under rocket attack, Jews around the world came under attack not fire of rockets and guns but tsunami of hatred. For many Jews outside Israel, this was first time when they really grasped that being Jewish can be dangerous again. They are seeing old prejudices reborn with frightening speed and sophistication. They see "never again" becoming again. The mask has slipped from the face of the world of liberal democracies. There is no going back to October 6, 2023. The genie is out of the bottle, and it will not return. We have seen the ease with which the world condemns Israel for defending itself, we have seen how truth can be distorted until the victim is blamed for the crime. The haters have been emboldened. The war for Jews and for Israel is never truly over. It seems that Israel will forever have to justify and fight for her right to exist, the same right taken for granted by every other people on Earth.

As Iranian-French filmmaker Raghu Kondori wrote: *During the Cold War, ideological solidarities were defined by stark lines of allegiance and opposition. Today, a different, far less coherent convergence is emerging: segments of the American and other Western left have found themselves aligned with radical Islamist movements.*

This partnership does not stem from shared values but from shared adversaries. Progressive activists still champion sexual freedom, secularism, and individual autonomy, while Islamist groups advocate strict Shari'a law and death to homosexuals. So, the hate of Jews is an effective bridge between the disparate movements built on historical ignorance and shared antagonisms: anti-imperialism and anti-Semitism. Israel, with its democratic institutions and pluralistic society became a symbol of Western power and perceived injustice. It is mindboggling to see the LGBTQ activists enthusiastically supporting movements and countries in which they would rotten in jail or simply killed under Shari'a law. As someone said – chicken vote for FKC.

The statement that Israel has done very little wrong in Gaza will make the usual candidates foam at the mouth, but it is the truth. I think the opposition leader Yair Lapid said it best in his greeting of President Trump in the Knesset session: "*You were misled. There was no genocide. There was no deliberate starvation. The truth is that there was an army fighting under the most complex conditions against those who sent their own children to die and used them as human shields. They sold you the absurd notion that radical Islam represents a liberal value. But there is good and evil in this world — and when you stand with radical Islam, you stand with evil. When you stand with Israel, you stand with good.*"

The IDF has undertaken unprecedented measures to protect civilians: warning leaflets, phone calls, text messages, humanitarian corridors, and pauses in fighting. There is no precedent in modern warfare for this level of effort, especially in a combat environment like Gaza, where the civilians cannot flee and Hamas is set to maximize the numbers killed.

Most Israelis, and Jews, generally, view the deaths of innocents, especially children, the way Golda Meir did: "*We can forgive the Arabs for killing our children. We cannot forgive them for forcing us to kill their children. We will only have peace with the Arabs when they love their children more than they hate us.*"

The "deliberate starvation" narrative was the most grotesque example. UN officials claimed a famine stalked Gaza, yet food aid continued to flow in daily. No genocidal army ever imported 14,125 tons of aid in one weak alone or deployed soldiers, including relatives of mine, risking and losing their lives, to protect humanitarian convoys. And no genocidal army ever had own lawyers accessing military targets or officers aborting missions to minimize civilian damage.

As an American presidential historian Gil Troy wrote – the newly diluted definition of genocide applies to any military conflict that kills civilians. By these standards, anyone marking Lincoln's birthday celebrates the "genocide" of 50,000 civilians during the Civil War, anyone honoring WWII veterans salutes "genociders" given two to four million German and Japanese civilians killed. And any Israel critic over 30 who remained silent as America killed over 940,000 civilians during the justified post-9/11 wars was complicit in their own country's "genocide".

Hamas and his Jihadi partners understand the West better than the West understands itself. Its strategy is not only military as they know it cannot defeat the IDF head-on. As Harley Lippman wrote, Hamas entered the battlefield with a sophisticated information strategy. It weaponized images of suffering, positioned military sites within schools, hospitals, mosques and other civilian areas, and ensured cameras would capture the aftermath. It is exploiting Palestinian suffering as a weapon, flooding the media with images, and distorting reality until Israel is portrayed as the aggressor and Hamas as the victim. One child's body on camera outweighs a hundred Hamas fighters off-screen, even if this body of a genetically sick child and not of a starvation victim. Hamas has turned death into PR, and the world swallows it whole.

After Israel left Gaza 20 years ago, residents themselves overwhelmingly voted in Hamas. On October 7, 2023 the "civilians" actively participated in October 7 massacre, hiding rocket launchers in their homes, weapons in children blankets and cribs, digging and supplying the terror tunnels, and engaging in activities that make them combatants. Now we know that many hostages were kept, humiliated and sexually abused in civilian homes, including families of doctors of Gaza hospitals. Many combatants were women, and many are 15-year-olds who fired rockets and shut guns.

We know about a number of conscientious Germans who were saving Jews during WWII, but we know Not a Single Gaza resident who helped Israel with an information about the whereabouts of the hostages! Not a single one! In Gaza there is a hardly separation between civilians and combatants. Israel should have all the rights to treat Hamas, Islamic Jihad and Hizballah the way the Allies treated the Nazis and the imperial Japanese. These terrorists must be totally defeated, and only then should their cities be rebuilt, as German and Japanese cities were. Just as peace wouldn't have been possible in 1945 if the Nazis and imperial Japanese were allowed to survive and remain in control, so too Hamas and Islamic Jihad must not be allowed to survive.

Bombing of Gaza was necessary just like German and Japanese towns and cities, to stop aggression. President Harry Truman ordered the atomic bombing of Hiroshima and Nagasaki being fully aware of the civilian casualties to deter the Japanese from further aggression. History has generally not condemned the Allies for their successful strategy in ending the war, though the civilian deaths they caused were intended rather than collateral. Yet Israel is being condemned despite its extraordinary efforts to reduce civilian casualties.

"Israel Derangement Syndrome" is a spreading sickness, and it is fully metastasized across the West. What we are seeing is not "criticism of Israel". It is a new, globalized anti-Semitism. When Israeli athletes are shunned, when Jewish students are harassed on campuses, when fences are smeared on synagogues and Jewish facilities, when kosher restaurants are vandalized from Paris, France to Jackson, Mississippi-it is not about Gaza. It is about Jews.

Hamas and Hizballah were defeated despite UK's prime minister Keir Starmer, French president Emmanuel Macron, Canada's prime minister Mark Carney and Australia's prime minister Anthony Albanese, who have been so dishonorably doing to ensure that Israel lost this desperate war of survival. And what about Spain's Prime Minister Pedro Sánchez utterly unhinged wishing his country had nuclear weapons to use against Israel. The West's attack on Israel and the Jews can only be explained by its attack on its own core values and identity.

For the past two years, they and others with a similar world-view are desperately trying to appease a Muslim population that is threatening their own countries no less than Israel. Too many western "progressives" are determined to blame Jews and Israel for their own demise and gradual extermination.

Eight Front

The fight for Israel's survival extends beyond the physical battlefield. The eighth and perhaps most dangerous front (besides Hamas, Hizballah, Iran, Houthis, Lebanon, Syria and Iraqui KH) is the Media, the source of the most information consumed by the public, and especially by the young people. Today, many kids seen by Jihadists as an easy prey as they raised in the families with no Jewish or Christian traditions and values, with no knowledge of history and indoctrinated by leftist ideas of their prestigious school faculties. And when one flips through the pages of the (left's Bible) New York Times, or The Washington Post, or tune into CNN or the BBC, you would think Israel woke up one morning and decided to go on a bombing spree for sport. For many young Americans-the future voters, journalists, and policymakers, Israel's story no longer resonates as one of people's rebirth and resilience but of domination. The Pew data showing 61% of young adults sympathizing more with Palestinians is not passing fluctuation; it signals a possible long-term realignment.

But being a Jew means to be an eternal optimist and see the glass have full. The horrors of October 7 created an opportunity. Across the United States, Jews who had drifted away from their identity came rushing back. As Adam Milstein observes, the "October 8 Jews" rediscovered their Jewish identity and connection to Israel in the face of an existential threat. Thirty-one (31) percent of American Jews (according to UJA-NY 2025 study) are more engaged in Jewish life than before the attack. In Israel, on battlefields we have seen thousands of secular soldiers, who probably never visited a synagogue, putting on tefillin and prayer shawls while joining their comrades in prayers. We also read and I personally met a former hostage, secular young lady, who kept Shabbat and laws of kashrut while in Hamas captivity.

According even to the left-leaning The Jerusalem Post Israel has become more conservative, more right-wing, more religious, and more traditional since October 7. The Jewish People Policy Institute found that 27% of Jewish respondents observe more traditions since the war, rising to 33% among those under 25. Faith in G-d increased among 28% of Jewish respondents and 35% of young Jews. The hard Right grew from 11% before October 7 to 19%. The Pew Research Center found that only 21% of Israeli adults now believe Israel and a Palestinian state can coexist peacefully, the lowest figure since 2013.

A Midgam poll in February found that 75% of first-time Israeli voters identify as right-wing. People in Tel Aviv or Herzliya Pituah, the most secular and left-wing addresses in the country, are telling about their own children or their neighbors' children who started keeping kosher or observing Shabbat. Parents mention, sometimes in disbelief, that their son or daughter will be voting for Netanyahu while they are voting for Yair Golan.

Israel has been successful in its regional relationships, superpower backing, and the resilience of its citizenry—the areas that are critical to her ability to remain powerful at home and abroad. Despite the contempt directed on Israel in Arabic media during the Gaza war, not one of the five Arab states with ties to Israel—Egypt, Jordan, United Arab Emirates, Bahrain, and Morocco—broke ties. Moreover, Jordan and Saudi Arabia were part of the US-led coalition working with Israel to thwart the 300 projectiles Iran launched on April 13-14, even if none of these Arab countries issued a statement confirming their participation in the effort. During October 2024 strike, in which an estimated 200 ballistic missiles were fired at Israel from Iran, Jordan issued a public statement saying they were part of the effort to ensure Iranian missiles did not enter its airspace.

The anti-Semitism and radical Islamization are not problems for Jews alone. They endanger all Americans, as well as French, British and others as undermining the moral foundations of societies. United Arab Emirates (UAE), being well aware of the dangers of Jihadi propaganda, just announced that it will stop financing the education of its citizens in the British schools and universities to prevent their radicalization.

In 2019 a former UN Rapporteur Ahmed Shaheed described Anti-Semitism as the canary in the coalmine of global hatred and Deborah Lipstadt called it a canary in the coal mine of democracy.

History has shown that what begins with the Jews never ends with the Jews. The Islamo-Leftist alliance that targets Jews today has a broader aim; its main target is dismantling of the Western civilization. Look at the bombings of Christmas markets in Germany and cancellation in December 2025 of what would be 60th annual Christmas Concert at Champs-Elysees in Paris out of concern of terrorist (read Islamic) attack.

As Israel is now emerging from a long nightmare, Western nations are descending into theirs — fruits of self-inflicted "war on itself," failing defend their core principles and own culture.

Qatar

We live through a global civilizational conflict between the Free World and the forces of Militant Islamism, like the Muslim Brotherhood, a movement that seeks not coexistence, but domination.

Qatar, much disliked by UAE and Saudis, has become the leading global patron of the Muslim Brotherhood with a strategical goal of reshaping societies from within. The Muslim Brotherhood and its affiliates have mastered the art of slow infiltration, cultural manipulation, and institutional takeover. Their weapon is not the suicide belt but the ballot box with the Muslim voter turnout often *doubling the average national levels, securing seats in municipalities and other governing bodies.*

Qatar continues to conduct one of the most extensive foreign influence operations in modern history funneling estimated at up to a trillion dollars, into Western universities, research centers, media and political networks. The Muslim Students Association (MSA) — founded by Muslim Brotherhood activists operates on over 600 of US campuses, the MSA works closely with Students for Justice in Palestine (SJP). Just as an example of Qatar's pouring extraordinary sums into elite American institutions:

Cornell University: Over $10 billion in total funding for its Doha medical school, averaging $156 million annually since 2012.

Georgetown University: More than $1 billion, heavily influencing Middle East studies and diplomatic training programs.

Texas A&M University: $1.3 billion, including hundreds of research projects - at least 58 with potential dual-use military applications.

But the infiltration doesn't stop there – it spreads even to K-12 schools. Qatar Foundation International (QFI), Doha's US affiliate, has penetrated American K-12 schools. In one notable incident, a QFI-sponsored classroom map replaced Israel with "Palestine" in a Brooklyn public school. QFI's curriculum material and grants give Qatar access to the political formation of American children. Qatar's funding is not benign philanthropy; it is a strategic investment in Islamist soft power, with far-reaching consequences for the United States, Asia, Europe, and beyond.

Partisan Issue

Israel is not becoming a partisan issue as I wrote previously. Since October 7, 2023 Israel now *is* a partisan issue.

A Gallup poll in earlier of 2025 found that Israel's support among Democrats has collapsed to just 7%. That is a political earthquake. According to the Times/Sienna poll in September of 2025, only 12% of Democrats say they sympathize more with Israelis than Palestinians; 54% say the reverse. Among 18 to 29-year-olds, 19% side with Israel, 61% with the Palestinians. Fully 73% of Democrats oppose further military or economic aid to Israel, compared to 20% of Republicans.

As a famous life-long Democrat Alan Dershowitz wrote, "The Democratic Party has become the most anti-Israel party in U.S. history. In April of 2026 all but seven Senate Democrats voted for an arms embargo against the Jewish state, and an avowed enemy of Israel, Abdul El-Sayed, is gaining ground in the Democratic campaign for U.S. senator from Michigan. There is no denying that the hard left, anti-Israel wing of the Democratic Party has moved from the fringe to the mainstream. Until recently there was an age gap, with younger voters more strongly opposing Israel, but recent polls suggest that the trend now includes Democrats of all ages. Republicans have their own antisemitic fringe, but for now it remains a fringe."

Herb Keinon wrote, when 47 Democratic representatives signed a letter urging recognition of a Palestinian State, this was not and isolated gesture. This is a sign that supporting Israel is no longer the safe political choice for an elected official in America and standing with Israel may in some districts even be a liability. The Democrats are deeply in debt to their anti-Israel, anti-Jewish far-left and growing Muslim population in major cities likely making them enemies of Israel for the foreseeable future.

In alarmingly large and increasing numbers we see support among young and not so young Democrats of the extremist left-wing positions over private wealth, privileging "oppressed" groups and punishing their perceived oppressors — of which Israel and the Jews are fingered as principal villains. These supporters applaud its obsessive hatred of Israel which they regard as "moral clarity".

We see the results of these historical shifts in the Capitol of Capitalism and center of American Jewish life electing a vindictive Communist Islamist Mamdani as its Mayor. Do people in the largest American city still believe in socialist paradise? As Milton Friedman wrote back in 2013 *"The only cases in which the masses have escaped from grinding poverty in recorded history are where they have had capitalism and largely free trade. If you want to know where the masses are worst off, it's exactly in the kind of societies that depart from that."*

The politics of left-wing vengeance never take into consideration the effects of their policy. It doesn't matter whether defunding the police gets more black people killed or whether supporting Hamas dooms Gazans. It doesn't matter whether a taxing the "rich" helps or hurts the city like New York. So, in the same city where UnitedHealthcare CEO Brian Thompson was shot and killed by a radical activist less than two years ago, the new radical mayor targets a hedge fund CEO as a villain who's ripping off the little guy. And at almost exactly the same time, we've got Mamdani's friend and supporter Hasan Piker appearing on a *New York Times* podcast talking about revolutionary violence as it applies to CEOs committing "social murder."

And here comes one of other reasons which compelled me to edit the first edition of this book.

While support of Israel has long been a hallmark of the Republican party, a June 2025 poll also found that sympathy for Israelis has dropped within GOP over the previous year. A small fraction of isolationists, conspiracy-theorist, antisemitic crazies has grown and become vociferous thanks to social media in the last two years.

The greatest shock of all to me personally was the person I admired for her standing on racial issues and whom I quoted in my previous book edition. After the October 7 Hamas attack, Candace Owens espoused increasingly explicit anti-Zionist and antisemitic views, calling Israel a "cult nation" and spread conspiracy theories about the conflict, suggesting Israel forces Muslims into segregated quarters. After her separation from mainstream conservative platforms as well YouTube, and the establishment of her own independent media presence, she continues to spew bigotry. She has become the unhinged conspiracist repeatedly insinuating that a "small ring" of Jewish people in Hollywood and Washington, D.C., control the media and other aspects of public life in a "sinister" fashion. In a July 2024 podcast episode, Owens questioned mainstream Holocaust narratives, referring to historical accounts of Nazi medical experiments by Josef Mengele as "bizarre propaganda" and an "absolute lie", also saying Adolf Hitler "just wanted to make Germany great". She liked a social media post asking a prominent rabbi if he was "drunk on Christian blood again," a reference to the centuries-old antisemitic blood libel accusation. In a December 2025 podcast, she held up an English copy of *Der Talmudjude* ("The Talmudic Jew"), a virulently anti-Jewish German book from the 19th century, and encouraged viewers to read what the Talmud says about non-Jews.

In "recognition" of these statements and actions, the U.S.-based advocacy group StopAntisemitism named Candace Owens their *"Anti-Semite of the Year" for 2024.*

The same "prestigious *Anti-Semite of the Year"* was awarded to Tucker Carlson, who had been ousted from Fox News earlier in 2023, and uses his independent online platform, "Tucker on X," to express a critical stance regarding Israel's military response and U.S. support for it. This position has been a major point of contention within conservative circles. Concern over Carlson's repeated platforming and promotion of vicious anti-Semites, Israel-haters and Holocaust revisionists exploded when he hosted Fuentes on his podcast expressing a mutual love. Fuentes has repeatedly said that Adolf Hitler was "awesome and cool," and has called for the "annihilation" of perfidious Jews" and others "when we take power". Carlson is also leading the attempt to peel away Israel's principal source of support in America—Evangelical Christians. In an attack on Christian Zionists, such as a Senator Ted Cruz (R-Texas) and the US ambassador to Israel, Mike Huckabee, Carlson claimed that they had been seized by a "brain virus" because they support Israel, even though they aren't Jews. Ted Cruz has been warning that if conservatives-and Republicans-don't call out this poison in their own ranks before it corrupts more young minds, the right and America are entering dangerous territory.

And here another victim of some twisted minds. Winston Churchill who has long been hated by the left, blamed for opposing socialism and communism, breaking Britain's general strike of 1926, supporting the British Empire and so on, lately became a target of a new hostile strain of Churchill-hatred broken out on the ultraright on both sides of the Atlantic, where he is blamed for a quite different set of supposed crimes. The American podcaster Darryl Cooper, who has never written a history book but whom Tucker Carlson calls "America's most honest historian", has claimed that Churchill was the "chief villain" of World War II. Cooper's remarks on the Tucker Carlson show led the Holocaust-denying podcaster Jake Shields to conduct a poll on X asking "who was the **biggest villain of WWII**." Sadly, among his almost 136,000 respondents, 40.3% gave that distinction to Churchill, with Stalin at 25.9% narrowly beating Hitler at 25.3%.

Are you shaking your head? These were not Hitler or even Stalin sharing the credit for 50 million graves?!

Is Israel Beneficiary or Benefactor of the US —
The answer is BOTH

Israel's role in the uniquely intense use of advanced US military systems is shown on the previous pages of this book. Here are some developments since the 2023 publication.

First, Israel's integration into the US regional military command for the Middle East, CENTCOM, is a game changer. Geographically, Israel naturally belongs under the Central Command, CENTCOM, with an area of responsibility covering the broader Middle East. But for decades Israel was placed under the European Command, EUCOM for political reasons since Arab states opposed normalization with Israel and refused to be grouped with it under the same command. No more such objection. As Eitan Shamir of Bar-Ilan University writes - It is not a formal alliance, yet provides many of the advantages of a defense treaty: stronger deterrence, coordinated defense with other US allies in the region, deeper strategic depth, and the capacity for joint action, while maintaining Israel's freedom of action. Israel thus became an official component of the regional security architecture that the United States had been building in the Middle East, designed to counter Iran through shared intelligence, integrated air defense, maritime cooperation, and coordinated operational planning.

For decades, Israel grappled with the question of whether or not to pursue a formal defense treaty with the United States. Successive Israeli governments hesitated out of concern of the potential loss of autonomy and fear that a treaty would restrict Israel's freedom of action, requiring American approval for sensitive military operations that often require quick responses. The current arrangement creates a "hybrid model" in which Israel enjoys the strategic advantages of quasi-alliance integration while retaining independent decision-making. Still, it was only after Hamas's surprise attack of October 7, 2023 that the full meaning of Israel's integration into CENTCOM became clear. The US responded with a rapid, large-scale deployment: aircraft carriers, missile defense ships, electronic warfare aircraft, and enhanced intelligence assets. In effect, the US provided Israel with a strategic umbrella that reduced the likelihood of a northern escalation and signaled unmistakable deterrence toward Iran and Hezbollah. The most dramatic development took place in the context of Iran's missile and drone attacks on Israel in 2024 and 2025. For the first time, CENTCOM activated the emerging regional defensive network. US aircraft intercepted dozens of drones over Iraq and the Red Sea; American, British, and French ships shot down cruise missiles; Jordan, Saudi Arabia, and the UAE provided air corridors and shared tactical intelligence; Israel synchronized its Iron Dome, David's Sling, and Arrow systems with US command elements. The result was an unprecedented multinational defensive effort that largely neutralized what could have been devastating strikes.

During 2023-2025 wars with Hamas, Hizballah, Houthis and especially Iran, Israel enhanced the capabilities of American and own defense systems. Moreover, it has exposed the vulnerabilities of Chinese and Russian military systems, which are deployed throughout the globe; thus, highlighting the superiority of US and Israeli military systems in the global market. According to the Ambassador Yoram Ettinger, this has yielded mega billions of dollars of US exports, expanding the US employment base (2.5 million people employed by the US defense and aerospace industries), generating billions of dollars of corporate and individual income tax revenues, while serving as the leading battle tactics and training innovation center for the US Armed Forces (e.g., maneuvering combat aircraft, overhauling engines of combat aircraft, facing car bombs, suicide bombers and IEDs, hostage rescue, precision raids).

The export appeal of the US-made F-35, F-16 and F-15 has been significantly boosted by the Israeli Air Force's combat track record, which has demonstrated the superiority of the US-made aircraft, as well as their precision strikes capabilities, advanced avionics, sensors, electronic warfare systems and deep penetration missions. The 50-55-year-old F-15s and F-16s have remained in high demand, globally, due to Israel's sustained battle-tested performance, which has systematically upgraded their capabilities. Lockheed-Martin has benefitted from the recent increased export of the F-16 (Turkey, Denmark, Bulgaria, Romania, Bahrain, Morocco, Jordan, Slovakia, Taiwan and possibly Ukraine) and the F-35 (UK, Canada, Germany, Italy, Finland, Switzerland the Netherlands, Norway, Australia, Japan, South Korea, Singapore, Denmark, Greece, Romania, Poland and Belgium). Additionally, Boeing exports the F-15 to Saudi Arabia, Egypt, Japan, South Korea, Singapore, Qatar, Indonesia, etc.

The uniquely intense Israeli experience in multiple combat theatres and over many thousands of hours has upgraded and highlighted the F-35's combat effectiveness. It has dramatically enhanced the F-35's reliability, maintainability, electronic warfare, weapons integration, countermeasures and overall survivability.

In 2025, Lockheed-Martin reported an F-35 backlog of $173–$179 billion. It worth noting, in 2018, Israel was the first country to use the F-35 operationally, when top experts doomed the F-35 to failure. But, the Israeli battle-tested laboratory, jointly with Lockheed-Martin, overcame critical technical (software) and mechanical (hardware) glitches, transforming the F-35 from the bane of a high-risk venture to a mega-billion-dollar boon. Over 1,200 F-35s have been exported since 2019, accompanied by an F-35-related 35% expanded workforce, reaching 290,000 employees and subcontractors.

The last two years also demonstrated the growing global demand for Israeli defense technology, particularly in air defense and unmanned aerial vehicles (drones). In 2024 and 2025, major buyers of it included Germany, the United Arab Emirates (UAE), Romania, Serbia, and India. Israel's military exports reached a record high of $14.8 billion in 2024, partly due to the demand for "battle tested" systems. Key recent purchases include:

Germany signed a $6.5 billion deal for the Israeli Arrow 3 air defense system and other equipment, a deal approved by the US because it was jointly developed. Germany has also purchased Spike anti-tank missiles, targeting pods for its Eurofighter jets, and components for its naval frigates from Israeli-linked companies.

The United Arab Emirates (UAE) was the secret buyer in a $2.3 billion arms deal, and has invested in Israeli anti-drone technology companies since the normalization of ties in the Abraham Accords.

Romania purchased Spyder air defense systems for $2.2 billion.

Serbia has a deal in place to buy drones and long-range rockets worth $1.6 billion from the Israeli defense manufacturer Elbit Systems.

India continues to be Israel's largest arms market and has produced Hermes 900 drones for the Israeli military through a joint venture with Elbit Systems. Documents also revealed that India exported rockets and explosives to Israel amid the Gaza war.

Slovakia signed a $583 million deal to purchase the Israeli Barak air defense system.

Jew-Hatred. How to solve it? You don't.

Jew-hatred exists because Jews exist. Anti-Semitism and philo-Semitism are two sides of the same coin; the Jews inspire both greater hate *and* admiration precisely because we are the inheritors of G-d's covenant and because of our contribution to the Western civilization. Jews must accept that being unapologetically Jewish will inspire more hatred—but will also command the respect of the righteous non-Jews. The only alternative is to shed our Jewishness, which I hope, is no option at all for you, my dear reader.

So why the fixation on my Jewish heritage and Israel itself? Although growing up and through all my life I always felt my Jewishness through being strongly attracted to the Jewish history, religious traditions, culture, in all things called *Yiddishkeit*. But what occupies my Jewish conscience the most—

is Israel, her security, life and achievements of her people and their increasing role within the Jewish Peoplehood. After all, the majority of the world Jewish population today lives in Israel. As the years went by, I began to feel more and more that, as a Jew, I should distinguish between the *sanctuary* and *homeland*, and whereas America has provided me and millions of my brethren with the most welcomed and comfortable sanctuary, the homeland is perhaps less comfortable, more demanding but miraculous Land of Israel. Indeed, the people of Israel (just like all Jews throughout our history) is often divided and always argumentative but bound in a common fate. Because, as former Chief Rabbi of Great Britain, Lord Jonathan Saks *zt"l* said…"It was the sense of family that kept Jews linked in a web of mutual obligation despite the fact that they were scattered across the world…. Argue, with your friend and tomorrow he may no longer be your friend, but argue with your brother and tomorrow he is still your brother…".

Israel is a beacon of Democracy in the Middle East—bright and brilliant and standing alone—the most faithful and grateful American ally anywhere in the world. And yet in the midst of this it is still a nation in peril, ever in a struggle for its survival to this very day. Surrounded by neighbor nations that are mandated by charter to annihilate all it stands for and raze it to the ground, it has since its inception been aware that its survival is in its strength. As a great British historian Paul Johnson wrote: "While 100 states came into being in the 20th Century, only Israel's birth counts as a miracle."

There is very much a parallel here. Because the young state of Israel, in so many ways, mirrors the beginnings of America: a nation whose traditions were born of a flight from religious and ethnic persecution, dedicated to the equal rights of men and women, to Democracy and to the Common Sense of self-determination. An infamous demagogue once privately noted to his inner circle: "If you truly want to destroy a nation, you must first attack its traditions." (His name was Adolf Hitler. He is no longer with us. But his Nemesis, the Jews, remain…and they prosper!)

So far, Israel has held onto those values. And so America, its inspiration, must also do the same.

The previously mentioned political thinkers Strauss and Voegelin warned us back in 1950s that the liberal democracy in the United States required a reinvigorated idea of purpose.

The question remains: Can those of us in the USA still find the resolution to do so?

In 1948, noting that Great Britain, dominated at the time by the openly anti-Zionist Labour party of Clement Attlee, was refusing to acknowledge Israel long after its recognition by the US and USSR, opposition leader Winston Churchill delivered the following words to the British Parliament:

"…The coming into being of a Jewish state in Palestine is an event in world history to be viewed in the perspective, not of a generation or a century, but in the perspective of a thousand, two thousand or even three thousand years. That is a standard of temporal values or time-values which seems very much out of accord with the perpetual click-clack of our rapidly changing moods and of the age in which we live. This is an event in world history."

Characteristic of Churchill's affinity for, and understanding of, the need for Jewish statehood—when Israel was finally recognized by London and Israel's first President Chaim Weitzman sent his note of gratitude—Winston Churchill simply responded with a three-word telegram: *"The light glows!"*

And so it does…

Index